STRENGTH OF MEN AND NATIONS

To create, today, is to create dangerously.
ALBERT CAMUS, *The Rebel*

STRENGTH OF
MEN AND NATIONS

A Message to the USA *vis-à-vis* the USSR

WILLIAM ERNEST HOCKING

HARPER & BROTHERS PUBLISHERS NEW YORK

CONTENTS

v

The Ultimate Issue of Religion
Changing Attitudes in Russia
The Descent into Hades
Science Looking beyond Its Borders
The Arriving Answer of Philosophy

PREAMBLE

In the course of a lifetime of imprudent undertakings, one maxim I have been led to adopt is that no task must be evaded merely because it is impossible. The relevant questions are: whether it requires to be done, and whether the circumstances point a finger in one's direction.

In public affairs the task now to be done exempts nobody. The radical quandary of our time does indeed involve the specialists—executives, diplomats, jurists, experts in military and economic affairs. But it is an odd feature of the present world predicament that the skilled technicians are as much puzzled as are we, the commoners. The traditions of statesmanship, the time-tried formulas, furnish no sure guidance in a situation that has no precedents and no parallels.

No precedents: Because for the first time in history the physical security sought by every civilized society has vanished—driven out by the unleashed physical powers invoked to achieve it. And with the vanishing of physical security, mankind faces the necessity—awkward indeed but hardly deplorable—of finding nonphysical grounds for world order —moral grounds, in a world uniquely unsure of its moral convictions.

No parallels: The unit-actors in the political world picture are indeed familiar. Here are the nations, "sovereign" as usual; each nation with its nondiscussable "vital interests" backed by military muscles hopefully presumed ample. Yet,

1

with a world-split between major powers and in precarious balance, no one wishes to see those muscles—the nuclear variety—in action. No one knows certainly under what circumstances we ourselves, or our opponents, would be willing to use them. And the dilemma is: *no one has an adequate substitute* for conflict, in order to reach settlements that must be achieved.

The natural substitute for conflict *within nations* is the appeal to law, to pre-established law applied by pre-established courts. For conflict *between nations*, the code is unfinished, and willing resort to the Court still dubious. The staples of international law, valid for many more issues than the nations are presently disposed to submit, falter precisely at the threshold of the situation-without-precedent—the changing world map, the "nonjusticiable" issues of status, of merging or dividing national entities, of imposed control of backward peoples. The "right of conquest" remains on the books—the USA has appealed to it for rights in Berlin —likewise the kindred appeal to *fait accompli*—each of these pleas subordinating law-and-reason to the history-making powers of force-and-continuity. There is a code of international law to be finished—no public business is more pressing —but the world processes now in action are the very ones that must complete the work.

Meanwhile, we hold to the military muscles—for our "security," we say, knowing full well that this security has become world-wide insecurity. The familiar picture of man mechanized by his own machines now becomes that of man intimidated by his own defenses!

Intimidated, yes. But perhaps also *emancipated*.

For since warfare with total-destructives is suspended— at least pro tem—the actual contest, continuing, must take place on another plane. The arms race thus shows itself simply irrelevant to the real issue. Perforce, the contest between the Western powers and the Communist bloc returns to its original character, an argument between ideologies by way of experimental demonstration. What we seem largely to witness is the forcible imposing of an ideology-in-action upon unwilling peoples; but what we—and they—begin to see is that *an ideology cannot be imposed* (I state this dogmatically, and shall duly undertake to support the statement). And the corollary is that *the contest for men's minds is the essence of the actual world situation*. The stalemate of arms thus becomes the renewed opportunity, perhaps our last, for carrying on a stern campaign, in the realm of thought and feeling, for the suffrage of the free human spirit throughout the world. The time is now.

It is for this reason that the experts everywhere are newly disposed not alone to propaganda-flooding but also to careful listening to "the public" whose allegiance or nonallegiance is their Judgment Day. The problems of diplomacy become the problems of the common man, as court of final appeal.

And the problems of the common man are *ipso facto* the problems of philosophy—philosophy being nothing else than everyman-thinking-over-his-world-problem. It thus becomes the duty of those whose business is with "Ideas" to concern themselves intensively with "Facts," those tough facts of the common lot—needs, labors, fears, losses, resentments— whose *parti pris* interpretation is offered by the battling ideologies. Ideas and Facts have always belonged together —there is no such thing as a pure "realm of ideas"—but now the philosopher has less right than ever to live solely in a context of generalities: as an interpreter he must seek knowledge of the facts to be interpreted, not through report alone but through experience and, by way of experience, through feeling.

For the contesting ideologies—*i.e.*, views-attached-to-programs—involve ideals stirring collective passions capable of putting human destiny itself in jeopardy. And "in order to dominate collective passions," as Camus says with penetrating precision, "they must be lived through and experienced."[1]

This demand may help to explain why that finger-pointing first referred to may have turned my way.

It so happens that my life's journey has taken me into certain situations in which the present world-split was being generated, not as a combatant but as inescapably a participant. As an example: the Munich crisis, perhaps the most portentous single event in shaping the existing alignment of powers.

During 1938 and the early part of 1939, I was in Europe, lecturing in England and Scotland, spending some time in Yugoslavia, Austria, Germany, passing through Nuremberg during Hitler's *Parteitag*, resident in Cambridge, England, when Chamberlain returned from Munich with the triumphant announcement of "Peace in our time; peace with honor." There we were fitted by the government with gas masks, in case of surprise attack. The topic of my lectures in Scotland was "Fact and Destiny." As holding an Idealist conception of the world-process, namely, that there is a governing purpose at work in the cosmos and history, I had been accusing Idealist philosophy of inadequate attention to the pervasive role of brute fact in the actual world. As the pact with Hitler began to bear its baleful fruit, I realized that a newly ominous pattern of man-made brute fact was entering European history. And with the shortly following maelstrom of World War II, with the wider use of "strategic bombing" and the new potencies of atomic warfare released upon civilian centers by my own government, there emerged a deeper challenge to any faith in a world-meaning than I had hitherto entertained. I was prepared by this experience to understand more completely the widespread rejection of faith, the despair of reason—often the nihilism that drank in Nietzsche's judgment, "God is dead"—to which many a courageous voice of that time gave assent, with the inference that man must trust to his own resources to create what values can be wrested from existence in a world devoid of inner sensitivity or meaning.

As a particular item, I had learned during the Munich days that the USSR, in the person of Stalin's ambassador, Litvinov, had sought to be included in the negotiations over Czechoslovakia, with the reputed intent of co-operating with Britain and France in resisting the eastward push of Hitler, a matter of importance in judging Soviet statecraft at this juncture. The mystery surrounding this proposal and its rebuff by Chamberlain and Daladier—Sir Nevile Henderson brushes the matter off with the words "Soviet Russia talked vaguely of supporting the Western Powers"[2]—indicates another phase of the interpreter's responsibility to the common judgment. The crucial question of all diplomacy refers to the *motives and purposes* of the other world-half; and motives and purposes are precisely nonobservable. The realist in politics knows to his cost that motives are the most formidable reality he has to deal with; and at the same time, as invisible and intangible, they elude his need for certitude. Must they, then, be guessed at? And does this reduce diplomacy to a game of chance? Have we not been involved in precisely this perilous risk-taking over the question "What are the motives of Khrushchev in his demands over Berlin?"

If diplomacy could proceed on Facts, it might become a science: no period of history has been nearly so well informed about facts; and officers of state, with the aid of intelligence agencies, have immense resources not available to the public: but what do the facts mean? The interpreter of motives becomes an indispensable adjunct to the fact-collector. And who is qualified to interpret? The common assumption that the interpretation comes with the facts is deadly.

If the interpreter is overcredulous, or oversanguine, or overpugnacious, or oversuspicious, or—worst of all—victim of some fixation as to what the facts *must* mean, he can give a fatal slant to the best informed State Department. True interpretation, pearl without price, can come only from an insight into the realities of human nature; and this gift is not the prerogative of any caste of medicine men—specialization tends to warp judgment. The ancient Egyptians shrewdly referred heart-weighing, as test of honesty, to a god! Lacking this resource, the advantage lies with an equally shrewd and sensitive simplicity: in the public pulse, uncommitted human nature tends to speak for itself.

But the worth of that voice depends largely on the public's own experience. To win the understanding required by a perceptive diplomacy, the suffering of the world must in some way become a shared suffering—shared by the interpreters and by the peoples.

Through these and other such experiences I receive a glimmer of light upon one phase of weakness in the American outlook, reflected in its diplomacy. It is only the direct experience of humanity-under-stress that can supply the clues for understanding the behavior and motives of other humanity-under-stress. There is such a thing as being too fortunate for judging the less fortunate. The USA—by nature, I believe, the most spontaneously out-living and generous of all great peoples—suffers under this handicap at just this juncture. For an intelligent response to other nations' policies conceived under strain, nothing can take the place of having lived through the turns of history in which those passions, prides, rebellions, outrages, those images, myths, ideals, ideologies, were developed.

We of the USA cannot indeed wish ourselves unfortunate in order to understand misfortune. But we can learn humility and respect. And we may note another source of national weakness that conspires with our natural complacency to deprive us of that mental and moral force now demanded by the world situation:

We have *weakened ourselves* by softening our entire system of education and its cultural standards. We have as a people become averse to the rigorous work of thought essential to a just realism in any field of action. We have, for example, even in our university life, become so prevalently anemic in our capacity to think as to assume—quite generally—that because there are important relativities in truth, morals, taste, we must dispense with all "absolutes," and indeed with all firm convictions on matters of principle. The obvious truth is that no relativity can be defined without the assumption of an absolute; and the absurd aversion to certitude weakens the fabric of every phase of life, including the judgments of our courts.

The very terms "principle," "standard," tend to grate on the ears of a public whose concept of democracy inclines to judge truth and right by weighing ballots. It is just these standards—in life, in art, in law—whose sense we must recover if we would regain our due national strength, the rugged fabric of a sound democracy, the *grit* that knows how to grasp *principle without rigidity*, through awareness of the Absolute within the relative.

This national strength we must and can recover. I am speaking as a common citizen of the USA, grateful for and proud of my heritage—speaking *for* the common citizen and *to* the common citizen. The man of the street has always a deeper-than-current-opinion ground of judgment. He may lose his *grip* upon his own certitudes; but he can never lose his *felt connection* with the central human realities in which our standards of truth, justice—yes, and of beauty and decency—have their perennial sources. I write in the hope of reviving his awareness of these standards so that they may become once more forces—sledge hammers if you will—implements fundamental to our national strength.

This piece began as a pamphlet, an informal statement of convictions without systematic argument. It is still in spirit a pamphlet, a tract for the times, though it has refused to stay within reasonable pamphlet limits. I remain heavily aware of its defects, done as it has been in undue haste. I am by necessity entering a field of battle, offering contentious judgments, stating conclusions without detailing all the evidence, conscious of incurring criticism. More than once, I have been tempted to put the essay away as *ultra vires*, which of course it is.

But an imperfect piece, offered without dogma, may find its place of usefulness. As written largely out of personal experiences which have given me, here and there, clues to what various turns of history during the last half-century have meant, it is done with a certain sense of obligation. The feeling of duty, even of urgency, persists.

Let me say that urgency does not mean anxiety or fear. Judgments reached under the stress of fear are not the judgments of free men. For free men can control events: they are not free nor worthy of freedom unless, refusing to be browbeaten by events, they *take control*. This expression of freedom is my conception of strength. It is in the belief that my beloved country is capable of rising to that freedom and that strength that I speak unsparingly and without despair.

For no man who knows reality as purposeful, and history as therefore significant, can have a right to ultimate doubt, nor to ultimate fear, nor to ultimate condemnation.

NOTE ON THE AUTHOR'S POSITION

It will not be amiss for me to remark in closing this Preamble, that on the merits of the ideological issues between the USA and the USSR—between capitalism and communism or between individualism and socialism—my views have for some years been publicly stated, and that I have had no inclination to change them. They can be found in *The Lasting Elements of Individualism* (Yale and Oxford Presses, 1939), especially pages 115-27. That book was an outcome of a debate or symposium with John Dewey and W. P. Montague, on "The Future of Liberalism," held in New York in

1934, and printed in the *Journal of Philosophy*, April 25, 1936.

I hold entirely to the view then stated that the sources of all creativity, and hence of every cultural advance, are to be found not in collectivities but in human individuals. The society as a whole, especially if it is a nation, has its quasi-personal character, its individual *esprit de corps*, its forward impulse and direction: it maintains what we may call a moral momentum in which its members share. Through its education it ushers them to maturity; it remains a stimulus and a conserving receptacle for the creative energies of individuals. But it is not itself a person; it can act only through persons, itself incapable of specific innovation.

The still-powerful current of thought bent to reveal the "social origins" of ideas and institutions has worked from an important truth, namely, that the human individual is not a self-enclosed atom, a monad. His very existence is derived, not self-made, a continuous being-in-relationship with something not himself which he learns to call "reality." He means by this that his experience is not an assemblage of subjective sensations—the common fallacy of Positivism—but from the first an "objective" world in which what is true for him alone is true for any and all others who may happen along. But note that this objectivity is prior to the presence of any specific others: it does not depend on "society"; it is there, as the germ of all possible sociability. It implies that what we mean by "reality" is the presence of a pervasive, non-centered, Other-self: and because of this continuous private intercourse with a non-intrusive Thou-art, individual experience takes on the character of universality. Prior to all the "social origins," aloneness from men, which is aloneness with the Real as Other-self, is the sole source of a genuine fertility of mind.

The principle of this observation, which we might formulate as the *universality of private experience*, furnishes the philosophical clue for the answer of this essay both to meta-physical communism and to an abstract individualism morally solipsistic. It is, I believe, the characteristic philosophical advance of the present century, disposing once for all of the hitherto unresolved dilemma of solipsism. It is the basis of my first book (1912) and of all my subsequent work.

But I see today more clearly than I had seen prior to the second World War that "Communism versus Capitalism" fails to define the issue we have to deal with. In January, 1945, at a Cleveland Conference on the proposed charter for a United Nations Organization, I undertook to show that there are in the world of advanced societies no purely capitalist and no purely communist economies—all are "mixed." The wide differences in the proportions of the mixture are due to the more essential issue of the *pattern of freedom*. This proposition, at that time contentious, is now a commonplace.

The economic issues between the USA and the USSR remain not only important—they have a certain primacy. For we must agree with the economic determinist that a viable economy is a necessary condition for any civilized living, and economic advance a necessary condition for progress. But in that assertion, the economic determinist has already agreed with us that the economy is a means, not an end: the fundamental issues relate to the ends, the qualities of a civilization. For today, prowess in discovering and harnessing the apparently limitless energies of physical nature has become an indispensable factor in national power. But no nation, our own or other, can carry its due weight in the counsels of mankind until it rightly identifies, and stands upon, the deeper grounds of strength. To identify them is our present task.

WILLIAM ERNEST HOCKING

Madison, New Hampshire
July 4, 1959

I

THREE TYPES
OF DIPLOMACY

SYMPTOMS OF WEAKNESS IN STRENGTH

NATIONAL power may so handle itself as to develop national weakness. Not that "power always corrupts": if that were true there could be no states and no statesmen at once strong and honest. There are such statesmen. But it is true that national power, taken as external evidence of an inner perfection, has an extraordinary capacity to mislead its holders, and in time to corrupt them. Through failure to identify and understand the conditions of its own power, a truly great nation may find itself mysteriously enfeebled.

World influence, for example, certainly an element in national strength, is a far subtler thing, and more swiftly variable, than the factual picture of economic and military power. Apart from large-scale catastrophe or the sudden unlocking of nature's energies, the physical potency of a nation has the momentum of all physical things: it varies but slowly. By contrast, the world influence of a nation, its "prestige," is subject to swift fluctuation. Of this truth we have had recent and startling evidence at several centers of power. Among them, the USA.

That the moral position of the United States has experienced a major downward shift needs no saying: current observers, official and private, agree on the fact, and prescribe

11

remedies for the most part according to their political bent. They incline to assume that the matter is temporary—a dip of our stock in the world's moral stock market, fully recoverable by a change of policy, a more adroit psychology in dealing with friends or backward peoples or the opponents, a better analysis in stating our case.

I take a more serious view.

Foreign policy is indeed at the center: as a name for our direct action on the outside world, it is the all-important vehicle of our will and thought and feeling. But foreign policy is not a ready-made organ on which the virtuoso-secretary can at will change the stops—pull out the *vox humana*, step on the pedals, give us something more affirmative! Policy, while from above it directs national action, has its springs in the convictions and purposes of a people, and especially in their judgment as to the meaning of their own ideals, and of the issues that constitute the public conflict.

Here are the sources of our weakness. They lie in the basic temper of our democracy—our orientation in world affairs, our conceptions of the good life, and withal in what we consider the meaning of our professed public principles—say of liberty, of free enterprise, of democracy itself. If in this region of our unformulated but daily-lived ideology there are maladjustments to the changing realities we have to meet, we can understand a loss of fitness for the leadership our position implies and requires.

AS ONE OTHER SEES US

It so happens that we have the exceptional advantage of comment from a friendly and capable observer who, seeing —as many see—certain defects in our foreign policy, sees also the folk dispositions from which these defects arise. Some remarks of the Canadian statesman, Lester B. Pearson, precisely illustrate the point I am here making. Writing in an American biweekly,[1] he observes that a progressive weakening of NATO, whether by a breach between France and the rest of Europe or by a subtle alienation between all of Europe and the USA, could so far advance the relative power of the USSR as to destroy the equipoise in which alone the cold war status can be maintained—not as against peace, but as against enforced retreat.

Quite apart from the cold-war issue, I ask why the USA should be losing caste in NATO. Pearson mentions some sources of silent offense: a prevalent unwillingness among our people to accept individual sacrifices for a wider good, whether domestic or international—holding out for tariff barriers against imports from nations with which we have reason to make common economic cause; pushing for advancing wage scales and consequent prices in presence of an inflation imperilling our own foreign markets—both pressures a form of fiddling while Rome burns. And meantime assuming that the USSR will someday crumble internally, because it ought to, and commit unconditional surrender without unconditional defeat.

Pearson judges that we tend automatically to oppose every Russian proposal on the ground that such proposals are attempts to obtain obvious or concealed advantages for Russia —perhaps an axiomatic assumption—and that this policy of ours means permanent stalemate. If we are not prepared from our own side to discover or devise proposals offering *mutual* advantages, the USSR being pure evil, our self-righteousness cancels in advance any possibility of settlement, and becomes a deadly rigidity. If every recognition of common interest is to be condemned as "appeasement" we are foreclosing, by an a priori attitude, the sole alternative to war.

Pearson's judgments strike close home. If our influence in an important joint effort in Europe is being injured by a shortsighted interpretation of "free enterprise"—our proud banner—we must look behind the slogan to its legitimate meaning, and shall do so. And if he is right that our policy toward the USSR is condemned to futility by a barren rigor of first-rate principles, we are again put on guard against assuming that the excellence of an ideal guarantees the wisdom of its use.

In this vital matter of principle versus appeasement, a central theme of our study, let me note at once that this alternative, so generally taken as defining the actual issue in our dealing with the USSR, fails to do so. If our choice has to be between appeasement and principle, we hold to principle come what will: and a logician might well tell us that as between yielding and not yielding there is no third course. True enough. But note an apparently irrelevant fact:

As between divergent national purposes of any two nations there are fundamental identities which no oppositions obliterate—identities which hold good over every chasm, of capitalism and communism, of tyranny and freedom, even of right and wrong; and a recognition of these identities may begin the repair of a seemingly hopeless cleavage. I raise the question whether we of the USA have lost sight of these healing identities, and have therefore missed the sources of a *third type of diplomacy*, neither appeasement nor rigidity. Appeasement and rigidity are both ways of national weakness; this third type is the way of national strength.

A THIRD TYPE OF DIPLOMACY

Complete definition of this third type can only be reached with the conclusion of our study of the factors of national strength. But a sketch of the general position may help to sustain the journey.

"Appeasement" and "Rigidity" are, of course, critics' labels for positions involving yielding or not yielding.

Around the pole of Appeasement, strictly a sacrifice of primary principle for the sake of peace, we find policies of "Flexibility" or simply "Realism," and "Compromise," a policy of mutual concession which has at times been praised as the peculiar merit of British political genius.

Around the pole of Rigidity, the current bad name for "sticking to principle," refusing to be driven by fear to the surrender of moral dignity and freedom, we find beside the fighting fraternity of the knockout blow, an unimaginative "moralism" in statecraft devoid of human understanding—a radical weakness masquerading as strength.

But if, between the opposing powers, there are common goods—aims which by their nature are necessarily accepted by both—it is clear that *to affirm those aims can be neither Appeasement nor Rigidity.* What it is easy to forget in the clean, good-versus-evil definitions of strife is that there are identical elements of purpose implied in human nature itself. For example—beside the all-human preference for being alive rather than blasted to atoms, and for order rather than for chaos—concern for full human development, aversion to futility, will to participate in a history having total significance, demand to know the total scientific and beyond-scientific truth about the world we live in and the place of common human values in a noncommittal universe—these common elements of purpose, relevant to no one special issue, are relevant to all issues as framework and perspective.

And because of them, another factor of diplomacy absent from both Appeasement and Rigidity may enter, the *Remaking of Motives.* The practitioners of the two staple types of diplomacy ask the question, "What is the Kremlin's motive?", assuming the motive to be a fixed fact like the Kremlin's geographical area. This assumption is a latent materialism and a confession of passive impotence at the point of maximum opportunity. For a motive is a living thing, not only malleable but *makable.* It is makable by way of those necessary common aims which bend the goals of all national policies inexorably *toward convergence*—an element of historical necessity as yet uncharted, with which this essay will be much occupied.

It is our main task to define and prepare the way for this third type of diplomacy. The type has no specific name as

yet. It might be called the Diplomacy of Remaking; it might
with literal accuracy be called Creative Diplomacy, though
I shun the descriptive too often used as calling for a miracle
of creativity on the part of someone else. To define its present
task in the world will be in some measure to define its process.

PROGRAM OF THE INQUIRY

The inquiry will take us through several fields in which
our guiding ideas stand in contrast with those of the USSR
—economics, law and rights, group morality, the meaning
of democracy, the forces governing history, the realities of
our present condition of fearsome international hostility—
somewhat in that order. Since national policy is the attempt
to control history, and national strength is, in simplest terms,
the capacity to direct historic change, the clouds of recent
world history will be all about us; and I shall offer interpretations of these tangled events, here and there unorthodox
—but without historic detail except at points where my own
observation might throw some light on forces actually at
work.

Before embarking on this analysis, however, let me call
attention to certain symptoms of our national weakness in
two fields wholly apart from either diplomatic or military
equipment and yet directly pertinent to the intangible ar-
senal of the cold war; namely, education and the fine arts.

Since education is the process of pouring a living civilization into new vessels, it necessarily reveals that civilization's
grasp of its own meaning and world role. And the fine arts,
whose essence is creativity, must with equal necessity reveal
the quality of a nation's dream, the meaning it assigns to
its own future, and therefore the meaning it can offer to new
life in other lands. If there is no nobility in a nation's art,
then there is no possible lift in the diplomatic promise it can
spread among the nations. Art in its full sweep, including
literary as well as graphic art and music, is the one fully
free expression of the outreach of a nation's spirit. If, then,

a nation's art—an international language more immediate than any other—has nothing to offer to the universal aspirations of mankind, that circumstance declares that the civilization there expressed, whatever its efficiency, has exactly nothing to contribute to the dignity of the race.

Both in education and in art, we are interpreting our social and political foundations, that set of ideals—chiefly Liberty, Equality, Democracy—which, in spite of a considerable investment in the sociologies and philosophies of change and relativity, we rightly regard as permanently valid, a light to mankind. We are convinced that we have largely realized them, for does not our nation attract by its polity as well as by its prosperity? And is not our prosperity deserved— largely a fruit of those ideals—thought out, worked for, fought for, achieved by courage, faith, free enterprise, and invention? We surely know the meaning of these ideals, else how could we realize them? In sober truth, as a people, *we can hardly claim to know.*

And because we do not clearly know, what we have actually achieved is partly the real thing and partly counterfeit. It is the counterfeit ingredients—the loose-running liberty, the fraudulent equality, the inwardly spurious democracy—that are today counting against us, bringing about a national texture tending to the flabby, the self-indulgent, the soft.

These inner weaknesses will appear most clearly in the fields of education and fine art, whose task it is to express the spirit of our civilization—their immediate relevance to the diplomatic task will appear as we discuss them. We shall then turn to the outward and tangible aspects of the tension between the USA and the USSR, beginning with the economic contrast that gives the entire conflict its current if inaccurate name, "Capitalism versus Communism."

II

THE COLD WAR
FOR MEN'S MINDS

WE ARE dealing with world movements. The world is moved by its concrete interests, by its thoughts, by its ideals, by its passions. Nothing becomes important until it touches feeling and aspiration. In the cold war, the thought-and-feeling of peoples—the ideologies and the emotions stirred by their impact on existing circumstances—is the determinant of allegiance.

J. Donald Adams, writing in *The New York Times*, has expressed a pertinent insight: "The cold war is fundamentally a battle for men's minds," and the determining factors will not be arms or money, but "what we have intellectually and spiritually to offer these peoples, even more lost in the twentieth century than ourselves."[1]

Both in education and in art, I have said, we are interpreting our social and political foundations. How does our work in education speak for us?

AMERICAN EDUCATION AND NATIONAL STRENGTH

The public school of the USA represents a great ideal, essential to a working democracy, and greatly exemplified. Its early success in creating a literate and well-informed people has spread widely the cause of "mass education." In our own half-century we have seen a movement in China, not without the incentive of this nation,[2] lifting millions (from

18

1920 onward) to new levels of participation in world culture. In the same period, we have seen the home enterprise curiously lamed, as by a creeping illness, failing in vigor and effect.

Concern over the lapse is general, already creating a literature of its own; diagnoses are many. Let me swiftly summarize the factors that concern our national strength.[3]

Broadly speaking, the trouble may be traced to a pervasive anemia in our conception of Democracy, inducing false lights of Freedom and Equality. Well-meaning leaders of educational thought have persuaded us that freedom is synonymous with release from discipline, and equality synonymous with a costless right of all to "be educated"—as if education could be bestowed as a commodity or gift—and on a platform on which the easy and the difficult are spread out as equivalent in value for amiable "elective" choice.

The prehistoric conception of education, embodied in the rite of Initiation, involved hardship for the candidate for Rebirth. He was about to enter into a unique heritage. All his aspiration to reach mature status, to share the great Lore which gave the tribe its power, was in high tension. He expected, and wanted, exertion and pain. But with us, far advanced, to be "progressive" was to relax; while the instructor must cater to our existing "interests." The thought that youth is eager to *take an interest* in things beyond its horizon did not occur to these advisers. Initial difficulties were therefore evaded; and the two disciplinary topics of primary education suffered. The multiplication table must be spaced over four or five years; and language analysis—the strait gate to clear thought and expression—is abandoned under the despised name of "grammar."

As a natural result, we—teachers and taught—consider labor over the anatomy of language too great a burden; actual study of foreign languages falls off heavily at a moment when the USSR is able to staff not only many diplomatic offices but the foremen of working gangs in foreign

parts with men speaking the language of the country. But
there is a wider casualty: the man who knows only his own
language does *not* know his own. We see that fact in our
graduates. Liberty not-to-know is not liberty.

Education in its full sense is the sum of our efforts,
through all agencies, to hand on our life-vision. That means,
for the USA, to foster in growing Americans their faith in
the Good Life as American experience and goals conceive
it. We must confess with humiliation that our success is
slipping: our youth, taking its own lessons from the tumult
of the times, tends to find our definitions lacking in contem-
poraneity, to strike out for itself, aimlessly if need be. We
have failed to take the measure of our task. What we have
to convey is the *impetus of our civilization*—its ongoing
drive coming out of our whole past, moving toward our whole
future. The essence of that *élan* is *struggle*. Can we convey
the meaning of that impetus *without* struggle on the part of
the learner?

Let us be more explicit. Our Western civilization is the
result of various types of struggle, but especially—in the
field of tangible obstacles—of three main efforts involving
mentality. The struggle with the secrecy of Nature's ways
—our achievements here recorded in mathematical *physics*;
the struggle for a livelihood, recorded in *economics*; the
struggle for reason in the strife of interests, recorded in *law*
—these three "tough disciplines" are the recapitulated history of the race, in its quest for a civilized way of life. If
anyone is going to understand his civilization, he must have,
in addition to the narrative history and to a philosophy
epitomizing the race's struggle for a whole view, a grasp of
the principles of these three tough disciplines. A "higher
education" which omits any one of these is imperfect; one
which omits them all is a farce. I raise the question: How
many of our higher institutions do not allow a candidate for
a degree, via substitutes, to omit them all?

The incredible array of "courses" and of options in the

usual college catalogue, each college apparently aspiring to multiply its "offerings," indicates at once that our higher education has in the main surrendered essentials for "equivalents." And if we face the reality that for essentials *there are no equivalents*, we are forced to the unhappy conclusion that our higher education has largely lost its stamina, sold its birthright for the pottage of a misconceived democracy.

The loss of integrity begins in the primary public school. It is a consequence of the dry rot in the grades that the later stages have to work with a mental material conditioned to painless advance. At the same time, the growing prosperity as well as the growing population make swift increase in the demand for "higher education" in which a desire for knowledge mingles pleasantly with other interests common to youth and fellowship. Four years of college life, once the prerogative of the financially fortunate, are now—so far as time and money are concerned—within the reach of an unprecedented percentage of our youth. Some quarter-century ago, Ernest Barker estimated that in the USA there were eight times as many college students, per unit of population, as in England. (England has much enlarged its percentage since then, but the ratio is still notable.) Our conception of democracy now proceeds to work with engineering efficiency.

There are entrance requirements, of course. But on the general assumption of a "right to education," implying that those who want a higher education have a human right to it, the volume-pressure makes its way. But *to what* is this aspiring multitude admitted? Democracy again speaks: "In substance, to what it wants." There are "requirements" in every honest institution; but for those who do not aspire to be scholars, it is still possible to be gentlemen and ride through on a "gentleman's C." And of course the scholars—looked on as a special odd breed—find in the presence of the gentlemen an important part of their own education. The curriculum is only a large fraction of the value of the total experience in which, in their intimate groupings, youth

deeply educate one another. But the enclosed sphere of
teaching activity within the curriculum has its own problem
of integrity, internal to its declared purpose. The influence
of the democratic ideal on collegiate opportunity can never
imply equality of standing, but only equality of *standard*.
The standard for all alike must be: a competent grasp of
the impetus of our civilization as revealed *inter alia* by the
tough disciplines, in their contribution to the total aim
and meaning of human life.

This is the truly liberal education.

In principle, such an education qualifies us to meet on
its own ground—more widely than at present—the in-
tensely specialized education of the USSR, so technically
proficient, without falling into its narrow identification with
"science" nor cheating ourselves by the loose ambiguity of
that term, and without the cloak of philosophical indoc-
trination thrown over the whole nation as a captive audi-
ence, removing thereby from discussion those ultimate
aims which ought chiefly to be discussed. In its tough
parts, this our liberal program is quite as severe and as
path-breaking as the pretechnical studies of the USSR.
Further, it does something to save for us a merit we have
squandered while they of the USSR drive it to excess—
the unique value of *paucity* in the total program. A certain bleakness in the main outline, with rich branching
into collateral channels, gives a unity and surveyableness
to the broad field of learning, lost in our formless surfeit.
This paucity promotes the priceless vision of a *whole*—a
whole of thought, dealing with a whole of reality. Such a
vision of wholeness is the natural fruit of education, essential at once to self-command, to citizenship, and to meeting
the unique challenge of our time. Without it we are weak,
and without it we promote weakness of fiber in our youth.

EDUCATION VIA PUBLICITY

Our educators are not solely to be found in the schools.
Education in *values* is surely a major part of the total task.

The schools offer courses in ethics and esthetics and, now, a general theory of values. But as consumers of goods, we are constant practitioners of value-judgments, and as constantly in need of teaching.

One aspect of our major educational lapse lies in this perhaps unexpected quarter. We have a rising standard of living—the highest in the world, some say. As a companion piece to the rising standard—rising in terms of multiform easings, cushionings, amusings, and toolings for our various original and multiplying desires—we have also a rising *cost* of living. This cost is greatly swollen by a newly inflated factor, that of advertising, a presumably necessary expenditure if ever-changing goods are to be made known to potential users. (A market of staples needs no advertising; we always know where potatoes are to be had: it is the "improved model" that requires public education.) Advertising is now magnified in importance in order to present the multiplying novelties to *the entire market area*; but, mind you, to present them in such a light that each competing novelty can be made to appear *superior to every other*!

Consider the logic of this effort. "Superior to every other" is mutual. The task thus defined is inherently infinite, self-expanding—an ideal professional occupation, in which every success requires a greater effort from the competitor. The calling enlarges itself by dint of its own achievements. There is no ceiling.

I do not here speak of the resulting clamor for our limited fund of attention. The right to invade our peace through conventional channels is part of our national liberty, including the sacred right of a free speech and press to mislead the misleadable and to distract the already distraught. I do not speak of this ubiquitous intrusion, pressing to destroy even the peace of the rural neighborhood and the beauty of an unspoiled nature. I speak only of the radical and unalienable interest in *truth*.

I point out that the immense advertising bill—running

toward billions and borne, of course, by the consumer—
while beckoning us to genuine new facilities as well as thrills
and ticklings, has become essentially a *bill for falsehood*.
Not that advertising lies in regard to facts—this it hesitates
to do—its falsities are *lies of emotion*. Thumb through our
best newspapers, our once-responsible magazines: let the
flood of pictured ecstatic grimaces run over you until you
are exhausted by sympathetic rapture with the portrayed
purchasers of every product, from the most ancient wines
and whiskies to the newest wrinkle in bras. You notice perhaps that this emotional jag is offered you by artists (for
some reason they are not abstractionists): the publicity man
knows better than to rely on his own feelings and imagination. Purchasable "artists" of drama or television are em-
ployed to blow up these too-tame emotions to sky-height:
the fraud is not concealed, it is flaunted: it is none the less
a lie. And my point is that in any civilization *falsehoods
of feeling are more deadly than falsehoods of fact*. They are
also more insidious; for they are irrefutable—they do not
argue, they infect the mind. Are we perhaps becoming an
infected people?

The Sophists of ancient Greece were accused by occasional
rebels like Plato of being willing, for hire, "to make the
worse appear the better reason." The art of publicity today,
also for hire, tends toward the revival of systematic sophis-
try, making the worse emotion—or none at all—appear a
bit of Paradise. Our society is being led toward chronic emotional inebriety.

One phase of this unbalance which runs deeper than the
artificial emphases of the persuaders is the matter of *selective
importance*—one of the essential services of all the media of
mass communication—the headlines, the boldface signals for
excitement or alarm. Since no human being can be all-in-
formed, the adult man must be selectively informed, and the
obligation to select rests heavily on his news agencies. The

postulate, commercially useful but psychologically ominous, that every day shall have its crisis, its call for maximum tension and response, elicits a protective reaction, with more or less effective individual screening. There persists a sense of too-muchness, a revulsion against the incessant drumbeat, and a call—as yet hardly formulated—for a new and significant aspect of truthfulness which is at the same time an aspect of fine art. It is not simply that our news services—and our storytelling services as well—shall speak with honester emotional adjustment, but that they shall speak from a background of serenity and moral steadiness, rather than from the sense of frenzy and breathless motion appropriate to a world in which everything is sensed only that everything may be forgotten. Where all is important, nothing is important. Where world peril deepens, only firm quietude can convey its gravity.

Where press enterprise is free, a nation has the press it wants, and deserves. The national character can be read (at home and abroad) in the type of press it supports. A nation's strength speaks not from a chronic press-flutter of alarum and excursion but from the measured energy with which it confronts its emerging tasks. It is to the credit of the USA that beneath a temperamental yen for excitement, the press-quality now winning durable favor is not sensationalism but *vitality*; that the "yellow" press tends to vanish; that—vying for public interest with business, politics, and social happenings—important events in science, medicine, art, religion, law become news. It is to be charged, I believe, less to closed-mindedness than to immaturity within its widening scope of information, that public judgment, with editorial complicity, clings to its stereotypes and party slogans; that it tends to a national orthodoxy and intolerance—signs of our educational failure to develop a robust *power to think*.

But it is to our discredit, I fear, that more than a touch of the salacious, the violent and the cynically sophisticated become growing factors in best-sellership. The self-indulgent propensities, sexual and other, of a highly productive nation make tacit conspiracy with a venal promotership to intensify, through press, screen, fiction, drama—often under a corrupt plea of "liberty of the press"—their insidious onslaught on national virility. Under the flags of "freedom," "realism," and "modernity," we tend to cover a creeping moral unrealism becoming visible in all our arts.

Here, then, we note a continuing under-cover civil war for the American mentality, which plays its part in the cold war for men's minds everywhere, and marks a point of national weakness.

THE ROLE OF FINE ART IN NATIONAL STRENGTH

Herewith we have touched upon a too-little-recognized factor of national strength. The relevance of fine art to a nation's world influence is direct: it lies in the fact that nothing of import in the world happens without *feeling*, the motive power of all ideals political as well as personal; and art is the language of feeling.

Like the thought of the thinker, the emotional drive of the artist claims universality—his only excuse for displaying or publishing his work. He thus undertakes to engage and shape the feelings of others, first of his own milieu, extending perhaps to his nation, possibly beyond. And whatever a nation accepts as giving valid and effective expression to its feeling —its song, dance, poetry, graphic art, architecture—in that, it avows something beyond its ideology but wholly pertinent thereto, namely, the quality of its purpose, its dream-of-worth, pointing beyond what it is toward what it aspires to be.

Hence what a nation prizes, exhibits, embodies as its art, becomes a public confession of its soul, and therewith of the qualities which its special version of the good life would recommend to mankind. If indeed the battle is for men's minds, it is for any nation and its ideology a vital question whether mankind will or will not be drawn to desire, or at

least to respect, the qualities visible in that art. Woe to that
nation—and its diplomacy—whose art inspires puzzlement,
or aversion, or a hostile query as to its status within civilization.

It is the spirit of the USA to believe in and welcome
experimentation, in the arts as well as in the sciences. Dogmatic certitudes are at a discount; and relativity counts for
far more in matters of taste than in matters of engineering.
In the sciences, novelty submits to rigid tests, and the false
lead is decisively rejected. In the arts, the distinction between
a novelty of advance and a novelty of incompetence and
decay has no such firm screening. The meretricious can only
be sensed at once by a man of intuitive genius conscious of
his standards; but who will identify the man of genius? One
by one our American museums yield their judgments to the
pressure, let us say, of a current. We of the public feel that
we are being misled by a loose mixture of vagary and serious
exploration needing, but lacking, a firm discriminant or
catalyst. We have our own view; but we suspect it: we dare not
trust that inner guide which leads every human being to raise
his intuitive feeling of esthetic right to the level of a universal principle. The bedlam of wayward tastes tends to
destroy our faith in the existence of any "right" in matters
of art: let personal choice and the drift of fashion decide the
matter![4]

Yet, with all due respect to the drifting connoisseurs, let
me point to the residual certitudes in art, never wholly surrendered by the common people. There is a native authority
assumed by every civilized people to know what is good and
what is less good in its own art product. Without that
authority, confident of the universally valid power of its
own literature, drama, architecture, music, graphic art, a
nation forgoes one major element of strength far from
negligible in the most realistic diplomacy. Side by side with
the common authority of science, now concretely binding
men's minds, there is a common authority of those man-

created images of life's meaning we call art, universal only by consent, capable of forging a unity the more significant because it is devoid of compulsion.

The recent award of the Tschaikowsky Prize in Moscow to an American pianist may serve to illustrate the point. Irrelevant to every specific issue between the USA and the USSR, the presence in Moscow of an artist-interpreter of Russian music, who could make his meaning speak across every barrier of idiom and ideology, has done more than all our diplomacy to alter the temper of the two peoples toward one another, durably, and in a way that must facilitate any further statesmanship in the direction of our third type of diplomacy. For the American public, and for our present argument, the striking thing in the Russian response to the Van Cliburn performance is its uninhibited spontaneity, with the complete and normal certitude of popular judgment. We had given him earlier a kindly hearing and some praise, and had let him pass on: it was the Moscow public that estimated his true proportion. Why?

Among the arts, music has the political advantage of being essentially *un*political. It is not empty of national character; but the national element is lifted into the region of universality by the language of music: we do not circumscribe the *Marseillaise* because it is French, nor localize the *Recessional* because it is addressed to the British Empire, nor discount the majesty of Brahms' *Requiem* because he called it German. Indeed, it is a unique quality of art that its national tang becomes part of its universal appeal: who would want Chinese painting to be un-Chinesed? For the heavy task of world-unifying, a genuine art is an indispensable resource: and the assured, discriminating pride of a people in its own a necessary background for diplomatic strength.

This certitude of the people has its message to the hesitating relativities of the experts: faith that there is a "right" in art, and the discipline to find it, is the way of true liberty and of true democracy.

Since the battle is for men's minds—and the minds hold the springs of those collective passions that must be tamed— I have placed these intangibles of education and art first in our inquiry. It is within the frame of the available certitudes of thought and feeling that any judgment of the tangibles must move. But the world of the tangibles must now be met on its own ground.

We begin with the general field of economy.

III

OUR ECONOMIC
PUZZLEDOM

IN SPEAKING as I have done about our education, our fine arts, our less fine arts of persuasion, I do not forget that as a people—taking a canny-wise attitude toward hard thinking —we make it a principle to sit loose on "principles." We have faith in the ever-fertile leadings of experience, in exploration, flexibility, in the sacred liberty to challenge all fixed standards.

Everyone speaks of standards, but who knows surely what they are? Apart from mathematics and the sciences, our definitions of the good, the true, and the worth-painting are debatable. In these matters, accordingly, we are modest, not presuming to lead, even eager to go along with the deviators, who for aught we know may be on the track of something!

After all, what is abstraction in art but a reach behind appearance toward the inner scheme of things, the mathematical—

> Euclid alone has looked on Beauty bare.
> Let all who prate of Beauty hold their peace.[1]

—the topological, the subconscious sources of design, décor, symbol, arabesque?

This philosophy, inquiring, shy of commitment, definitely

not pragmatic—let us call it a philosophy of Genial Vagrancy—has the merit of openness, not only toward the future but toward novelty in general. It is distrustful of its own intuitions; it conspires with the eternal unfinishedness of school philosophy to make the USA, in matters of culture, feebly docile, standing for nothing, where decisiveness is essential to strength, where native sense speaks with certitude if one would listen, and where,

> . . . brushing debate aside,
> the moral *nose* should be the instant guide.[2]

THE NATIVE STRENGTH OF THE USA IN PUBLIC ACTION

In fields of public action our attitude is different. Here we have an original national strength, and feel it. As an active, geography-conquering, self-organizing folk, we are here at home. In fields of tough and characteristic USA achievement—in industry and labor, in the market place as swappers and traders, in politics and law inheritors indeed from England and the Continent but improvisers to world-wide effect—we are prepared not only to defend our ideas but to teach the world, are we not? Here we know the meanings of Liberty, Equality, Democracy, in practice!

We speak of "free enterprise" not as a theoretical fancy but with proud after*klang* of the immense task of taming the Western stretches, not discounting the earlier immense task of mastering the Eastern seaboard. Look at the stone walls of New England, built of boulders painfully dug out of the reluctant clearings.

Stopping for breath, knocking sweat from his forehead, and leaning on his crowbar, a neighbor, wrestling with an extruding rock in a hayfield remarked: "They say it's arguin' with these fellows that makes us folks so stubborn!" Very likely! But with some native stubbornness to begin with. I take off my hat to the memory of an early settler hereabout, Isaiah Forrest, of whom it is recorded that he "built eight miles of stone wall" during his lifetime. They were men. Working for themselves individually, they also worked for a collectivity, the New England "town" in the New England colony: they and their likes elsewhere built a nation.

This habitat-shaping spirit enters into what we call our "capitalism." Some of its post-Civil-War phases are still within recall. In my boyhood in the eighties there was an office at 91 Lake Street, Chicago, western office of the Cleveland Rolling Mill Company. I used to dangle my small legs over a big chair in that office, over which Uncle Nelson Pratt presided. Barbed-wire fencing had recently been invented. On treeless prairies wooden fences were prohibitively expensive and stone walls could not exist; yet fencing for horses and cattle was necessary. Cleveland Rolling Mills, fencing miles on miles of prairie farms, were "doing well"— so were the farmers. The federal government at Washington had surveyed and mapped that region from the 1820s onward, but there was no wit in Washington to solve the fencing problem—that was a job for private heads—*ergo,* we thought, for private rewards. The *ergo* was not questioned: if somebody got rich, that was as it should be, provided the inventor got his share, which often happened. Robert Frost's poem on the New England theme, "Good fences make good neighbors," holds good in principle for the barbed-wire country, including another of his sentiments, "Something there is that doesn't love" a barbed-wire fence.

Nation-building has meant the building of an economy, of which this boundary-marking activity is a sample, including at every step improvised understandings of what is "fair and right," the economy's market-manners, its (easy or wrangled) employer-employee adjustments, its free field for invention and for patents on ideas. My lifetime spans the arrival of the telephone, bicycle, electric light, transportable electric power, automobile, each one involving large experimentation, swift altering of early models, hence large capital risk, with notable accumulation of wealth at points of success and often elaborate suffering at points of failure. Here (with the aid of free access to natural resources not too promptly marked for public ownership) we witnessed the beginning of eye-popping private fortunes, due in part to the wit of the enterpriser, in part to luck, in part—quite often—to hard playing, and in part to the growing breadth of the market which he certainly did not make.

It is this surge of human wit, energy, courage, grasp (not unmixed with graspingness), shrewdness, in a responsive natural domain, amid a wide community with a common language and a common ethical sense, partly inherited and partly made to fit the occasion, a free-for-all struggle with survival of some-kind-of-fittest—the best and some others—it is this that we designate by the term "capitalism." The economic strength of this nation is its product—a reality, not a debatable cultural standard.

IS "COMMUNISM VERSUS CAPITALISM" A VALID LABEL?

Whatever confidence we have in our economic way of life, let me repeat, is not due to any preconceived theory, economic or other. *We built from life*, not from an ism: we built from common sense, from the problems set by soil, climate, vegetation, resource, and from the neighborly ethics of men who need to co-operate on terms of mutual respect under common pressures and dangers, and with common hopes. There was no Adam Smith in the world when we began, nor any Ricardo, nor any Thomas Jefferson: if the Manchester school of economics expressed any part of our sense of market prices, of labor and capital, that was subsequent and, for us, imperfect. "Capitalism" is a word we never heard until our outlines were well drawn. It is a partial fit, but no more. And misfits in names can become public dangers.

As a convention of current speech, "Communism versus Capitalism" names the basic cleavage in the public life of

mankind today; as a ready handle, the phrase will do, and
we shall use it when convenient. As a guide to the real problems before us, it is profoundly out of joint with the facts.
If we are seriously concerned with actual issues between the
USA and the USSR—and there are such issues—our first
duty is to observe that these terms fail to describe them.

Their failure is obvious, and indeed is often noted; but
our concern is with what is not often noted—the necessity of
this failure. It may be seen at once by way of a simple illustration. An imaginary society of pure Communists, having
everything in common, like Plato's guardians, or some early
Christian commune, or a group of Tolstoian Dukhobors,
could by united efforts set up a working tool-using industry.
The tools, workshops, materials, finished goods would constitute a common capital. They would thus become a *capital-
istic communism*, or a *communistic capitalism*, as you prefer.
The illustration is not fanciful. In the 1870's, General Red-
stone founded in Kaweah Valley in the southern Sierras, a
colony on the scheme of Bellamy's *Looking Backward*. By
labor in which all took part, men and women alike, a fifty-
mile road was built for the export of lumber. The trees and
the road constituted a common capital—until Government
pre-empted the grove and took over the road without compensation. Deprived of its communal capital, the colony dis-
banded; it has been called "the only socialist colony in the
USA which did not die a natural death." For us, it raises the
question whether there can be any such thing as a noncapital-
ist communism. And the answer—if the economy moves beyond the most primitive agricultural handwork—has to
be no.

The corresponding question has to be asked: Can there
be any such thing as a capitalist society without an element
of communism? Again the answer is no: there can be no
civilized economy without a background of community of
goods, and a common concern of the whole for each individ-

ual. This point must be dwelt on. But I state in advance the thesis emerging:

In the world today there is *no pure example either of Communism or of Capitalism:* all actual economies of developed nations are *mixed economies.*

Let us look more closely at the facts.

The economy of the USSR, of no single type, approaches a state capitalism more nearly than an ideal communism. The economy of the USA, largely dependent on capital accumulations, has as its background a vast common-wealth, a public domain, a far-flung system of roads, rivers, harbors, national forests and parks, reserves of natural resources, a shared general welfare (including with an immense credit an immense debt), all severely limiting the possible results of a free-running private competition. Our heavily graduated income tax, as well as a tax on corporate profits, pays into a public purse, implying a compulsory sharing of material fortune. I do not say that either mixture is good or bad; for the moment I simply point out the fact that we have in neither economy a pure example of its professed type.

But I may indicate further that this mixture is inevitable. Karl Marx, while regarding the problem of *distributing* the product of industry as unsolved in the prevailing capitalist economy, gave Capitalism credit for doing well in the problem of *production:* indeed, the theory of economic determinism implies that advances in productive technology become imperative, because of the unremitting pressure of population on consumption. And advances in technology involve increase of capital—no escape.

In point of fact, the situation in Russia is openly avowed. In 1958, under an exchange agreement, an American delegation of nineteen members toured Soviet Union steel works, under the leadership of Edward L. Ryerson, formerly of Inland Steel. They were impressed, reporting among other things that some of the Soviet operations are "superior to

anything known in" the USA. If one asks how this is possible, an answer was given by Secretary of Defense Neil H.
McElroy, who, after stating that the USSR economy was
growing at a rate "roughly twice that of the USA," com-
mented that "Russia is plowing back a larger percentage of
her gross national product than America into capital investment for industrial expansion."[3] The word "capital" is
McElroy's, not Khrushchev's, but the term is correct: there
can be no such thing as a great modern state without commensurate capital. Once we emphasize production, we demand industry; and once we "industrialize" we commit
ourselves to capital and to capital increase.

The phrase "Communism versus Capitalism" is thus a
thoroughly misleading labeling of the issue. There can be no
clear "versus" when each economy has ingredients of both
types. The proportions of the mixture are, of course, very
different in the USA and the USSR; and as the isms identify
themselves with the ingredients on which they place the primary weight, there is still a "versus." But if the issue were
merely one of proportion, it would hardly justify the gravity
we attach to it: there are matters of principle at stake. The
injunction of Confucius is timely: begin by "giving things
their right names."

PATTERNS OF OWNERSHIP, CONTROL, AND MOTIVATION

The important contrast between the economies of the
USSR and the USA certainly does not lie in the *mechanisms*
of production.

In the startling progress of the USSR in recent years in
this field, the processes, materials, and equipment are much
the same as with us. The capital required for plant, materials,
and also for services, is comparable with ours in its ratio to
the net value of the product. It is true that the outlay for
labor and for technical services can be controlled by political
fiat in the USSR, as we cannot control it. But this control is

limited in the USSR, as everywhere, because productivity is keenly sensitive to the morale of the workers.

The obvious contrast lies in who owns the capital. And then, as a corollary of ownership, who controls management, finance, and the distribution of net income from the product. The problem of distribution requires decisions: what fraction of net income is to be marked as profit, or held as reserve, or plowed back into plant-and-growth, or perhaps shared with workers as part producers or as part of the consuming public? In the USSR these decisions are (in effect) made by the State as owner. In the USA they are made—after the State has taken its tax quotas—by the private enterprisers, as owners or as delegates of owners.

As an immediate consequence of this difference, while the *factors* of production are similar in the USSR and the USA, the *motives* of production are widely different. To put it baldly and in the rough: in the USA potential consumption governs production; in the USSR potential production—in the national interest—governs consumption: the consumer takes not what he wants but what the producer supplies. More in detail:

In the USSR, the State as monopolist producer in *all* domestic industries (and in the absence of a brisk foreign trade) shapes the major part of Soviet consumption. Not that the consumer's wishes are forgotten: he is keenly aware of what is *not being produced*, and government, aware of his hopes, becomes paternal-and-maternal administrator of his standard of living to a degree we hardly conceive. The Soviet State has a direct motive to raise that standard, beginning with needs and moving on through comforts and vanities, but with the *dominant motive of national power*, in interest of which the Soviet consumer practices an involuntary austerity. He looks forward to the improvement of his lot, while relating his frugality to the national necessity and to plans well advertised to him, with a measure of confidence based on tangible progress hitherto. The USSR controls production to a proclaimed national plan assumed to be generally accepted.

In the USA, the *national plan*, if one exists, is to the economy as a whole *practically subconscious*. Public necessities and projects claim, indeed, a large share of the citizen's dollar, and involve much private industry. But the characteristic spirit of the USA economy appears after the taxes (authorized in a total package by the citizen's token assent via Congress) are paid.

Here the consumer enjoys the result of a competitive struggle among a multitude of private producers—to supply what, and for what motive? To supply the needs and wishes of which the consumer is aware, plus a spectrum of wishes of which he is unaware but can, by due psychological strategy, *be induced to feel*. The motivation of the producer is, in a word, the profit motive—his own profit, not the nation's, not the consumer's.

The profit motive is legitimate. It is not identical with greed or cupidity. It represents, normally, a sense of contribution, of effort-deserving-reward, identical with that of the farmer rejoicing in a good crop due in part to his efforts and in part to good luck and sunshine which he did not produce. The profit motive does not deserve the slur implied in the phrase "private vices, public benefits." But the proportions of the mixture of self-administered reward-for-services-rendered and common greed are not assignable by law, nor by any economic chemistry. And just because they are not assignable, they constitute the ground on which *humanity as a whole passes judgment on any type of economy as a whole*. It belongs to the honor of the situation that the element of service-rendered shall be dominant, and the element of self-controlled reward be subservient, in due proportion.

This motivation lends at present a peculiar emphasis to the role of the artfully engendered desire. Free enterprise now thrives not alone by devising new satisfactions for known wants, but also by developing new appetites, exploring new wants-and-appeasings, *creating a demand where none existed* by supplying a good which the inert imagination had never conceived—television, perhaps. If private rivalry in these adventurous arts is well aimed—easing our labors, implementing our powers, supplying us with magic carpets of transportation through land, water, air—it can and does produce extraordinary advances in the scope of living. If it lurks at the level of the cynic, the results can be what we see, under the false flag of "giving the public what it wants" in the arts, letters, amusements, addictions. In point of fact, free enterprise *does both things simultaneously:* it builds, and it corrupts. And neither the free State nor the free economy is, per se, capable of distinguishing between the services of the philanthropist and those of the panderer.

The love of liberty, lighting on producer and consumer impartially, offers no solution, and no criterion.

Liberty, taken alone, throws the burden of discernment on the consumer's judgment, the plain integrity of virile human nature sensitive to the note of decay. *Perhaps it should remain there*, the discernment of free men? Admitting State control at the level of the more definable public poisons —narcotics old and new, etc.—the faith in liberty holds toward the more subtle, psychologically feathered, insidious commercial concoctions of free enterprise the principle that *self-limitation is better than authoritative limitation*. And so it is—provided self-limitation takes place.

But what if it does not take place? And what if, with the ideal of liberty, there goes an amiable doctrine of relativity whereby there is no firm standard, no clear line between the honest and the meretricious? Could there be—and is there— a silent, pervasive seduction and softening of the American fiber as an incident of its admirable system?

There is definite clinical evidence that the acme of American prosperity, with its mass access to the newer artifices of

cushioning, has been attended by a pronounced decline in
what psychiatrists refer to as "integration."

A recent paper by Dr. Bertalanffy calls attention to the
correlation of that prosperity with the excessive proportion
of all beds in American hospitals occupied by mental pa-
tients. He comments on the presumption that mental de-
rangement is occasioned less by economic hardship than by
the gropings of affluence, unorganized in their goal.

There is further evidence that the influence of Freudian
psychoanalysis, greater in the USA than elsewhere in the
world, has had not alone the natural result of increased attention to the psychoses resulting from unsatisfied cravings,
but the further result of increasing the psychoses themselves.
There is reason to believe that it is not so much the unsatisfied craving that makes us ill as the anxious *search for an
unsatisfied craving to satisfy,* a morbid inquiry for obscure,
residual longing.

Such residual longing always exists. For there is always
a gap between any current sum of partial satisfactions and the
total fulfillment of any human will: it is this gap which
motivates the continued aspiration toward "happiness," the
Faustian restlessness, or the stimulus of William James'
"ever not quite"! It is a permanent factor in the religious
quest for peace. It is certainly not of itself a specific craving,
such as the sexual impulse emphasized by Freud, or the
libido of Jung. But there is one craving which has its locus
in just this gap—yet seldom noticed by psychiatrists—the
craving for hardship. I see here one factor making for the
persistent return to soundness in the USA. While this taste
for the tough assignment, which drove Richard Byrd to
Antarctica, is still strong among us, the current soft spot
may be considered a temporary aberration. It is there.

CONTRASTS IN ECONOMIC EFFICIENCY

Purely on its economic side, the contrast we are concerned
with, roughly summarized as a contrast in ownership and

direction—in the USSR unitary-and-national; in the USA plural-and-private—reveals certain significant differences for the interests of consumers and producers.

For consumers, the USA setup has large advantages. The increasingly costly experimentation involved in each further step of man's command of nature has hitherto been carried, whether in private or in corporation research laboratories, in the stride of anticipated reward. Applying these results, the broad-front improvement in living standards, calling for the most varied, untrammeled, risk-taking enterprise, has readily found its volunteers. Mass production, with competition, brings the fruits to all doors. The casualties and the shady incidents of exploiting folly, the use of blind-alley lures, moral confusion, esthetic distortion, may in total— if we work through them—be charged to profit and loss as a cost of self-education. The consumer learns what he really wants, and has it.

For the producer—especially the producer of staples— the perspective is naturally different. Our seasoned steel-producers found marked advantages in the USSR setup, among which (strange to say) the first-mentioned was *absence of competition!* "The government-controlled industry did not have the competitive problems of individual American companies." Further, with set quotas, USSR steel-works know well in advance how much to produce in any season; they can work on a year's schedule, with quarterly adjustments. But most conspicuously, for sheer results, Mr. McElroy saw a further advantage not open to the USA: "the Soviet Union can at any time make her 'hard choices' without advance consultation with her people." For them there is no congressional check on postponing the consumer's hope.

For production planning there is a clear advantage, though the quota system has its open invitations to inefficiency. But is the advantage in production, with its unitary thrust free from sidelong glances at numerous competitors,

wholly at the expense of the consumer? Or is it possible that
this consumer accepts the deferment of his hopes with something better than grudging necessity? Is it possible that, in
spite of the publicity pressure of national planning, he
achieves genuine sharing in the national objectives? What
our reporters have described as the low standard of living,
hitherto carefully shielded from outside comment, is now—
if Mr. John Gunther is right—an occasion for some pride, as
token of the people's willingness to abstain, through their
confidence in the long-term purposes of the Presidium. The
sense of a world contest is in the air; and underneath its
traditional tension as a life-and-death struggle, the game
spirit enters the scene. For example, the prosaic business of
steel output gains an emotional backing from the prospect
that before long the USSR's product, with an abundant if
rather low-grade ore, may enter the world market as a direct
competitor with the USA's product—a situation that would
not be lost on the Soviet public.

It is in the nature of the case that consumers in the USSR
are more intelligently involved in the progress of their well-
publicized production efforts than can possibly be the case
with the USA, where production, immensely complex and
varied, remains so largely a private mystery, and the new
models that appear from year to year—so demanding of
forgetfulness of what was yesterday so best and so up-to-date
—are creatures of an almost mechanized art of invention,
commercially profitable as long as the public will bear the
costs of change. Its occasionally important results quickly
become the property not of the USA alone, but *of all lands
capable of the construction, which have been spared the
enormous costs of experiment.*

On this account alone, whatever the advantages of the
central control of the USSR, the world—including the
USSR—could ill spare the dispersed and fertile initiative of
the USA. And if this involuntary world-function of the free
—and prodigal—enterprise system of the USA were recog-

nized as such on all sides, we could consider replacing the "versus" in "USA versus USSR" by some symbol indicating "USA indispensable to, or at least supplementing, USSR"! This suggestion, I submit, is not wholly fanciful: I present it as an aside, but I raise the question seriously whether it is not beginning to be a part of the felt situation. With perhaps a touch of reciprocity in view of certain wastes of competition, now definitely shirked in major business associations.

But the fact remains that the issue is not solely, nor even primarily, one of economic structure and advantage. Perhaps the chief failure of the label "Communism versus Capitalism" is that it presents as economic an issue involving our deepest convictions regarding the normal bond of social and political organization. It is this which gives the opposition its gravity, and leads us to refer to non-Communist regions as "the free world," with the profound concern that will always surround the concept of Liberty.

REVOLUTION AND THE CRISIS OF LIBERTY

The USSR defines itself as a union of republics and also as a dictatorship; we are chiefly aware of the latter character.

Within the economic system, unitary control of production means that the worker cannot choose his ultimate employer —an absence of choice not wholly redeemed by the fact that this employer is "the worker's state." There is no alternative top authority to whom a dissatisfied worker might shift. The Soviet worker has his unions, but no right to strike; his liberty of motion and of contract have been measurably increased by recent decentralization of industry and by newly opened industries, with local shortages of labor. But the comprehensive and detailed nature of State planning carries with it a definite circumscription of opportunity. The hand of authority is upon every functional choice of the Soviet citizen's life.

But let us avoid a prevalent mistake at this point. If we

consider that the contrast is between liberty, on one side, and no liberty, on the other, we are wrong. The Soviet community is indeed regimented; it tightens its belt at State command. The USA community is not regimented: we have rather firm views about tightening our belts at all; but if we are to do so, it shall be with our consent, after strenuous governmental efforts to persuade us of the necessity. This contrast—let us say of govern-most versus govern-least—is real; but what it signifies requires two further reflections:

First, that the USSR is a *product of revolution*. All revolution is, in its nature, a *drive for freedom*. Camus puts it well: "Freedom, 'that terrible word inscribed in the chariot of the storm,' is the motivating principle of all revolutions."[4] We should know something about revolutions; we conducted one, not two centuries ago. We were driving for freedom— freedom, of course, *from* something. So with Russia: there was a bondage to be thrown off. Not precisely a bondage of serfdom—technically abolished in 1861; nor yet precisely a bondage such as Marx denounced, subservience to dominantly industrial capital—Russia was still merely toying with industry. But the whole flowering and lordship of the nation was still squeezed from a miserable laboring class which, incapable of free movement, was also incapable of either effectively remonstrating against or respecting its overdom. This overdom, ornamental, proud, notable in the arts, was incompetent in practice, habitually humiliated in wars with lesser powers, recently with Japan, and now in 1917 in retreat from the beleaguered Germans! The exploited Russian masses could indeed be herded into spiritless armies; but these armies, feeling shame, could also be fired in a cause of their own, could hold the secret and the sinews of revolt! There was, I say, a bondage to be free from. And *that* bondage, at least, has been thrown off.

The Romanoffs are gone, the nobility and the old intelligentsia, the ruling classes and those of liberal persuasion who might have ruled and ruled well, those of the Dumas and the

Kadets, émigrés in number enriching many lands, noble souls many of them, none better on earth—all are gone. The broom has swept over-clean. But it has swept. The private economic taskmaster is today hard to find; the USSR has its steel plants but no U.S. Steel Corporation; its sales-places, but no private merchandise chains; its state banks, but no stock market. Its landlords have vanished; and the large-scale farmer, the kulak, pinched to death by Stalin on a larger scale—five million or so—is replaced by the collectives and state farms. Let us say that *the negative freedom sought* by the Revolution, freedom *from, is largely achieved.*

Negative freedom, it is true, is not enough. A state must live, think, and act. *Revolution is decapitation;* and it takes time to grow a new head if, indeed it can be done at all. The freed community, shorn of its sustaining habits and deferences, can keep its hard-won freedom only by a rigorously imposed order, till the new head grows its nervous system and the new heart its coronary arteries out of plain cellular tissue! Neither Marx nor Lenin held out hopes for the speedy completion of the new social organism, conceived as in struggle—especially during its infanthood—with a hostile world. Meantime—as Stalin read the ambiguous Marxian program —there must be an intensification of state control preparatory to the apocalyptic moment when the State itself could begin to wither away. What, then, of this preliminary dictatorship: is it not a renewed slavery? Is it perhaps an exchange of many minor taskmasters for the Gigantic Taskmaster? Many an observer, many a penetrating thinker, had interpreted the course of history this way: revolution as a path to liberty devours its own children. Camus, who knows revolution better than most of us, sees this catastrophe as inevitable. He touches its logic with precision:

> Every form of collectivity, fighting for survival, is forced to accumulate instead of distributing its revenues.

It postpones justice for a later date in the interests of power. . . . Revolution, in the dilemma into which it has been led by its bourgeois opponents and its nihilist supporters, is nothing but slavery.[5]

This dialectical reversal, this nemesis of the high hopes of freedom-from, sufficiently illustrated in the political crimes and police terrors of the initial struggle of the USSR for survival, extending through the Stalin period, appears to confirm our usual judgment of its regimented life as, if not in Camus' drastic term a "slavery," yet literally devoid of liberty.

It is here that our second reflection must enter.

Regimentation may be a one-way or a two-way affair. Beside the one-way regimentation of tyranny, there is a regimentation that is demanded *by its subjects*. In any fight for survival—assuming the privates are for the fight—what they want is no gentle looseness of rein but a strict and determined command: recall the traditional preference among midshipmen for the captain who "keeps a taut ship." His rigor is a necessary instrument—not for *his* purposes but for *his and theirs*, a tool of affirmative freedom for all concerned.

Whether in any given case regimentation is tyranny or liberty depends not on the structure of authority but on the factual picture of purpose: tyranny is regimentation *for the purpose of the tyrant;* liberty calls for authority—possibly for regimentation—in the execution of a *common* purpose.

Of which type is the regimentation in the USSR?

Perhaps of both types, in process of change? In Soviet theory, dictatorship is not concealed but professed: the ultimate governing power is concentrated, presumably for the benefit of no one class, old or new, but for the ideal goal in which, with the classless society, the State with its police apparatus evaporates. To what extent this theory corresponds with the facts (and Djilas' comments are pertinent)

I have no direct means of judging. What we can all observe is that the external conditions calling for the internal co-hesion and discipline of the Soviet state—the stresses of what Camus calls "the bourgeois opponents"—persist in the mutual demarcations of the cold war, frequently invoked, no doubt, by government propaganda for the express purpose of sustaining the public will-to-be-regimented. We aid this process by our stereotyped assumption of unmitigated Soviet tyranny.

My own opinion is that the ingredient of tyranny, still present in spots, is on the way out; that the point of greatest dictatorial stress is passed, and—barring war—will continue to diminish; and that a substantial proportion of the public is affirmatively with the government's visible and tangible objectives—allowing for much inertia in the non-Party masses. Just to this extent, the Soviet people expect and welcome regulation (reserving the human right to protest when it hurts too much); and just to this extent are *free because they are regimented.* This, I say, is my guess, not my dogma; and if I am right, the element of affirmative liberty present in the mixture will be increased by our recognition of it.

THE PATTERN OF LIBERTY

Whether this guess is on the mark or not, of one thing I am sure: no one who fails to see that liberty at times actually calls for regimentation has the slightest chance of under-standing either the nature of democracy or the major move-ments of history.

And I say with regret that blindness at this point, danger-ous at this moment, is a prevalent weakness in the USA. It pervades our misconceptions of education. It sustains the common prejudice that there is more liberty in disorder than in order, more in separation than in union, more in dissent than in agreement, more in cacophony than in harmony, more in private property than in common property.

The truth does not lie in swinging over to the opposite prejudice: holding with Hegel or Spinoza that there is full freedom only in the glad consent to necessity; that liberty lies solely in order, union, agreement, harmony, the love of law as embodied reason. Reasonableness is certainly an ingredient in liberty; but there is also a creative freedom which gives laws to reason, and may take a temporary form of the arbitrary—perhaps the lawless.

Liberty, as I shall later undertake to show, requires an *organizing of these opposites*—the powerful order and the powerful innovation. For our present argument it is sufficient that we recognize the inner complexity, the occasional paradox, of liberty. It is no simple essence, for which a hearty hurrah settles everything. Its inner diversity is part of the puzzledom that continues to invade our economic problems. The ideal of free enterprise is inseparable from the American heritage, a part of our world function: but this liberty does not imply a preference for the chaotic in production, nor a condemnation of all proposals for authoritative order.

It becomes clear that the contrast we seek to define is not a purely economic contrast in ownership and control, not Capitalism versus Communism, nor yet the Free World versus a wholly Unfree World. It is a difference in the *pattern of liberty*, together with a divergence in the philosophy that defines Liberty.

Of the pattern of liberty, note as a matter of course that the liberty that *may become* regimentation, the liberty of obedience to law and to the State's purpose, is present in the USA as well as in the USSR. It is the right and duty of each citizen to serve with his own life and fortune the existence of the republic. The radical difference is that in the USA *external hostility has not been habitually assumed*, and the closing of ranks has therefore been seldom called for (except when a new-bred fear of subversion throws a palsy over the

American citizen's normal freedom of speech, writing, travel). In the USSR, however, the sense of being on the defensive in a hostile world has been unremitting, and the corresponding call for the over-all loyalty incessant.

As a result, in the USSR the wider liberties of the citizen are drawn into the pattern of the economic process: they are for the most part concentrated in the governmental drive, whereas in the USA, liberty lights first on individual destinies and choices: we have a *pluralist versus a collectivist pattern of liberty*. Among the current isms, the most approximate labels seem to be Individualism versus Collectivism.

But the pattern in the USSR includes for each citizen a share in the usual freedoms of civilized communities, spelled out in detail in the Russian Constitution of 1936, with further additions in the UN Universal Declaration of Human Rights, in whose formulation the Soviet member of the sub-committee entrusted with the drafting took an active part.[6]

We are driven to the conclusion that the patterns of liberty, identical *in profession* at the top and at the bottom —at the level of State purpose and at the level of individual rights—diverge as widely as they do in practice partly for historical reasons, but chiefly for reasons of fundamental philosophy.

For the USA, individual rights come first in authority, and governments exists to secure them. We allow ourselves the pragmatic boast that free enterprise "works well"; but its first justification is that it *ought to be*—which is why it works. Hence the freedoms we care about under the name of free enterprise—the right to choose one's field of action (shall I say "the right to work"?), to gain and own property, to devise and invent, to form companies with the (bourgeois?) interest of gain, and with the sportsman's readiness to take loss for misjudgment and folly—these rights belong first not to the economy, but to the moral ideal of a self-developing human life. And whenever this broad liberty is clipped or threatened—whether under the name of Socialism,

or the Welfare State, or the Labour Party, or the Planned
Economy, or the New Deal—the free enterprise spirit scents
danger, and sees red, and counter-acts.

The USSR, having a preformed social ideal, is actually
more consciously philosophical in its attitude than the USA,
whose nation-building spirit, as I have pointed out, was
shaped in pioneering experience long before it was expressed
in theory. The USSR has the rather cumbersome advantage
of authoritative scripture, and therefore an orthodoxy, well
shaped prior to experience, and attempting to guide an experience of revolution, never fully tamable to formulae. But
however rough-hewn in the struggle, the main thread of its
philosophy is sure: that history is shaped by the development
of economic techniques and necessities—the ultimate world
powers are in this sense material, not moral: the "rights of
man" are desiderata, not prior demands on either law or
economy. No one can doubt that Marx himself was deeply
moved by the injustices he saw in the industrial situation;
but, like Spinoza, he judged the capitalist order as a part of
the reigning necessity of history, destined to bring about its
own reversal by way of the climactic excess of its own principle: this is the "dialectical" necessity.

We continue our inquiry with a look at the foundations of
the notion of rights.

IV

BASIC RIGHTS IN THE
LIGHT OF EXPERIENCE

THE language of "rights of man," firmly embedded in the original documents of several western nations, especially of the USA, is inescapable in the common speech of all peoples. Where is the tongue in which there is no equivalent for "standing up for one's rights"? Yet at the same time this assertion is challenged or denounced by certain jurists in all nations that have jurists: as a basis for legal theory it has the discomforts attending all "axioms" presenting themselves as absolute principles. Experience finds them awkward: an "unalienable" right to life? Yes, but after a few murders? Our own reservations about fixed principles are peculiarly vigorous in contemporary American legal thought: Jefferson's absolutes have few defenders among us. The fact remains that we fall into the language of rights in spite of ourselves: there is no good substitute.

THE LEGAL STATUS OF THE RIGHTS OF MAN

We are much disposed to agree with Pashukanis, the great and unhappy Russian jurist (who had to recant in 1936 doctrines he had published in 1926), that all law arises, like British Common Law, in experience; but we have to add that *what experience reveals is a set of rights*, and that Pashukanis' own words imply as much. He saw the market place

as the original law-teacher; here men reach agreements and
make contracts, which law arises to protect. In their bargaining, both buyer and seller assume, says Pashukanis, that
"a man has a right to do what he will with his own." A right!
Embedded in the very notion of *property*. If there were no
property respected as such, how could there be a market
place instead of a raw scramble for possession? The notion
of property marks one beginning of civilization. It is a
notion as essential to the order of the USSR as to the whole
meaning of free enterprise. Property is the goal post, without which there could be no game. Consider the meaning of
property.

PROPERTY, PRIVATE AND COMMON

We recall that Locke's triad of rights-of-man is not identical with that of Jefferson: Locke speaks of "life, liberty,
and property." And property, for Locke, means *private
property*. And private property is property from which
others—even the State, under ordinary conditions—can be
excluded (*jus prohibendi*); property which one can use as
he will, or abuse and destroy if he will (*jus utendi* and *jus
abutendi*); and property which—just because of this absolute ownership—one can sell, or give away absolutely
(*jus disponendi*) and feel that he has truly made a gift.

Thus interpreted, property could be described as a small
realm of kingship—of complete control (which is why
human beings can never be property). Its significance is in
this quality of control, not in its extent; and because of this
limitation of extent, it can confer upon innumerable human
beings the qualitative experience of being ruler over a bit
of Nature—as builder, shaper, artist—or even as recluse.
But this relation to Nature is natural: it is a realization of
the human calling to be master of the inanimate, to find himself in that capacity, to discover his own quality as reflected
in the thriving or nonthriving, the beauty or ugliness, the
order or disorder of the small segment of matter subject to

his will. Private property, in this sense, is a genuine province of liberty, and a necessary factor in arriving at human maturity.

It is equally essential that for each person there be a region of *common property:* indeed, man comes into a world of common property as he comes into a family, and his private possessions are at first, like children's toys, tentative entrustments, withdrawable in the common interest. They move toward a mature absoluteness, but never reach it except in legal abstractions. For the more tangible property is, the more surely it has location in a physical world; and the space of our physical situation is both infinite and incurably communal. However much I own, I have a next-door neighbor: he is "mine," and by the same sign I am "his." Every propinquity is full of interactions as pervasive as radiation, and seldom as silent. There is no ideally private property except in sleep.

It has been said that the USSR "is the first state in modern history to have declared in its constitution that it is founded on the basic principle of the public ownership of property."[1] If so, we shall find that in the USSR, which certainly claims title to all land, much public property is "affected by a private interest," just as in the USA we find that much private property and enterprise are "affected by a public interest." So far as the shadow of public concern falls over what we call private property—as in the famous Slaughterhouse Cases of earlier days—it will cease to be true that a man can "do what he will with his own" in any absolute sense. If you own animals, you are not at liberty to starve them, though you harm no living person. And it is equally true that the shadow of private concern may fall upon a public claim.

In Yosemite, in 1907, there were vanishing remnants of an Indian tribe. Near our camp was an empty cabin; an Indian of the Yosemite tribe had died there within the year. The cabin contained a store of acorns, some clothing, a few tools, a rifle, all usable and useful to the poor remnants of the tribe. Why did they remain there untouched? After a man's death, his personal possessions are taboo to everybody for a year: the habit of private use conveys a post-death sanctity toward which the tribe will hold itself in check. This primitive feeling, the inhibition of public intrusion on private ownership, carries over into all civilized societies: the Englishman's home, his castle!

What we can say without qualification is that for each human being some experience with common property and some with private ownership is essential to a normal growth to personal maturity. Property law, everywhere, must be based not alone on economic utility but on the moralities of normal human fulfillment—useful because right.

If this is the case, every actual economic system will find itself under pressure, as by a semiphysical necessity, to find room for *both types of property.* What do we find? On the one hand all extant Ownership societies are compelled by widening recognitions of what property is "affected by a public interest" to check the private exploiting of natural resources, and remind self-enclosed owners everywhere of a latent "eminent domain." Even an intangible like natural beauty is finding means to defend its communal status in the USA as against the drive of the blatant billboard.

On the other hand, all extant Communal societies are driven, not alone by the primitive "instinct of appropriation"—as irrefutable as a dog's claim to his bone—nor by the "magic of ownership" which, transforming property by art, transforms the owner, but by an equally rooted need for the rhythmic swing from fellowship toward loneliness and privacy (there's a magic of solitude). These societies are driven, I say, to alter their collective-farming plans to the extent of providing "home plots" and to revise their communal domestic architecture in order to make place for the mine-not-yours requirement of a healthy domestic and individual mentality. In the new suburbs of Stalingrad small homes are being built, Mr. Harriman reports,[2] by aid of government loans, on individual designs, which "seem to reflect the yearning of the owners for individual self-expression, and above all, privacy."

It is thus not by argument, nor by concessions to the opponent, but by the quiet workings of experience on one's home soil, that ideologies, let me say, *concrete* themselves, find room for their own antitheses *without dropping their theses,* and so, by a tacit dialectic, with all banners flying, effect a degree of *rapprochement.* Property in the USA and property in the USSR, let me say, tend not to identity of meaning, but toward mutual understanding: they converge. There remain differences as to the kind of property that is allowable, and as to the extent of property and of the power which property represents.

LIBERTY AS ABSOLUTE AND SELF-CURBING

Nothing is more important for our self-judgment than to understand the self-curbing nature of Liberty, whether in the economic sphere or elsewhere.

Liberty is an inner life working outward in numerous ways of action. In its outward expression it is not a single right but a cluster of rights, including, with the freedom of enterprise we are now discussing, freedom of speech, press, religion, association. All such outer freedoms are rooted in the inward freedom of thought and conscience. This *inward freedom is absolute,* because thought and conscience *can only exist as free;* and no outer compulsion, no police state, can ever find them or trace them to their hidden springs to arrest or question or banish or destroy or compel them to be other than they are. No outer freedom can be absolute in this sense. All are conditional and any one can be curbed by the State. But my present point is that each outer freedom *curbs itself,* in order to realize the inner freedom from which it springs. In our present instance, if liberty of the economic man's self-

interested struggle for power through wealth had an un-
checked scope, nobody would be satisfied, not even the top
survivors, individual or corporate. When self-interest ran
its fairly free course, in the early years of the Industrial
Revolution in England, it was not labor alone that demanded
the Reform Bills of 1831: it was a good part of the nation,
including not a few of the factory interests.

The self-curb is due to the fact that individual "rights"
in their nature *universalize themselves*. A "right" of property
taken as a private perquisite, satisfying greed, ceases to be
a right and becomes a mere fact of power. Hence the successful free-enterprise individual, however justly proud of his
contribution to public good (like a self-willed bee in Mande-
ville's *Fable*), finds himself obliged to look around, think
whether the rules of the game are perfect, examining his
situation under such other heads as Equality or Justice.

I mention Justice and Equality together. Not that justice
necessarily calls for equality, on the contrary, our belief in
competition, which is meaningless unless some pull ahead of
the others, implies that the game is such as to show which
one or ones *deserve* to win. If there is cheating, or a large
ingredient of luck, or a bad set of rules, the worst man may
win; but since the rules were worked out by experience, there
is a presumption of a certain average justice in the winning
and hence in the losing. It is not equality of result that
justice demands, but equality of opportunity and fair play:
given these, it is the significant measurement of unequal
merit that is just.

At the same time, unlimited inequality does raise the question of justice. We have accustomed ourselves to magnificent
differences in personal wealth, and take a certain pride in
ignoring the gulfs that separate the extremes: our democrat
eyes the plutocrat with toleration and says of him, if he is a
good sort, regardless of the disadvantages of wealth, "A
man's a man for a' that"—his excess may be overlooked if
he himself ignores the chasm!

There is nothing wrong in wealth-difference: there would be something radically wrong if the existing rules of acquisition registered no difference between capacity and incapacity, application and neglect, service and nonservice. But there remains a query against the limitless accumulation, if only because there are limits to any man's power to use or administer, as well as to "earn." If our successful brother says, "I earned it," we raise the question, "Did you then create this broad land and open market which made you what you are?" The answer is fated: there is no such thing as a self-made man; no wealth is "just" in the sense of having been created by the owner, in independence of the given setting of his activity. All earning is in an unearned world! We cannot eliminate, nor do we wish to eliminate the element of "fortune" in fortune-making: it can be a happy aspect of the odd world we live in, provided we recognize that the differences of fortune in the upper brackets are relatively independent of justice, and *unimportant except for the uses made of them.*

It is at the other end of the scale that we most firmly question the justice of system-begotten inequality. When need becomes poverty, and poverty becomes destitution, a public concern enters which is not a matter of charity. We say to the losing brother, "However your faults enter the picture —your idleness, wastrelsy, stupidity, refusal to fit—there is a limit below which you shall not fall." Losses may be just, but indigence is unjust, because it closes the way to recovery. The ancient principle, "From him that hath not shall be taken away even that which he hath," accurate as a factual picture of the mercilessness-on-principle of pure enterprise, is deficient in the wider justice which recognizes a continuing right to a new start, and to decent subsistence.

We have here another call for clarity as to the meaning of our easily-spoken ideals. Liberty, yes; Equality, yes; both together, impossible. And the puzzle enters directly into the perilous world situation.

TENSION BETWEEN LIBERTY AND EQUALITY

It was Leslie Stephen who most vividly reminded our democratic age that Liberty and Equality are incompatible. In the economic field, Liberty is pertinent primarily to Production, Equality primarily to Distribution. Marx and his followers incline to separate the two: from every one according to his ability, to everyone according to his need. (And human needs are far more comparable than human abilities.) But the separation is unworkable. Suppose we go all out for the attractive ideal of equality in distribution: no rich, no poor, no upper-middle-lower "classes" in terms of income or wealth—a complete realization of the human joy-in-brotherhood unbroken by gulfs of status-in-market-values. What becomes of the incentive to rise, yes, even of the incentive to *produce?* Incentives are differentials.

In pioneering conditions, which thank God are always with us somewhere, there is no problem of incentives and not much of equality. The omnipresent concern for dear life, family and neighbors, and the mastery of forest, stream, wild life and winter throws an immediate brotherhood and equality over the scene. Except for certain phases of army life, this is the purest fraternity men ever know, and fraternity is equality—each involved in all. Capitalism is also present: if a man has an extra-good rifle, or scythe blade, or breeding bull, it is up to him how much or how little he lends it. And nowhere does native inequality of intelligence, resource, persistence make more immediate marks on the differential picture of a man's "place"—his property. But this is mixed with the other inequality we call luck; and when it comes to the common perils and the hard-hitting individual disasters, there is an immediate sharing of fortune and mutual help: the ultimate equality in the total venture shows its head. Every man's surplus becomes a common fund: in the conflict with Nature we are comrades, equals.

INCENTIVES: THE WELFARE STATE

It is when the economy becomes highly technical and impersonal that the notions of equality and incentive split apart. The systematic attempt to equalize distribution almost automatically lowers production.

As the London *Economist*, in view of England's continuing experiment in planned economy, has put the matter: "Under the Welfare State, everybody is deprived of the farmer's cudgel (result varies directly with effort) and also the farmer's carrot. It can give no reward and threaten no punishment. Nobody stands to gain by effort, and nobody stands to lose by lack of it." And as a result, a leader of the British Labour Party is quoted by Whiting Williams as saying, in regard to the expectation that "every worker, as part-owner, would give his best to his job . . . We have been greatly disappointed. Instead of the expected profits, our railroads, mines, and other nationalized industries have run up deficits running into many, many millions of pounds . . . the working man has let us down!"[3] Perhaps not the workingman himself has let them down, but rather an artificially equalized return, together with a premium on moderation of effort by each, to spread the good wage-fund to all.

This reaction is not limited to the Welfare State: within our own free-enterprise economy, the labor-union movement conducts a limited experiment in equalizing incomes, conceived in the first place, I believe, in a genuine spirit of brotherhood within the union. That (informal and almost spontaneous) experiment consists in easing the effort of each, so that the total job will provide work for the maximum number of workers. No one who has not been a member of a working gang—as I was for a time in San Francisco in the months following the disaster of 1906—can appreciate the naturalness of this "care of each for all, and of all for each" within the union. Looking at a measurable phase of

labor effectiveness over a number of years presents some
startling data. In 1906, a bricklayer's daily stint for straight
work was 1500 bricks per day. What is it now? New England
may not be up to date on these matters; but I hear whispers
of 750 or less. And I personally know masons in this neighborhood who evade the union régime in order to be free to
give full value for wage received—the core of soundness in
any economic system. The opposing principle, evident in
featherbedding, and the steady diminution of the working
day, in complete negation of the spirit of workmanship in
production, is also wholly contrary to the natural temper
of the American workman—there is no better workman in
the world. It is due to his concern, through the union, for
the spread of jobs, as the specter of unemployment looms
ahead because of technical improvements and automation.

As long as unemployment remains an unsolved problem,
within our free enterprise system, there will be an artificial
clash of interests as between the natural co-operators Labor
and Employer: management rightly insisting on increase of
productivity for increase of wage; labor concerned for tenure
and continuity for all, and hence unnaturally averse to spurs
and measures for increased per-man production. There
creeps into the situation the unwelcome ghost of the Marxist
doctrine of class war, which we justly refuse to recognize: the
clash is there; it is not due to anybody's ill will, whether
of labor or management; it is an artefact of the system. And
while labor, *faute de mieux*, resorts at times to the back-
handed devices no one wants, responsibility falls back on the
community as a whole. In spite of our strong preference for
a self-adjusting economy, we are obliged to invoke community concern for the fair participation of all in the necessities and in the common welfare-advance.

Here the ideal of equality finds its valid meaning: the
equal dignity of men of good will; their equal consideration
(not equal share) in distributing the total product on *principles to be determined by agencies of the whole*, rather than

he equality we stand for
al identity of income; it
als of reward, as natural
es not decide for us what
ution remains unsolved.

roborates this result. The
tted as a humanly neces-
d spurring, productivity.
at is common knowledge.
n income tax, graded ac-
ne; it exempts the lowest
summit than thirteen per
acceptance of inequality;
urements here and there,
s for the rarer types of
Stakhanovism, piecework
own; but bonuses are fre-
he efficiency of milkmaids
to mothers who give birth

f the USSR opposes wide
most no nonworkers living
inherited fortunes. There
ar artists, novelists, musi-
of managers of industrial
earch, officers of govern-
ment: these are all for actual functions in the ongoing life
of the nation. The proposition "everybody labors" comes
close to the fact. And there is of course no private employing
class whose possible exploiting temper could renew revulsion
against these functional inequalities.

It might be possible to formulate a set, not so much of
fixed principles as of desiderata, in which the USA and the
USSR could concur, in some such terms as these:

No fixed over-all equality of reward, canceling incentive;

No destitution within the reach of community aid;

No extreme group inequalities of income, creating social chasms, and inviting functionless indulgence;

No individual accumulation without corresponding responsibility.

ENTERPRISE AND THE GAMUT OF REWARD

There would be wide differences of interpretation, especially of the second pair of these desiderata. In the USSR there is no legal limit to personal accumulation, though facilities of investment outside of government bonds are limited. In the USA there is also no limit, and most conceive it as part of our national lure of "opportunity" that there should be none; the more so since accumulation, with us, is usually largely in terms of securities that involve the owner with the business community, and discourage that epitome of idle luxury, the "bloated bondholder," the bourgeois *bête noir* of Communist abhorrence. We are to some extent preserved from the corruption of Veblen's "conspicuous waste," not by the economic system, but by a traditional and temperamental taste for labor. In contrast to a maxim left by Jowett, Master of Balliol ("for statesmen and others"), "Never drudge," we believe that every man should master his own drudgery by going through it, as one destined head of Standard Oil of New Jersey, after his Cornell degree, put on jeans and went to work in the oil fields. This is an unlosable element of our instinctive democracy; and an understanding of labor through participation is a national strength able to act as ballast to a considerable overspread of financial sail.

With this proviso, in contrast to the USSR, we believe in *wide differences of personal fortune*, corresponding to the wide differences among men in function, responsibility, and capacity for administering a complex property in such wise as to do credit to the human power to create beauty in the mastery of matter. We cannot compel men *by law* to use

wealth in such a way as to honor human nature—it is in the
nature of property that it can be abused; we can only maintain the silent censorship of indulgence, folly, decadence,
and know that the survival of our way of life depends on
what free men customarily do with their resources.

Whether we achieve *justice* in distribution is a question
we must duly consider. In the rough, we trust to a fair system of property law, which tends to "render every man his
due" by giving him a chance to show what his due is. The
hidden differences among men we believe to be very great—
to the advantage of all—including the differences in imagination, in creating the picture of liberal human living. We
accept as a highly imperfect measure of these differences the
gamut of tangible services: in the business world, services to
companies, corporations, boards, councils, actively competing, combining, splitting, reuniting under the management
of heads commensurate with the interests involved. The economic strength of the nation is made up largely by its wealth
in these heads: they do not live to themselves alone.

For their success, they must apprehend, not alone the
nation's complex of enterprises, but the world complex; our
changing status depends much on their world sagacity or un-
sagacity. Are they equal to the load? No: no one could be.
Are they disinterested in their advice to the country? Not
entirely, or let me say not unanimously—they supply the
nation with an immense amount of honest counsel, from the
standpoint of a specialized phase of experience; we cannot
expect pure wisdom. And we are aware of the peril to our
policy from the circumstance that the total mental power of
"business" in the USA today exceeds the total mental power,
in terms of the mastery of world-affairs, of the nonbusiness
political nation. It is our fault if we do not supplement their
invaluable services by a completer philosophy. As it is, our
future as a nation depends largely on the moral orientation
of "business," of which I shall have more to say. But for
the present question, "Does justice sanction the considerable

differences in income in the USA?" I should say—up to the
present time and simply as an abstract proposition—yes.
Does justice require an upper limit of personal wealth? The
answer must be, "Of course": endless wealth is meaningless;
and no man has a moral right to more than he can wisely use;
but what that limit is depends on the man, not on a prescrib-
able statute. If we remember that an impersonal system,
based on a reasonable law of property and contract, can in
no case pretend to do justice to the intangible merits of the
human heart, our gamut of wealth-difference, admitting certain weird anomalies, is not extreme.

THE RESIDUAL ISSUE OF JUSTICE

The foregoing comment is subject to two reservations:

First, that all wealth has an unearned increment in its
creation. As we have observed, it is the nation which helps
make the wealth, never the man alone: the nation, its extent
and its liberties, however his "right," are not of his own
providing.

Second, that all wealth is outlined by what we call, with
perfect precision, "fortune." And law, for the sake of order,
must in our economy protect the fortune—the lucky break
—with the deserved achievement. We cannot objectively
separate the element of luck from the element of solid service:
the psychological implications of this mixture are far-reaching, and move history.

For those that gaze at fortune may learn from it either
the honor of service or the gambler's hope, or a mixture of
both. It is a question of fact whether for our American public
"getting rich" is a part of our working ideal of the good
life, and one ingredient of our love of "liberty," as a right to
enter a wide-open lottery for the highest stakes. For those
at home, and for those that seek us from abroad, the "land
of opportunity" may mean chiefly the open chance for a
good break that might set one beyond care, limitation, even
labor, a providential union of intelligent courage with the

secret arbiters of luck. From this point of view, the men who get ahead are not necessarily the able: they are the lucky, the shrewd, perhaps the sly—objects of envy, or perhaps even of resentment.

On the normal level, this means the entrance into the economic system of an element of adventure, which I believe plays a considerable part in the psychology of the labor force.

We need feel no surprise if labor's imagination finds a certain regular "earning" a fairly prosaic outlook. Its plea for justice may be, subconsciously, a wish for the game and its chances. To keep up a due excitement in the round of life must there not be a wide gamut of possibility for each worker —something between the income of a TV star, a Texas oil magnate who "struck it rich," a baseball indispensable, down to that of a dull old college president? Factory labor lives always in the down-risk of loss of job, cushioned by union and other insurances; but the up-risk—the gamble and the prize, something beyond mere security—that is missing. Factory labor has not even the risk-and-enterprise element in farm life, still the most natural of all occupations, an eternal game with weather and soil and seed and stock, and yet with a sobering cause-and-effect relation between effort and accomplishment.

With this understandable factor of discontent with the monotonous and safe, we can understand that justice is not a sufficient ideal. And the movement upward, in equipment for living, becomes not a reversible phase but a mental fixation, a regularized substitute for the game-and-prize excitement:

> Count that year lost whose low descending sun
> Sees from the Company no nice fat Package won!

Expectation begins, as always in human nature, to constitute a right. Correspondingly, a downturn, always possible in a game, would be a wrong, Psychology has its own logic; and I know from experience that the temper I am here depicting is not purely speculative. On confessing to a worker's group in San Francisco, in 1919, that I had come to the University of California in 1906 for $1000 a year, I was told that this was clear proof that I belong to "the servile class"; for "There's not a guy in this room that would work for a thousand bucks a year": no visible inducement—too tame!

I do not regard this craving for the game element as re- proachable—it is part of the American atmosphere. I say only that we must distinguish it from a concern for justice. And it borders upon a materialism of motive more earth- bound than that of the USSR, whose workmen have a na- tional cause to scrimp for. American labor has its own latent joy in workmanship and pride in production, its own capac- ity to relate its efforts to national ends—*provided the na- tional ends are discernible in the total temper of its industry.* If the industry as a whole has no aim beyond its own income, labor could not be expected to hold a higher goal. Let gain- at-all-costs become the ruling ambition of business, then the USA is indeed weak in a vital spot, and poor in the midst of riches.

The test will come when we now look at the moral fabric of our public life, a matter essential to our own strength in world affairs, and also to our judgment of other nations, and to the possibility of an effective international law.

V

OUR DOUBLE
MORALITY

I SPEAK of the moral fabric of our public life. I refer not alone to business, but also to our political groupings and understandings—parties, congresses, courts—and our social institutions, dependent as they all are on the mutual confidence among members and on a certain integrity of their corporate purpose. Their moral fabric is sometimes spoken of as "morale," the firmness and fire of that common purpose. But the "moral fabric" also implies personal reliability of the individual members, their "morals" in the usual sense.

It has been frequently observed of late that the moral tension of the USA—a vague quality like the "atmosphere" of a place, but quite discernible—is relaxed, lacking focus and serious drive, as compared with the temper of collective resolve common in the USSR, in schools, farms, workshops. We have ourselves been speculating on the subject of morale for a half-century in special fields, first of military units—their discipline, fighting fervor—then of labor groups, athletic teams, nations at war.[1] But the morale of a people at peace is equally significant: no morale, no strength for any common undertaking—no national strength. And while morale is not identical with morality, *a divided morality is fatal for morale.* Let us go to the roots:

67

PERSONAL MORALITY AND GROUP LOYALTY

Our notions of "morality" are mainly personal, draped around familiar precepts of behavior calling on us, from childhood up, to check the free run of natural impulses likely to make us a nuisance to others, the burden of the second five of the Ten Commandments: "Thou shalt not . . ."

But as one moves beyond the family circle, there is another morality everyone encounters. He discovers that the numerous groups-for-doing-things—as distinct from the central group for living together—groups of whatever size or texture from the boys' gang to the political party—have a code of their own, a code which begins and ends with an expectation not only of deference but of co-operation, an affirmative shaping of one's self to the group plans and efforts, a "Thou shalt . . ." for which later the term "loyalty" will be used. This reshaping begins, not with a set of rules, but with a *feeling of partial identification* of self with group, inclining the member to spend himself for the well-being of the group.

If one's group is in straits, one feels better if he hurts himself—more or less—on behalf of the ongoing corporate life with which his own life has become partly identified.

In any case, loyalty implies an intimate sense of *unity of purpose* with the group: a disloyal act, even a deception or silent reserve of the truth, disturbs the integrity of that inner sense. Royce, who has done much to give loyalty its due place in the list of virtues, used to say—thinking chiefly of the friendship group of two or more—that the disloyalty which destroys a "We" is as truly murder as is the killing of a person. It is not simply one's duty that is involved: one's happiness is involved also, since life with the group becomes part of one's at-home-ness in the world, and of one's self-realization. The code of loyalty therefore *runs deep*. And as distinct from the personal Commandments, Thou shalt not injure thy neighbor, it is affirmative: it calls for positive contribution and service.

But groups also are living things, and like persons they have their wills to live. They have also their ambitions and perils. The sentiment of moral identity naturally accompanies the adventures of the group—its cold wars, if you like, in which much of the courage, swift wit, resource of the individual are called out. Without these, we should be the poorer by much of the story-life of the Scottish clans, of Sicily, of the exploring, raiding, foraying groups of our own early history, not to mention the exploring spirit animating the tangled enterprises of boys' gangs in all lands, with fantastic loyalties within and fantastic defiances without. In all of this, the definite engagement, or commitment, of the individual's purposes with or to those of the group are parts of the eliciting of his powers, his character, his self-judgment.

GROUP CONTESTS AND THE CLASH OF CODES

But these group interests, especially those involving the destinies and ambitions of the group, are likely to fall into competition, possibly mortal conflict, with the interests of other groups. What, then, does loyalty require? Can a member retain intact that personal code requiring him to refrain from injuring others? If he is called upon to deceive, to aggress upon, to steal from, possibly to kill, members of the hostile group in order to protect his own, he finds himself involved in a double morality—his group morality stands versus his personal morality.

In all societies, even the earliest, this doubleness has presented itself. When the group in pursuit of livelihood or safety has fallen afoul of outsiders, it has become a matter of loyalty for the group member to take from the "enemy" fields, cattle, hostages, lives. The "enemy," though only self-defensive, becomes synonymous with the "evil one." To the Children of Israel, en route to the Promised Land, the command "Thou shalt not kill" applied to the in-group only. On occasion they were moved to carry out the injunction of Deuteronomy:

> . . . of the cities of these people, which the Lord thy God doth give thee for an inheritance, thou shalt save alive nothing that breatheth: But thou shalt utterly destroy them . . . [then, noting a basic moral reason:] That they teach you not to do after all their abominations.

And this attitude toward the outsider as contestant is not confined to the period of conquest of Canaan—the "enemy" becomes a functional character, a stage property so to speak, casting his shadow even into the most universal and beloved of all the Psalms,

> Thou preparest a table before me
> in the presence of mine enemies . . .

a symbol of their total discomfiture as part of the just Providence of Jehovah. The injunctions of personal morality —"Do no murder," etc.—are then seen to apply strictly to the in-group "neighbor"—that is to say, to fellow tribesmen, friends, and guests—definitely not to members of the "enemy" group.[2] This, I need hardly remark, is the historical attitude of most colonizing and imperial ventures in all ages, including our own implementation of our Manifest Destiny. Loyalty to group interest, whatever it involves to the outer impediment, becomes the *first and inclusive moral law.*

The fundamental difficulty here is that the personal precepts *press toward universality*: "Thou shalt not kill thy kinsman" seems to work toward becoming "Thou shalt not kill any human being." And when this universality becomes a clear-cut conviction, explicitly rejecting the in-group limitation, as in John Locke's great saying (with the American colonizing enterprise in mind), "Truth and the keeping of faith belong to man as man, and not as member of society" —you are to respect promises to Indians—we are touching the threshold of *a civilization potentially worldwide.* That is our situation today, now for the first time definitely confronted, and within the sphere of literal achievableness.

Today more than at any earlier time, the man of conscience, faced with the conflicting demands of a double morality—called on to lie, or cheat, if not to do murder, for his group—such a man finds himself in a quandary involving acute moral suffering. There are men, strongly sensitive to the good-fellow sentiment, who take this duplicity in their stride; the man who suffers is the only promising world citizen.

THE CLASH IN AMERICAN HISTORY AND TRADITION

It was our East-coastal colonies that were first faced with this issue in its most drastic form—shall the colony survive? The Indians themselves began to see this as the crucial problem in their relation with the growing numbers of the white settlers. Friendliness could be tried, but it had to be a tentative hypothesis. King Philip's War represented its abandonment on the part of the Indians; and their determined effort to hold their own necessarily evoked an equally determined effort of the colonists. The "Great Swamp Fight" culminated in a massacre, not of the Indian warriors alone but of their women and children. As a recent writer[3] has well put the matter: this massacre "was not the only instance of the New Englanders treating the native inhabitants of the new Canaan as the Israelites had treated the Canaanites of old. . . . If New England was to survive, it had to be this way."

"Had to be" is a hard saying. It is equally hard to dispute it. We recall that Roger Williams, whose humane principles were akin to those of Quaker William Penn, found himself reluctantly drawn into the war for survival. The issue of principle confronts us at every turn. Assuming that we surely know, without waiting for the raw test of survival, what is "higher" and "lower" in scale of civilization, are we then committed to the use (and approval) of whatever means appear necessary under given circumstances to secure sur-

vival of the higher? Kant poured a fine scorn on the type of
statecraft he defined as *Fac et excusa*: do what has to be
done, and find (as Frederick the Great put it) some pedant
to excuse the method. The plea of Manifest Destiny can
hardly be given dignity of necessity; yet its fruit, the conquest of the great Southwest, tempts us to waive scruples
over the trumped-up inception and strategy of the Mexican
War.

The entrance of moral doubleness into our judgments of
history refuses to remain a purely historical matter. It
affects our attitude as well to present *faits accomplis*, in
which desirable public results call for forgetfulness of the
facilitating procedures. It presents a problem for our own
attitude toward stock-piling of weapons for mass destruction; it will affect our attitude toward the crimes of revolution conceived as necessary by the revolutionists, and toward
the present inheritors of the results of those crimes. The
issue thus runs deep into the whole texture of the actual
international scene.

It is certainly not the case that loyalty to group interests
is intrinsically in conflict with personal morality. On the contrary, the moral individual is not complete until, entering
into group memberships beyond the family, he takes part in
a chosen rather than biologically determined social environment—one whose welfare and behavior depend to some extent
on his own decisions.

Yet, just because of the strong emotional identification of
the thus-enlarged self with the fortunes of its chosen group,
the possibility of moral clash is always present. And it is
striking, how little the latent conflict is recognized in our
moral tradition. While faithfulness to persons and trans-
mitted law is emphasized, and friendship is praised, the
claims of functional groups on affirmative loyalty are scanted
—the term "loyalty" itself was apparently not needed by
the King James translators of the Bible. Due fealty to the

state is recognized: "Render unto Caesar . . ." and "Be subject unto the higher powers . . ." And there is the great vision of the Kingdom of God to be set up on earth. But for the nation as carrier of laws and institutions, for economic cooperation, even for the family tie, the New Testament has no firm appeal. The Sermon on the Mount presents the majestic induction whereby all personal moralities are unified in their identical inwardness; but positive and vigorous effort to bring Nature under human control, taking thought for the morrow—the basis of all economy—is discounted. As for the spirit of enterprise, the love of adventure, the nobly power-conscious drive of nation-building, sportsmanship itself—all these seem to be relegated, with the greed for wealth, to the disparaged category, "after all these things do the Gentiles seek." The loyalties of group co-operation for tangible ends are an empty chapter.

We see today that the drift of the Christian movement was not world-hostile but world-deposing-from-first-place to make first things first, to the ultimate curing of a sick world. The early Christians walked the earth as strangers, owing another allegiance, communists, disenchanted: Christianity lifts its followers out of the tribal law, out of the Greek agora and the Roman forum, into the freedom of a single unworldly devotion: in this sense, it is *the ultimate revolution*—"I renounce the vain pomp and glory of the world." But it set aside the functional human group in order to make salient *the germinal person*, the "soul," bound to earth only by love of neighbor, and seeing in the neighbor, not the fellow citizen, nor the serviceable officer—scribe, centurion, artisan—nor even the "brother or sister or mother," but only the fellow soul vowed to the Eternal Kingdom. Christianity is the *disclosure of the individual*, free, tieless except to its absolute beyond the State, and infinitely fertile in freedom. Out of this discipline of detachment during three centuries of *contemptus mundi* (answered in kind by a resentful world

order) a new earthly civilization was paradoxically deposited. It was not against the world, but beyond the
world, to renew it.

DOUBLE MORALITY IN AMERICAN BUSINESS

The discipline of detachment, whether in Christianity or
in the Stoicism whose proud inner citadel stood beyond the
reach of imperial power, was not, I say, *against* the group
life of daily human concerns. But it could neglect them; it
could fail to give dignity to their positive drive. Care for
their vitality, including the concerns of trade and industry,
could be left to "the world," with a different scale of value,
and an independent ethic having its own claim.

In a remarkable essay by Chester Barnard entitled *Elementary Conditions of Business Morals*,[4] Alfred N. Whitehead is quoted to the effect that "A society run on strictly
Christian principles could not survive at all." Civilized life
calls for a certain security against wanton injury and destruction which can only be present where—quite apart from
the police—there is a generally felt responsibility to maintain the social order, a responsibility "almost entirely absent
from Christianity,"[5] concerned as the Teacher was to draw
attention away from the all-absorbing externals of life.

Barnard enlarges on the theme of this responsibility as it
affects business. For the extraordinary degree of smooth
running actually achieved by our intricate economy, much
depends on a wide variety of responsibilities carried in good
faith—i.e., with the "loyalty" we have been speaking of—
to the quality of the job in hand, to fellow workers, to stock-
holders, to the standing of the business as an ongoing concern. The momentum of such responsible loyalties often
presses hard on conscience. For example:

—how, while praising competition, to devise mergers with
    competitors to reach the optimum magnitude for effi-

cient production, research laboratories, and mutually helpful *sub rosa* understandings about marketing;

—where, safety for workers and users being imperative and safety devices costly, to limit their expense;

—when to destroy produce to maintain prices, and when to lower standards of materials or workmanship in order to facilitate an obsolescence of the product desirable for the producer.

I know no essay so enlightening as to the prevalence and the strain of the double morality in contemporary business. He makes clear that a modern economy cannot proceed without a complex co-ordination of responsible activities, whose ethical pressures present "a set of problems no one adequately comprehends" and yet whose solution is one of our greatest needs.

Some of these strains would be relieved by a centralized control of business—and we have seen certain of our steel experts finding advantages in the USSR's single-mindedness. But total unification becomes an impossible burden, with intolerable chokage and delay at the center, calling for the decentralizing recently begun in the USSR. A modern economy is unworkable without a widely distributed initiative and responsible loyalty. And with it, the problems of double morality.

Barnard does not undertake to supply the solution; he rests his case, calling on us, the public, to take over.

We can best do so, I believe, by considering the business problem as a special phase of our general problem—has the inclusive social order, whether as a national total or as a civilization, a claim upon the responsible loyalty of its members which may call for *breach of their personal codes?* For a nation's independence, it may, as we usually judge, become the duty of a citizen, signing away his own right to life, to cancel his duty not to kill, or to accept the moral torment of a spy—of a Nathan Hale or any other honest deceiver. The lesser loyalties involved in business enterprise present, of course, a far less imperative claim. But they involve the status of the same personal moral principles, which as entering into the fabric of Western civilization could hardly be subordinated *in toto* even to the survival of that civilization. For if they were surrendered, what would survive would not be Western civilization.

The problem touches directly that philosophy of public life which becomes explicit in the philosophy of law. I suggest a swift examination from that quarter.

THE PROBLEM IN WESTERN PHILOSOPHY OF LAW

The strains of double morality in all fields would be at once eased if the personal precepts, as of truth and good faith, were denied the absoluteness they seem to claim. In an era in which absolutes have largely lost philosophical status, why make an absolute of "Thou shalt not steal"— or lie, or bribe a friendly official? If "Thou shalt not steal" is simply a condition for social welfare, it has no other validity or obligation.

That personal moralities are, in general, necessary conditions for any civilized order needs no saying. Security of person and property, the validity of contracts, become not only the first concerns of law; if our prevalent sociological jurisprudence is right, these interests are the *whole* concern of civil law.[6] And since the nation, as the cultural in-group, is the most tangible representative of "civilization," it would seem to follow that the obligation of moral and legal rules, as conditions for its welfare, *ceases at the border* of that group. Conduct toward the outsider would then be rightly dictated by prudence or interest: dispose of the aborigines without remorse. Is this escape from double morality too facile?

I submit that this derivation of the personal code (and

the corresponding legal precepts) from group welfare is a
patent fallacy. In any human encounter whether in society
or in the wild there is an immediate and wordless adjustment
of man to man, wholly different from the adjustment of man
to animal or to physical event. Like all wordless adjustments,
it may require a galaxy of words for its full interpretation.
Let us attempt it:

Explorer meets savage, unknown as friendly or hostile.
There is something each instantly knows: "Here is a man;
I cannot treat him as log or beast; I must treat him as
capable of free action, aware of the possibilities of human
intercourse in a world identical for us both: apart from this
identity of situation, we can neither fight nor be friends."
While each must be on guard, caution itself *presupposes the
mutual involvement.* To this extent, each knows that to
injure the other is to injure himself.

If this interpretation is valid, there is in our most elemental will adjustment of man to man an intuitive universality that must traceably affect the development of both
ethical and legal thought. While Roman law was essentially
a law of social functions, from Ulpian's time onward there
was increasing recognition of this presocial relationship. In
Constantine's day the leap became explicit: gladiatorial combat, for example, was forbidden on the ground that slaves,
captives, criminals, outlaws—all technically exterior to society—have "souls" implying a status independent of citizenship. It is this step outside organized society that marks
the distinctive Western legal position, and constitutes the
basis of all legal individualism.

This non-political, non-social status later takes the form
of a "natural rights" theory whose complex story is more
often rehearsed than understood. While the historical line
runs through Magna Carta and the 1689 Bill of Rights—
through Hooker, Locke, Grotius, Blackstone—it is still the
odd Scottish-German Kant who most accurately formulates
its basis; and not in his treatise on Law but in his doctrine of

an inherent humanity which as end-in-itself must never be exploited as means to the ends of any person—*or of any group.*

And while, as Dean Acheson has effectively argued,[7] the scope of law in the world can seldom exceed the area of dominant power, the hope of mankind must rest not in restricting law to that area but in bringing power toward the normal area of law, inherently universal. And the double morality we have been tracing, the conflict between group loyalty and the personal code holding the germ of legality, remains as a dominant malaise driving to that achievement.

And though Camus is somewhat apart from our tradition, he has, I believe, added something of great importance to just this all-human Kantian picture, and hence to ours. Kant speaks of the duty of the possible *exploiter* not to exploit; Camus speaks of the duty of the *exploited to cancel exploitation by a positive act,* and thus to remind the exploiter of his own humanity. The Rebel of Camus creates solidarity, and thus restores the normal liberty of both master and servant.[8] Camus here adds a new chapter to the Western tradition of liberty, that of the affirmative correction of injustice through a creative deed, in contrast to the negative correction through revolution. This duty to create, existing in no list of Commandments, is likewise a universal demand, hence independent of group loyalties.

So far as the official position of the USA can be identified by the traditional documents and our Bill of Rights, there can be no doubt that we are fully committed to the universality of the personal code for all peaceful situations, while equally committed to the citizen's obligation in time of war. On this level the quandary of the double morality persists, unresolved.

And the problem is peculiarly ours for two reasons. One, that the double morality is especially rampant in our numerous interior groups, not excepting our political parties. Two, that we are inclined to insist on the personal ethical code in peaceful international relations, for our own officers and also for judging the conduct of other nations. We assume that the commitments and behavior of states toward one another must follow in principle the ethic of interpersonal relations, as a basis for a working international law.

Since double morality is the most pervasive enemy of national strength, we must look to its workings in both fields, and first to the international field where it appears—in the absence of a complete and accepted legal code—most nearly justified.

MORALISM AND ANTI-MORALISM IN USA FOREIGN POLICY

The double morality which suppresses personal scruple for the sake of a group's economic survival seems on the face of it far less defensible than a similar duplicity for the sake of a nation's vital interests or survival. If the stake were the survival of a civilization, the case for suppressing personal morals would seem to be at its height. In that situation, would we incline to utilize that "reason of State" which traditionally overrules all "weak sensitivity of conscience" on the part of the statesman?

The USA has not been inclined hitherto to invoke this special indulgence. It has been part of our national pride to promote in international dealings, not the actual morality of our political parties, but the professed principles of our public law, applying to nations the rights we seek for individuals in domestic law, and calling on others to do the same, as a condition of peace with justice. At the same time, we are as a people "practical"—not pragmatic; practical in the sense that we prefer concrete, empirical reasoning to reasoning from generalities. We have a distaste, not for morals in foreign policy, but for moral preachments as a mask for bungling statecraft, weak in building power. This may be what inspired Mr. Dean Acheson's recent criticism of "Moralism" in foreign policy.

Without going so far as Mr. Cordell Hull in his insistence
that our foreign policy is and ought to be based exclusively
on national self-interest, Mr. Acheson likes Mr. Hull's can-
dor. Our highest duty, he holds, is not to an abstract ethical
idea but to a concrete task, namely, to preserve the values
of civilization: if those values are threatened, our duty is to
protect them, even if we must overcome our indisposition to
use force or the threat of force to that end. His guiding
maxim is that "The ends of action are not, for the most part,
determined by ideals, but the other way around." This
sounds dangerously as if the "other way around" would be
"The end justifies the means"; but no: it is the *ideals*, not
the means, that he considers governed by the ends of action.
I should prefer to say, *involved in* the ends of action. In
other words, believing as we do in "liberty" and "peace," we
cannot go gunning for liberty or peace *per se*: we must keep
our eye upon the concrete situation, and give our support to
those movements, or nations, in which our conceptions of
rightness are most effectively embodied—to help them will
help liberty and peace. These ideals are not separable
pieces of split kindling: they are aspects of a total nobility
of life, a recognizable integrity of good will, in which the
proportions of freedom-and-dictation, pacifism-and-pug-
nacity, individualism-and-collectivism, will vary: fix your
eyes on the Integrity, the whole Humanity of the movement
or nation, and when you find groups whose ends are right,
work together with those groups, whatever their internal
structure—not for the names of ideals, but for their wise
incorporations in the texture of history.

In talking thus about the concrete "ends of action" as
taking precedence of an abstract "moralism," Mr. Acheson
is directing attention to a total loyalty, as significant as it
is vague. He asks us to be loyal not to an assignable group,
but to the world process itself, conceived as a movement toward civilized integrity in the international order. In loyalty
to this "end of action," comradeship of purpose must take

precedence of agreement on definitions of right and wrong in particular policies. We do not, for example, prove traitorous to our democratic faith if, in a world war against a threat to all international order, we join hands with imperial or dictatorial powers of various types, as we have twice done. "Moralism" might have kept us out; but it was moralist Woodrow Wilson who, as a prelude to nailing up the Fourteen Points on the wall, opened our way to participation.

This participation during the first World War, and our nonparticipation in the League of Nations after that war, have been equally embarrassing for the morally scrupulous.

Bird-limed in the secret treaties of the Sykes-Picot line regarding the Mid-East settlement, Wilson sought to rescue the USA's moral honor—in half-fulfillment of wartime promises—by way of the unilateral King-Crane Commission of 1919-20, seeking to ascertain the "wishes" of those ex-Ottoman regions that were to become A-mandates. But since the proposed mandates were already allocated, and since the USA, much wished-for, *refused a mandate*, Wilson could not so much as publish the report! The League became, willy-nilly, executor of understandings—including the Balfour Declaration—inherently crooked, and of a Peace Treaty inherently impossible, though floating in the medium of the noblest hopes of mankind. The moral defects of League and Treaty, maternal ancestors of the present Mid-East confusion, inspired our Senatorial rejection of membership in the League. And this rejection left us disadvantaged to assist those forces of healing that in 1928 could have steered Germany away from Hitler and World War II. I happened to be in Geneva at the moment when Briand's passionate refusal to meet Germany in disarmament turned the tide.[9] We, the USA, were not there.

Isolation, in moral rightness, is not the answer. I recall Stimson's historic note to Japan, in presence of her 1931 *démarche* in Manchuria, reminding her of our resolve not

to recognize governments instituted by force. A brave
resolve, but hopeless as from an absentee from the
League! Isolation is no remedy for palpable wrong in a
world now beaten into shared destiny by a thousand blows
of technical and economic advance. The second League,
the UN, largely our doing, has as its own basis a wide
moral generality, the "peace-loving" state—raising the
question whether there exists a state that will not profess
peace-lovingness; but the actual commitment at which
the UN aims is not subscription to a pre-existing code of
professional ethics for nations; it is rather the *necessary
commitment* of a civilized community—in the world civilization now arriving—*to the minimal conditions of coexistence* within a continuous history of experiment
through which the moral and legal principles of interaction can be formulated.

The UN can be in no sense a union of the already moral
nations: it is precisely for the development of a code of
international practice and of law, workable under present
conditions, that the UN exists.[10]

THE MORAL ABSOLUTE IN STATECRAFT

To recognize the dominance of the Great Aim in public
policy is commonly taken as an *ipso facto* repudiation of a
moral absolute. The inference is fallacious.

It is true that the Great Aim is still called upon to justify
the obliquities of *Realpolitik*, the crimes of revolution, the
mass destructions of civilians in total war, past and con-
templated. The notion of a law-within-warfare which inspired the work of a Grotius and the Geneva Conventions
seems to be at last gasp in presence of contemporary arts of
obliteration. But it is one of the services of destructive power
to reveal the minimum of civilization that the will-to-destroy
must respect. This minimum, the elemental logic I have
spoken of, must now achieve a commanding place in all international dealings.

Like all important matters, it is *the forgotten obvious*.

There can be no civilization, no world order, unless there is united acceptance of the identities underlying all differences: there is one world, one history, one truth in which the nations, their actions and hostilities, coexist. It is not relatively true that there is relative truth, but absolutely true that there is truth both relative and absolute, the absolute holding for all nations and providing explanations for its relative facets.

Because of this, *veracity* in what is publicly asserted will be one of the absolutes. Here private morals will not yield to the exigencies of statecraft, but on the contrary will give rules to foreign policy and to the conduct of membership in the UN—no double morality there! With veracity will be associated other absolutes: *good faith*, the keeping of *treaties*, a concern for *humanity* in the use of force, all identical in area with elements of personal morality. There are others.

Nations have always tried to deceive their enemies; in the logic of coexistence, they cannot consistently lie to the UN. They *will* lie there, and do. My point is, that in this connection they are lying to recorded history, and will be obliged by nobody's malice to experience the nemesis of the recorded falsehood. In due time, they will stop it.

As an example: Our State Department has recently published a 53-page pamphlet which, among other matters, accuses Mr. Khrushchev of misrepresenting the origin of the second World War. It corrects his statement by "the truth," namely, that World War II was precipitated by the Molotov-Ribbentrop Pact of 1939, the USSR being therefore directly responsible. The issue of veracity was raised. It was raised also editorially by the *New York Times* (Nov. 29, 1958) under the caption, "The Kremlin Lies." The Kremlin version seems to have been that the USSR was ready at the time of the Munich Conference (September, 1938) to join England and France in the

defense of Czechoslovakia against Hitler; and that it
was only after the rebuff of this advance that Stalin, in
defense of Russia, made the nonaggression pact of 1939
with Germany. It happens that Mr. Walter Lippmann
has recently reported a conversation, in which Mr.
Khrushchev had put forward "with passionate conviction"
this alternative theory, with the additional comment that
the Western negotiators, Chamberlain and Daladier, had
"wanted Hitler to attack Russia" via the convenient
Czechoslovakian corridor, and had therefore not wanted
Russia's help in keeping Hitler at home. Khrushchev had
been quite clear that "the Western peoples do not understand" this duplicity of motive in the catastrophic Munich
appeasement.

Now if Khrushchev actually believes his version of the
event, he ought hardly to be accused of lying (as I pointed
out in a letter to the *Times*, published December 4, 1958).
Nor should the State Department be accused of lying, if
it really believes that World War II was decisively let
loose by the Stalin-Hitler Pact of 1939, rather than by
the first consequence of the Munich Pact, Hitler's rape of
Czechoslovakia and the consequent threat to Poland, which
Britain was publicly bound to protect. It was this overt
act of aggression, with Britain's hasty rearmament, which
to common judgment actually began the war, and seemed
to precipitate the Stalin-Hitler Pact, as a result, not a
first cause—an effort on the part of Stalin, turned down
by Britain and France, to gain time for defense. If this
is the case, it is not the USSR but the makers of Munich
who directly released World War II; our State Department cannot be ignorant of the essential facts.

Having been in Europe during this period, my own
observations tend to confirm the judgment that Stalin
was ready to aid the Allies in September of 1938. The
matter is of considerable importance to our judgment of
the entire course of things since 1939, and to the present
state of feeling between the USA and the USSR. The
motives of the participants remain hidden; and I certainly
do not dogmatize. I surmise that Stalin's highly condi-

ditional readiness to co-operate in the defense of Czechoslovakia against Hitler was inspired less by a concern for
Czechish liberty than by a persistent Russian ambition
(long dreaded by the Czechs[10]) to gain a footing in mid-
Europe. My point here is simply that in raising the important issue of historical truthfulness it is exceptionally
imperative to allow your opponent whatever ground-in-
fact he may have for his view.

In respect to these absolute qualities, nations acquire an
individual repute, as Chinese merchants at one time held a
world repute for reliable merchandizing and accounting. If
through loyal lying the repute of a line of diplomats suffers,
their word, discounted in advance, fails to serve the national
interest: there's a logic here not erased by concreteness of
aim. A diplomacy wholly divorced from the standards of
personal morality becomes, by purely realistic measures,
simply bad diplomacy.

The strength of a nation in this field is measured by the
sustained character level of its representatives: its ability to
fill its consular and diplomatic posts with individuals who,
while mentally qualified and adroit (and knowing the local
language), carry the immediate impression of a personal
dignity incapable of chicanery.

Great Britain, uneven as its record is, stands high in the
number of such men. If it viceroys India with a Lord Lloyd
who makes his name by daring to arrest Gandhi, it also ap-
points a Lord Irwin who, keeping faith with Gandhi and
thus helping India toward its independence, earns a meed of
denunciation from certain empire patriots at home, one of
whom said to me that Irwin should be "hung to the nearest
lamppost." This type of loyalty-morality would have kept
India perforce within the Empire. Its rejection, to Lord
Irwin's credit and to Britain's, has led to the great international deed of this century—the emergence within the
Commonwealth of a free India without bloodshed between
contracting parties.

With the best will in the world, the ambassador must still represent the vital interest of his nation, as conceived by that nation; and this commonly means by the party in power. The security of the nation, its prosperity, also its honor, are in the keeping of the ruling party. And while a great ambassador, like a great prime minister, can at times compel his party or his nation to bring its power to the level of its honor, a weaker man can let both sink to the level of a Munich, and yet report to the nation that he has brought home "peace with honor." A double morality in the party tends to transmit itself to the nation's diplomatic agents.

But the public, whose morale depends on the confidence that its agents are acting in good faith, cannot as a rule be admitted to the duplicities of either the party or the statesmen. Just in proportion to the element of duplicity, a veil must be maintained between public knowledge and official purpose, and the words of statesmen take on the now-familiar accent of "propaganda." We learn to distinguish between the utterances that are meant and those that are "for home consumption." The auspicious side of this sometimes ludicrous and always painful disparity is that most publics can be counted on to remain close to the moral absolutes, which are no more than the common sense of human intercourse, and will ultimately control the course of official sophistications.

What I here point out is that in the relations of nation with nation, on the world platform, and in the relations between government and people, the double morality *tends to solve itself* through the recovery of the all-human absolutes. Until that occurs, the doubleness remains a public danger, and a forfeiture of normal national strength.

THE FRATERNAL GROUP AS CLAIMANT

Among the much-used freedoms in the USA is the freedom to associate. We form clubs, institutes, councils, committees, commissions, orders, fraternities, unions, bunds, blocs, boards without end, for all purposes and for none. There is no legal limit to the number that may be created, or that any one man may belong to. Since each one takes time, expects participation, involves expense, the spread per man is self-limiting. And for each man, it is likely that some one of them is his special concern.

For the made-group, as a small society in its own right, has one character of great importance to the inclusive community: it *absorbs loyalty*. The intimate group, in its inner variety, tends to symbolize mankind: what it claims from its members is a metaphor of what humanity may claim. Most such groups find members whose continuous attachment and service through many years gives them heroic stature—think perhaps of your college Class Secretary!

Thomas Hobbes well realized this loyalty-absorbing character of the small groups, likened them to parasites in the entrails of the state, regarded their existence as a menace, recommended limitation: his prescience was verified in later history—was not the French Revolution born in a cabaret; was not Hitler's first outburst born in a Munich beer hall? Radical movements are commonly begotten in social "cells," among cronies. Or put it in the converse: where cronies are gathered, there the world is drawn into the crucible of discussion and revision; and some of these fermentings become gestations of new world fancies, plans, programs, attempts.

I shall not raise the question whether there are among us, with our exuberant club-begetting powers, too many such groups within the nation group. We live in a period of too-much-ness in general—too many *good* things, even too many good books! Our capacities for appreciation are fatigued by our abundance. But I point out the *psychological necessity* of the smaller groups, drawn to a scale in which a man can feel a certain fraternity with all the fellows: if a group becomes too large it is bound to subdivide in order to maintain mental surveyability. Each person's social proclivities, outside the family group, tend to unfold themselves in some *limited* company, perhaps an occupational group, which nevertheless represents to him the human universe—Rotary, for example.

And because of this capacity to be at once intimate and quasi-total, the small group exhibits an egoism which is psychologically justified. It tends to exalt its own being and its needs, and the rest of the world—miscellaneous environment—is its fair prey. The Greek city-state was surveyable, not beyond the acquaintance-reach of a single individual: the modern nation-state is unsurveyable, the modern city a wilderness—New York, for homing purposes, an odd collection of ethnic villages, insulated by Sargasso Seas of mechanism and artificial mountain chains burrowed into by innumerable woodchuck holes of clubs, each its own sufficient universe relegating all the rest, like the roar of the streets, to a characterless blur of otherness.

I say we must not be either surprised or disturbed by the egoism of the fellowship group: it is impossible for such an entity, or its members, to intuit with identical sympathy the life and need of the heterogeneous Outside—a formless It, or at most a They. We must be appreciative of their indispensable services: the great society requires them for its fertility in ideas; its poetry, its art, its philosophy, its science, its medicine, its faiths have in all ages been the products of "cells," like the Pythagorean Brotherhood. In comparison with them, the nation as a whole is simply barren: that "public" to whom we commit our destinies, apart from them, is an idealess moron. With them, it becomes animate, and makes its shrewd choices of direction.

At the same time, we must see clearly the line-drawing that spontaneously occurs—the We-versus-They distinction which easily becomes an hostility, sometimes purely gratuitous.

If the We happens to be gathered around an illicit occupation, as let us say the former network of distilleries in hideouts of the Ozarks, no one has a right to the We sign unless he both condones the occupation and is ready to take part in its concealment: a double morality, involving deception of the innocent outsider, is of the essence of membership. And even if there is no tangible antilegal, anticonventional, anti-orthodox sentiment to enhance the warmth of union, there is a *certain impulse to exaggerate the in-out contrast for its direct emotional* flavor. The intensified domesticity of comradeship which results from the "we-against-the-world" situation supplies a craving for covert excitement very deep in some souls (and rather general in the teen-ager).

As a natural consequence of this group egoism, and the We-They prespective colored by a seductive conflict-sense, the multitude of fellowship groups becomes, almost unawares, a drain on the national life. What are our representatives in Congress for? If our fellowship group is occupational, and at the same time in its national extent numerous, it is likely to have a lobby, formal or informal, to present its case to government.

Take the farmer, for example, and his fellowships:

Without going into detail about the immense sums devoted to aiding the farmer as a group, at the expense of the national treasury, let me say broadly that the granting of this relief—genuinely needed—has not been wholly free from consideration of the "farm vote" in swingable sections of the Middle West; and that the reduction of the appalling burden of stored grain by new legislation has not been carried out without resistance from interests not identical with those of the nation.

I speak first of the group I belong to, and know best, the farmers, a proud and essentially clean group, whose welfare is necessary to that of the nation, and whose economic plight, in an inflationary period motored from other quarters, is still waiting effective analysis. I use it to illustrate the easy drift of the fellowship group toward the "pressure group" relation to government; in which the legitimate concern to inform the legislator blends easily with the will to achieve his favor with side play on his interest in re-election and party power.

In the absence of a moral vigor not now in evidence, the prevalence in the USA of the *pressure-group function* for all interests—as a useful institution of spontaneous growth—could mean the spread of a polite and plausible bribery subtly undermining our democracy. Recall the Fascist claim, voiced by Gentile, that Italy under Mussolini was the most truly democratic government in Europe: "Democracy consists in giving the people what they want; they do not know what they want; the Leader tells them, and then procures it for them." This handsome sophism has a certain sting; for we are acting as if democracy were indeed "giving the people what they want," and at the same time *assuming that the people know what they want*, a fatal policy when "what they want" is defined in terms of the double morality of pressure groups.

The terminus of such benevolence of all to all could only be a crash into Radical Denial, something like a Fascism of revolt, capable of denying group demands in the interest of a total solvency, the sober "what they ought to want" of a true democracy, imposed by overhead discipline. Such a resort to authority would amount to a confession of moral inability on the part of our actual democratic structure—inability to trim group claims to the nation's good. Must this confession be made?

If the double morality of pressure groups is incurable by themselves, and if the authoritative trimming is not achieved, we must acknowledge one deep-seated national weakness: a hemorrhage of "generosities" to a thousand claimant groups equipped with votes—in other words, a million polite bribes —in which case, as they say of rotting foundations in New England, one could "poke a putty knife into the sills."

The failure to do the trimming lies, of course, in the party structure of the American democracy. As an artificial organ provided for in no constitution, created in the first place by

natural antitheses of opinion, but living by the need to bring
intelligible shape to the unguided opinion-making of the
millions, the party must have its secrets, its "good reasons
and the real reasons." Originally begotten by issues, they
continue to exist by issues begotten by themselves. Current
platforms are devised in the attempt to assemble the greatest
agreement of the greatest number, and at the same time to
appeal to the interests of (right-thinking) potential con-
tributors, while careful to offend no (right-speaking) influ-
ential minority. The chronic vote-hunger of the party opens
its campaign strategy to the influence of vigorous minorities
with axes to grind: there are some important economic fields
in which, according to Professor Sumner Slichter, we have
never been able to pass a bill in the *national* interest.

The point is that the party "has to live": its own life problem must excite the compassion of any knowing layman. As
the Tammany story illustrates, the party has to survive by
service as a more personal local Providence than a federal
government could possibly be. This function is legitimate: the
nation can never lay aside completely its early role as the
extended family. But when Providence exchanges its bless-
ings for votes, we have the beginning of a pleasant neighborly understanding which, made general, means the abandonment of honest democracy by the Demos itself.

THE FRATERNAL GROUP AS COMBATANT

The call for group loyalty, with its possible strain of
double morality, is naturally most intense when the group is
engaged in combat. The social freedom we care about includes freedom to compete and, within the law, to fight. In
fact, contest is so far the spice of life that if it is absent we
invent it, as the whole area of athletic rivalry may testify.
The political party lives with contest in view. Competition
in business may become a no-quarter struggle for survival.
But with us it is chiefly the Labor Union that is committed
to combat as its primary function.

The pride in workmanship of the older Trade Unions and of the still older Guilds lives on with difficulty in our era of fast-changing tools and techniques, and with the general replacement of the craft unit by the industrial unit of bargaining. That pride still lives (and in Germany retains some of its rituals) ; it will never become extinct while skill and art are factors in the product. But as of today, the active function of bargaining holds the center of Union concern, calling for an intenser and harder-fisted loyalty, with stiffer pressure on private scruple. The Labor-Management alignment of collective bargaining, with the power of each side to injure the other at the cost of some injury to itself, suggests the temper of the Marxian Class-war, but under the very different flag of social justice as the professed aim of both sides. The quality of the contest is reflected in the leadership whose gamut runs from the statesmanship of a Reuther to the criminality which may here remain anonymous.

Almost alone in our social order, conflict in Labor-Management relations takes the rank of an institution with legally regulated procedures. Accepting the opposition of the interests in the distribution of the net proceeds of industry, the state undertakes—not to determine justice—but to bring about a rough equalization of bargaining power by legalizing (i) collective bargaining, and (ii) the union shop aiming to monopolize the available labor supply for a specified process: "Deal with us, or shut up shop." As Professor John M. Clark has put the matter, "Only in the case of organized labor has the government sanctioned the use of monopolistic powers and practices by private organizations in the service of private interests. . . ."[11]

The reason for this exception is well understood, namely, the helplessness of the individual worker in holding out for a fair wage, or for any wage at all, where labor supply— as is usually the case—exceeds the demand. For the uncapitalized worker, *his right to work is inseparable from*

his right to life. Yet his right to work imposes no duty on
any specific employer to employ him—and nothing is more
futile than a "right" with no addressee. And while for
capitalism the business cycle with its recurrent spectre of
large-scale unemployment remains an unsolved problem,
the free-enterprise community willy nilly must take over
responsibility for the livelihood of its members. Reluctant
to serve in its own person as residual employer, it presses
private employers to employ. The union shop is one such
device.

These policies, worked out not by prior theory but in
strenuous American experience, are successful in the essential
point: they put an end to the historic motive force of revolution, as pictured by Marx, namely, the unlimited power of
capital-as-employer to exploit the absolute need of the uncapitalized man for work and wage. *There is, in the USA, no
fuel for a revolution.* Revolution must get its explosive force
from suffering, from a suffering that knows itself at once
general and unjust: no such suffering here exists, and there
is no suppression of the normal activities of protest where
inequity is felt. There is nothing here to keep a Communist
Party alive and in good health: it quite rightly "withers
away."

But our rule-of-thumb correctives of the original unbalance in bargaining power are hardly in final form. Have
we perhaps reversed the unbalance? Have we overcompen-
sated the weaker bargaining position, at the risk of wasting
compassion over former sufferers turned hold-up men? These
questions are timely.

But I raise a more central question: have we lost sight of
the *underlying problem of justice* in distribution?

We, the public, often forced to suffer in the strife of Labor-
Management groups, are hardly prepared to consider the
strike as the final and perfect way to discover justice.

We agree in the fundamental principle that Labor is not

a commodity; and that it is not to be dealt with market-wise on the basis of supply-and-demand, even when the union shop relies on its control of supply for its power. We acquiesce in the strike, as a tug of war, not because it reveals justice, but because we prefer it to the apparent alternatives, decision by Ownership alone, or by the State alone.

The "right to strike" is not discoverable in any list of the rights of man: it is frequently interpreted by Labor as including the right to override public convenience, order, sometimes health and safety. It definitely involves the public. And the public, on the whole, is willing to be involved and discommoded if the process is indeed a method of reaching a more perfect justice. But is it?

Remembering that Labor is not all on one side of the contest, since wage-labor is by no means the whole of the hard work going into production—Management, too, is labor—we recognize that wage-labor is right in insisting on its status as the concern of the nation. Its standard of living is our democratic boast; its place of honor is our pride. It is not a "proletariat"—we have none; but wage-labor is the best single representative of the Demos in our democracy, and what happens to wage-labor happens to all America. As such, it deserves not a "living wage," but a *standard-of-living wage*, sharing in the total advance. In its capacity as producer, it deserves recognition for technical prowess, and for differential productivity with improving machines. These items, capable of objective measurement, could be standardized, eliminating the need of quarrel to secure them.

But has Labor, beyond these, any just claim on profits? And if so, ought a worker who does the same work in an unsuccessful venture receive less than his fellow craftsman in a prosperous plant? And does a claim to go up with the profits imply a willingness to go down with the losses? Further, if justice were the concern, would not the weaker labor-groups be considered in the demands of the stronger? And with them, the exigencies of the consumer, and of the nation's

export trade with its five million workers? The conclusion to
which we are forced is that current Union pressure is not
concerned for the nation, nor for the public, nor for Labor
at large, but simply for what it can get for itself—as a rule.
It has largely *outgrown its concern for justice.* It has, indeed
a concern for the total future of Labor as it sees automation
creeping in; but its immediate question is simply What can
we compel the employer to afford? Not alone is there here
no fuel for revolution: there is not in the entire American
labor movement enough public passion to draw up a united
program, not to mention a Boston Tea Party. The local
skirmishes evolve no major principle.

This situation—equivalent to importing a minor game of
power-politics into the economic order—implies not so much
an absence of concern for justice on the part of members or
leaders of combatant groups as a suspension of the issue. It
indicates, in part, a mutual response to the supposed temper
of the opponent: "If he shows no concern for the nation's welfare, why should I? If self-interest versus self-interest is to
be the game, let us play it with might and main." All games
abstract from the total background of reality, make their
own rules for their simplified world, and accept their gains
and losses as the counters of the game rather than the facts
of life. The game of business as of politics is a hard game; it
involves willingness to accept pain, and by the same sign, to
inflict it. That the loser loses is the plan logic of the case: to
mitigate this loss by mercy would falsify the record. Hard
consistency, if the game is straight, is a form of honesty as
well as sportsmanship. These are regions in which we can
say with satisfaction that the USA *is not soft!*

Only: the issue of justice will not down, nor the wider
concerns of the nation. And when we are obliged to admit that
—Adam Smith to the contrary notwithstanding—the free
play, or free competition, or free fight, of self-interested
groups has *no inherent tendency to produce justice,* we begin
to identify an inherent weakness of the free-enterprise system

when taken as self-sufficient. It attempts to make the "economic man," who is a fraction, do duty for the whole man: it can't be done.

The truth is that "economics is no longer a closed science" —I am here quoting Herbert Feis, as we met in Dubrovnik in 1938 after his trip through eastern Europe for the State Department—"there are no economic solutions without ethical solutions," nor, as I then added, "without metaphysical solutions." "Maybe," he replied.

The trouble is that the ethical, juridical, psychological, metaphysical solutions, particularly of the problem of justice in distribution, remain so difficult and contentious, that government itself evades the issue, and prefers that the contenders shall play their game as at least a peaceful substitute. It remains true that acceptance by government of the strike as a method of settlement—a method essentially uncivilized —is itself an abandonment of the issue of justice, perhaps a confession of *inability to think the question out!*

And as a consequence, we find a will to dictate to government, on the part of the Combatants. It is not simply that competitors on both sides combine to escape the competition that was to provide an objective test of their worth. It is also that government, in its effort to revise the rules of the contest through "labor legislation," becomes aware of pressure on the political parties to conform to the union demand or lose the formidable union vote. To submit to such pressure, or to a subtler counter-pressure from industry, willing to dictate terms to the nation, would be to accept *a hidden dictatorship* by fractions of the nation, *under the mask of a democracy.* An inversion of principle, and a falsification of our world-role.

In summary of our observations on the Double Morality which tends to conceal from us our most serious sappings of strength, we may well listen to the swift impressions of a sagacious observer from the East.

Prime Minister Jawaharlal Nehru finds the USSR wanting because of its "suppression of freedom," a suppression which he believes will not long be tolerated by the beneficiaries of its notable educational program. At the same time he judges that "The new Western civilization, with all its triumphs and achievements, and also with its atomic bombs, also appears inadequate; and therefore a feeling grows that there's something wrong."[12]

Nehru is to be thanked for that careful word, "inadequate," precisely pertinent to our problem of national strength. The West, including the USA, is somehow unequal to the promise of its great power. Nehru refrains from analyzing the sources of inadequacy—there is "something wrong"; perhaps we are now in a way to identify a part of that wrongness.

When we allow our group attachments and loyalties to dictate to our individual consciences—the sole source of genuine universality of judgment—we forgo our natural strength as persons and as nations; we surrender our dignity both of mind and purpose. We develop a technique of "adjustment" to the social situation, perhaps an American equivalent of "muddling through," inconsistent with clarity at home or with intelligibility abroad. The ruling motives of our society lose that resonance of integrity which is the birthright of our national spirit.

It is the integrated man, moral and political, who must give laws to the economic man, not the economic man to the whole man. It is only within an honest Democracy that the man of integrity can come to full stature. But Democracy—next to Liberty the most cherished of our ideals—is, I venture to say, the most widely misconceived. We turn to its examination.

VI

THE DEMOS AND
DEMOCRACY

DEMOCRACY is at once the most auspicious and the most difficult system of government.

All government is *of* the people—what else is there to be governed? All government professes to be *for* the people—even the Czarist autocracy was headed by the "Little Father." And, indeed, the pretense is never pure hypocrisy, for government itself is every man's necessity, and exists for the sake of the public action which shapes every man's destiny and may be every man's pride. What Caesar does, Rome does; and what Rome does, all we Romans do—it is *our* history, done for us! But how can government of the people and for the people be also *by* the people?

Literally impossible, since governors and governed must be distinct entities, with different functions and knowledges. Morally possible if—and only if—there is an *esprit de corps* which rulers can feel, interpret, and obey.

THE ESSENCE OF DEMOCRACY: *Esprit de Corps*

This *esprit de corps* is the element of democracy most forgotten, as vital intangibles are likely to be. We commonly think of democracy as embodied in certain mechanisms of distributed voting, representative bodies, separation of powers, referenda, and so it is. But the entity embodied in these mechanisms is invisible, a state of mind. We come nearest to *seeing* it in subhuman group action, say in a flock of migrating birds: we see no mechanism; there are probably signals, perhaps leaders, but they seem to move at the spontaneous stirring of a common impulse, a rule of the whole *by* the whole, an *esprit de corps* that defies analysis and yet governs action, as if telepathic and teledynamic. Such instant mutuality is unavailable to dispersed human communities; yet I hazard the assertion that unless there is in the animus of a community something corresponding to that spirit-of-the-whole, democratic machinery cannot produce genuine democracy—nothing but counterfeit.

Look a little closer. A human individual is or ought to be self-governing—a government of himself *by* himself. That capacity is his unalienable freedom: he irons out inwardly his own alternatives, doubts, conflicts; he "makes up his own mind." A human community, in contrast, can make up its own mind, assuming it is a mind, only by bringing its doubts and conflicts into the open—unless some benevolent dictator spares it the trouble—and what decision prevails is certainly not devised nor achieved "by the people" as a whole, but by a majority or leaders thereof, in effect commanding the whole. This process is vastly more cumbersome than decision by an individual dictator: its results, on the perilous assumption that majorities are likely to be right, may be as good as those of the dictator, or better, but that is not the point. The whole point of democracy is that we, the people, *consent to the method*, participate in it, and with good will abide by the result. It is in some sense *our* result, whether we win or lose, for we have been consulted, our diverse opinions expressed freely and without fear have been heard, our minds have been stirred together: we have become understanders of the issue, and co-makers of our destiny. Without this cumbersome and costly process, decision might be as good or better, but a public left mentally idle would be no partner in the result. A nation is self-governing just to the extent that it consents to and participates in the method of reaching decisions. Tenuous, but real as far as it goes.

And this consent is rational just in so far as there exists
an underlying *esprit de corps* whereby—to interpret its unspoken sense—each tacitly says to all the rest: "I trust you,
across all differences of judgment, to be acting honestly, as
you see it, for the good of all of us, and hence for me." Any
such trust implies a confidence—let us call it an unwritten
premise—that there is broad agreement as to what "the
good of all of us" consists in, a similar outlook and direction.
Government "by the people" is moonshine unless that confidence is justified; and how can it be justified in view of the
variety and relativity of all judgments of value?

The premise is simply false unless there is indeed something universal in the value sense of each member. Democracy
rests on a firm and immediate persuasion of all-human
brotherhood—metaphysical and inescapable, of which I shall
have more to say. But our *esprit de corps* as political beings
requires something more than the valid generalities common
to the genus Homo; it becomes vital and substantial in proportion to a certain at-home-ness of each with all in the
nation, due to kinship of purpose, a nation being *a specific
experiment in living and lawmaking*. This *esprit de corps*
confirms itself in proportion as that highly general brotherhood finds empirical concreteness in applying a specific common heritage to a specific common soil—Royce's "community
of memory and of hope."

As a national spirit, it has history in it—customs, the
stories of heroes, the pride of former victories, the bond of
ancient sufferings and defeats well outlived. It has in it goals
of action, national causes, fulfillments to be reached in the
total human scene, perhaps its own special version of Utopia,
a national myth. At every point, too, the specific soil and
landscape, the gifts and the refusals of Nature, the local
aspects of the seasons, the dreads and glories of sun, storm,
and ice fill the common language with their allusion and
poetry, and enter the premise as its *mise en scène*. All framed
within some view of the nation in the wider world, a role, a

destiny, manifest or not, giving the national character a *raison d'etre* in the total scheme of things, dignifying its demand on individual sharing of efforts and rewards, one's stake in the common lot.

One of the most deeply moving phrases of a student in defeated Germany-under-Occupation (1948), speaking of the bleak forward look both for the youth and for the nation, writing to me in trenchant criticism of the type of democracy we were recommending to Germany, was this avowal of a persistent national spirit:

"I reject a Russian socialism just as I refuse an American dollar-imperialism for Germany. I plead for, and will give myself for, a Germany which . . . can stand as an equal and free factor among peace-loving peoples. I believe in spite of everything . . . in the unchanging mission of a man and of a People, in a future Freedom, in a Peace, and in an understanding among the peoples. Perhaps I am wrong. Who knows?"[1]

"The unchanging mission of a man and of a people"— even of a people in the hands of victors, rebuked and ruined, yet conscious through its youth of an unconquerable strength and identity of purpose. "Unchanging mission," yet, in view of disaster, calling for a revised conception of its own meaning!

This revised conception, for Germany, can be achieved only by Germany itself.

This national specification of the spirit of human brotherhood deserves a name of its own. It has something in common with the General Will of which Rousseau spoke; but it is prior to all willing, the matrix from which acts of will are derived, a felt premise from which decisions follow. And while it is general, in the sense of being identical for all members of the community, what we have to note is its individuality, its quasi-personal character. It is an environing assumption of purposive direction from which both political decisions and also every personal act of will can start. Let me call this individual motive spirit of the nation "*the national premise*," the felt agreement of concrete aim, within which each member works out his personal life.

With this conception in mind we may submit this dictum: *No national premise, no genuine democracy*, however perfect the representative mechanism. And further, in proportion to the firmness of the national premise, a degree of government by the people exists without machinery. For no tyranny can permanently flout a firm national premise. When, for example, dictators lie in order to deceive not outsiders but their own public they thereby acknowledge the power of public opinion directly derivative from their own national premise. And in normal situations, while the whole apparatus of representation confesses that direct government by the people nowhere exists nor can exist in human societies, the anxious awareness on the part of governors of what public sentiment is or may be, what is wanted, what will not be stood, what is fair and right, gives a firm national premise effective legislative power. The *degree of effective democracy is proportionate to the firmness of the national premise*, under whatever form of government. From this position, certain consequences may be drawn pertinent to our problem of national strength and weakness.

THE NATIONAL PREMISE VERSUS THE WORLD STATE AND PANMIXIA

First of all, *the political world must always be a world of plural nations, not a world state*. For a world state, including everybody, could have no distinctive national premise; and therefore (with all due respect to elaborate constitutions drawn up for such a world state) could not possibly be a democracy. Nor could any democracy be a world state. The individual experiment in living and lawmaking implies distinct history, distinct organization, distinct character, distinct role and purpose—in a word, severalty. This severalty is based on the identity of the most universal principles of human order, the ultimate brotherhood of all men; for which reason, each several experiment is of interest to all the others, each valuing the uniqueness of every other. And each refusing to be absorbed in any other, unless its national premise can retain identity within the union.

Another consequence: *a random mixture of peoples cannot be either a nation or a democracy.*

A government of sorts can be organized anywhere with any kind of crowd—say a miscellaneous shipwreck-assembly pulled together by some Admirable Crichton. Or better, a Babel of gold-seekers on the Amur River in the 1880s (wasn't it?), loose items from all globe-quarters compelled to a common cause by oncoming winter, and brought into order by a few Russians who could use the simple formula of the *mir* or *artel* and establish a police. In such circumstances there is sure to be an undercurrent of democratic spirit, enforced by the exigency, a brotherhood of crisis in which the bare universal of humanity speaks the decisive word. The San Francisco Fire of 1906 made strange bedfellows in refugee camps, and brought to various burnt-out citizens of mark a revelation unforgettable and bright, a wholly unimagined experience of brotherhood in beginning again with nothing! The democratic vision lies at the basis of every social order, stable or improvised.

But for a community concerned for permanent nationhood, *panmixia*, whether of the imperial or of the melting-pot variety, is inconsistent with a strong democracy.

In the imperial variety, the national premise of the included peoples, never wholly suppressible, creates the chronic instability of the empire organization. The history of gradual enlightenment of empire builders, whether Alexandrian, Roman, or British, is one of moving toward the Commonwealth pattern, with increasing respect for the autonomy of peoples refusing permanent subjection. The relation of tutelage is valid—the mandate system as a whole had a factual justification in the realities of "backwardness" and partial

dependence during progress toward maturity; though its
actual history is colored by the cupidities and tyrannies of
mandatory powers.[2] The USA has on principle avoided imperial relationships, mandatory or other, but has been
involved marginally, as with the Philippines. The USSR,
on the spur of two motives, the Marx-Lenin mythos of world
revolution and the protective impulse of buffer regions, is
deeply involved: its imperialism must encounter the same
logic—the inner weakening, and the attendant drive at the
center toward greater and greater repressive violence, the
eventual necessity in its own interest of respecting autono-
mous national premises.

For such mixing, compulsory or spontaneous, brings with
it dilution of *esprit de corps* and dissipation of the national
premise. A loose co-presence of diverse ethnic groups, each
huddling with its own type in a voluntary segregation, for
the sake of an historically motivated fellowship without
which it is not "at home," confess thereby an alienness to the
national premise under which they live. This unhappy
separateness may be temporary: it may in time yield enrich-
ment to the host nation's premise. Thus Buddhism, at first
an invited stranger in Confucianist China, then spreading
and finding itself subject to alternate respect, discipleship,
and persecution, at last bore *Chinese* fruit in such neo-Con-
fucian syntheses as those of Chu Hsi and Wang Yang Ming.
Hu Shih, with the long story of Chinese civilization before
him, still judges Buddhism a perpetual alien to the Chinese
spirit, with its un-Chinese cult of asceticism, monkish with-
drawal, mystic folderol about the Void, self-torture, foot-
binding. Yet even Buddhism, nonhistoric in its spirit, in
contributing to the popular Chinese imagination such fig-
ures as the all-gracious Kwan-Yin, and to the nation's art
inestimable works and motifs—even Buddhism has entered
and enriched the national premise of the most history-con-
scious, and almost the oldest, of living nations.

An unchanging fixity of the national premise would mean

not national strength but national decay; fertilization by injected otherness remains a spiritual as well as a biological law. Yet indiscriminate and multitudinous otherness means dissipation of national integrity and ultimate non-entity. A plural frittering away of the specific character of the national premise, under the plea of universalizing the spirit of brotherhood, could result in a nondescript national life verging toward a vacuum of individual meaning, and the reduction of "democracy" to its machinery. Such a reduction results in pure counterfeit democracy; for there is on longer a "people" to be listened to—nothing but theoretical mankind!

The reality and national identity of a people are necessary conditions of every democracy.

The USA is not immune to the danger of dissipating its national being. Its hospitality, a matter of just traditional pride, expresses also a justified self-confidence: we can be almost endlessly hospitable and remain ourselves—almost. But we must *know ourselves* as a specific nation, and refuse to be driven by national fragments, nostalgic for former national premises, toward a fallacious ideal of the world state devoid of nationhood. Any national premise holds the vulnerable position of a vital organ incapable of legal formulation, hence subject to being sublimated away, through an ostensible flattery inviting it to the angelic existence of pure abstract brotherhood, by way of emasculation.

It will be sufficient to recognize this problem for what it is, and allow firmness in holding to our national identity to dissuade those entrants whose happiness depends on canceling our specific character.

THE AMERICAN NATIONAL PREMISE

In view of this problem, arising from a great virtue itself part of our national premise, let us dwell for a moment on what ingredients enter into that individual character of the USA.

It has long roots in history, roots in Palestine, Greece, Rome, in Alexandria, Byzantium, Nola. And because of these, it also derives sustenance from the rare flowering of civilized life during the rich confusion following the death of the Roman Empire. Christianity had lived underground, semi-alien to all, despised and despising with a fanatical *contemptus mundi*—an apparently impossible parent to any worldly state. Yet through the decisiveness of its social judgments it became a refuge of order, and bore within itself a germ with incredible power to generate a new civilization out of ruins. Its secret, its radical assertion of a spark of divinity resident in the human person however unlikely, demanding a type of reverence for which the gladiatorial combats, the exposure of infants, the procuring of abortion, the breeding of wars, possibly even (as Tertullian the lawyer feared) the practice of law itself, were sins against "the soul"—an entity undiscoverable by law, though a later law could protect its presumed existence in the name of what we now call "rights."

This civilization, the first in human history to be created by an Idea rather than by tribal bonds or rulers, was destined to breed its own critics, modern science, the independent arts, a secular law, the secular state. Rebelling against ecclesiastical dominance, and against the injection of purpose into the facts and laws of nature, the Renaissance and Modernity as humanist and post-Christian conveyed a twofold commission to mankind: to master the physical world—spurring the age of exploration, of rationalized industry, of capitalism—and to retain meaning for human life in a meaningless universe.

So far, the Old World: two affirmations and two negations. The affirmation of classical antiquity, negated by the Christianity of world-rejection: the affirmation of Christian man-dignity, negated by the spiritual force of objective science dedicated to the conquest of nature—including organic nature, hence man as object—by way of absolute mathematical obedience.

Colonial America, whose beginnings were almost exactly contemporaneous with those of the Modern Period in philosophy—say from Descartes, Locke, Grotius—built its several national premises on what its new task of nation-making could compose of these various and partly incompatible structures of inheritance (which, by the way, should be the substance of our historical education—"our" history begins not with Columbus, nor Jamestown, nor the Mayflower, but with them). Our national self-discovery, hammered out in the difficult conditions of wilderness-taming, paralleled distantly the European struggle of thought in which religion and science, slowly clarifying the grounds of their mutual hostility, unable to disparage either the growing utilities of technology or the insistent necessities of moral order in the self-shaping societies, attained an uneasy truce. The colonies needed both, applied science and applied faith: they needed both more than they needed the resolving analysis, only now being achieved. They worked, as men can, with unresolved polarities.

They built their economies on the groundwork of private property and individual enterprise, within a domain held in the name of, and paying tribute to, European sovereigns. They built their governments on the groundwork of respect for royal authority, but with individual rights, and with some wraith of a "social contract" whereby that authority, failing in its *quid pro quo,* could be called to account, and if need be cast off by revolt—the "right of revolution." They built their religion on the ground of the several versions of Christianity then available, with such reinterpretations as Pastor Robinson's, or Roger Williams', or Dean Berkeley's, or William Penn's, or whatever more indigenous thinkers, Jonathan Edwards perhaps, might find suitable to their consciences, and to their insistent new experiences and resultant convictions.

The emerging national premise of the USA could in no wise echo any European model. It could come into existence

only with the achievement of nationhood. Even if it had
been possible to transport from Europe an economy or a
frame of state viable in those social and physical situations,
it would have fared ill in the altered conditions. For as with
most animate beings, the life of a national premise is *always
in the making, a two-way process:* from the Idea into the
changing facts; from the facts into the Idea.

The meaning of this two-way process will appear if we
consider what a nation is. Let us recall Vico's words put
down while Europe was digesting the results of the Peace
of Westphalia which had carved out more or less durable
national shapes. A nation, Vico said, is "a natural society
of men who, by reason of unity of territory, origin, custom,
and language, are drawn into a unity of life and of conscience." The word "conscience" is of the essence, though it
is proposed as a product, not an original factor: if people
have a common background, and find themselves living together, they come to think alike on matters of right and
wrong; and it is this which fits them to carry on a joint experiment in lawmaking. A nation, we have said, is *a people's
experiment in lawmaking* while living together.[3]

We can always distinguish the ideological nation, which
thinks out policies and devises laws, from the grass-roots
nation engaged in making ends meet. The ideological nation
has an outfit of inherited notions and customary behavior;
the grass-roots nation, finding this outfit more or less chaf-
ing, proposes change. Living, which involves deduction from
inherited premises, *interacts with induction* from experiences
of fit and misfit. The result is a slow evolution of the national
premise, retaining its identity as the personality of the State.

"Uncle Sam" is not all a myth; but it is chiefly as a myth
that the national premise takes graspable form, with a mixture of conscious fantasy and serious purpose. It is the element of fantasy that leads serious thinkers here and there to
the conclusion that men are governed by myths and lies. "In
order to force the masses of mankind into submission," writes

Berdyaev, "It was necessary to inspire them with a belief in the sanctity of authority. . . . A fiction and a lie were required. . . . Myths unite, reduce to submission, and inspire. . . . Such myths are those of the sacrosanct character of kingly power . . . of the *volonté générale*, of popular sovereignty in a democracy."[4] But it was Plato who first suggested the efficacy of "one magnificent lie" in maintaining the difficult bonds of duty even in an ideal Republic.

My suggestion is that the element of imagination inseparable from the prefiguring of the goal of national purpose—I will not say the Utopia, but the valid social ideal—is not falsification, because it is understood as imagery; and is not deception, because it is invented if not *by* the presumed victims themselves at least with their collaboration. The impulse of duty is not from an *outside* source, but from within: otherwise it would not be duty, but compulsion. It is an unnecessary defaming of the moral *élan* of a people to call "obedience" by the name of "submission." There would be no leaders unless the masses had a native wish to be led. This wish may indeed be the parent of hope for the impossible; it is the trait upon which demagogues seize, luring dissatisfied masses by false promises of impending relief and ease. But every human purpose of far-reaching scope must steady its aim by a vision for which the realisms of the moment have no data to offer: Political vision is blood kin to other works of creative art.

The democracy integral to the USA's national premise shares this character of vision: it is not refuted by being shown impracticable. It is as irrefutable as the Statue of Liberty. It has nothing to lose and nothing to fear from being examined with an eye to eliminating the falsifications to which all great visions are subject.

THE MORAL CORE OF DEMOCRACY

When independence was achieved and the colonies became the USA, there were two prompt consequences. One was

economic: we ceased to owe taxes to Britain; for better or
worse, or both, our economy became *ours*. The other was
moral: we could begin to embody our budding national
premise, vision and all, in a constitution. Plural colonies of a
monarchy became a united democratic republic, the colonies,
now "states," retaining a measure of autonomy.

The "unity of conscience" which had precipitated the
struggle now spoke in the terms of this document, and of the
shortly following Bill of Rights. Each colony had already
outlined its own experiment in lawmaking, and (like Virginia
and New Hampshire) could offer fair models for the scheme
of rights, powers, and duties that citizens could expect. The
most characteristic expression of the moral spirit of the
young USA is to be looked for in the listing of this treasury
of rights. Including a distributed but not universal right to
vote—and what for.

Emphasis on rights was at that moment of history entirely
in order. But that emphasis has its well-known dangers, and
Mazzini came forward with a list of the Duties of Man to
balance the account. We have begun to outgrow the idea that
a right is a costless gift of power and privilege, and to realize
that by the logic of its definition a single claim of "human
right" implies as many duties as there are other persons
alive. But for the then-extant pass in human affairs, the
pertinent point was that rights of citizens were *ipso facto*
duties of government. And since liberty is simply the sum
of one's rights, the whole moral meaning of the political
event was the outlining of the free man's scope, not as *grace*
of the ruler, but as a *necessity* to which rulers must bow.

Now for some two centuries the legal fraternity in America, with guidance from a Supreme Court, has been applying this fundamental law to the million exigencies of an
unpredictably widening and self-complicating experience.
There have been amendments. The framework stands. Some
self-evident truths of the Declaration of Independence have
had to be qualified, in ways we have noted. And one truth at

least, *not* at that period self-evident, is becoming self-evident by dint of that qualification. It is the truth that *plural rights, taken as absolute, conflict with one another;* and conflicting, cease to be absolute. Absolute right, if any, must be one only: the root of the several relative rights.

The inner freedom of thought and conscience remains untouchable by any political power. The outer freedom of self-expression, by speech or personal writing, the natural output of thought, comes closest to an outward absolute, as inseparable from the active being of the thinking and feeling self. To kill expression is to kill all legal rights; for no legal right can exist unless it can be claimed.

Freedom of the press, swiftly following, finds itself limited —necessarily limited. There must be libel laws; there are public interests in case of clear and present danger; there is a consumer's right to truth in case of too-free-running right-to-lie in advertisement. But in its normal extension of the function of expression, by men of good will, the free press has proved itself indispensable. Its right includes the right to criticize every aspect of government. It thus becomes an instrument of each voter's right, since discussion in the press is a part of that thinking process in which the voter "makes up his mind." In the pursuance of this function, it becomes the agent of a further right, as yet unlisted, now assuming major importance, the right to be informed, or more generally *the right to know,* i.e., to have the data without which political judgments are blind. But precisely at this vital point this group of rights encounters an immovable obstacle, the government's necessary concealment of "classified" information, not to mention the citizen's right to privacy. No absolute right to know!

This right to privacy, now spontaneously invaded by every instrument of the press, photographers and all, whose cash rewards tend to be in proportion to their defiance of decent reticence as by an assumed "endowedby-their-Creator" privilege, leads a most precarious legal existence owing to the difficulty of definition. The temptation exists to put both the right and its defense into the category of the extralegal, let us say as a sort of gentleman's agreement that every citizen has a right to use something in addition to his dignity, some form of *force majeure*—some would recommend fists—in case of insufferable intrusion. I make no specific recommendation, but point out that such an agreement would be part of the unwritten national premise, in a people disposed to the free enterprise of self-help. As bearer of the spirit of the laws, this premise is prior and superior to what is formulated in law. Law must by all means civilize "self-help" but hardly eliminate it!

From this our experience one judgment emerges with considerable clarity: *the greater the number of listed rights of man, the greater the potential legal confusion,* and the greater the encouragement of all and sundry to put up claims, in the name of "rights," for unconditional privileges, egocentric and irresponsible. It is more workable to offer to unlimited human hopefulness a list of *three* unalienable rights than one of a dozen such; and a dozen are far more workable, in view of our limited powers of exact definition, than the multitude enumerated in the UN Universal Declaration of Human Rights. This declaration is less a bill of rights than an inventory of the normal functions of the well-rounded citizen of a modern state. For example, the "right to an education" (education not being a transferable commodity) and the "right to work" (addressed to no one in particular) are not legalizable "rights." But their listing has great significance for the meaning of democracy. They help to elaborate the fundamental postulate of all democratic states: *Every man a whole man.*[5] Or, to put it in the negative: no man shall be deprived by the social structure of exercising any essential function of fully developed manhood, including the functions of well-informed thinking, of earning a living, and of sharing in the control of his own destiny by way of government.

In sum, what our experience has brought us to see is (i) that there are no unconditional legal rights, and (ii) that there is one and only one absolute moral right, the right to become a whole man, or, in other words, to find one's task in the world and do it. As incapable of legal administration, this right is not mentioned in any of the official lists. Yet—as I wish now to show—it is the actual basis for the mechanism of the democratic process.

THE ABSOLUTE RIGHT . . .

For consider the links of this mechanism—free public discussion, participation through ballot in the choice of officers, of representatives, of platforms, constitutional limitations of executive power, etc. These are devices, the best we have so far lighted on—not for proficient government, but for the *unfolding of human powers* in all members; every man to some extent a self-ruler through stretching his mind to the whole.

These devices, let me repeat, are no recipe for swift, decisive, economical, adequately informed government. As the most difficult, democracy is also the most vulnerable form of government, open to numerous abuses. As trusting men's judgment and intelligence beyond the fact, it flatters, and risks incompetence; yet it induces growth. As trusting men's honor in seeking the common good rather than private advantage, it opens itself to every wile of self-seeking and of the double morality which claims favors under the guise of justice; yet it learns its perils, and through defining them and being compelled to wash its linen in public, consciously raises the level of public integrity. Democracy alone can cure the evils of democracy.

In this latter process—just now fairly active among us —the USA has overcome one of the judgments with which

Karl Marx loaded "the democratic republic," namely, that it "is the optimum political shell for capitalism," a mask for exploitation under the guise of public consent. How so? Through the necessary limitation of the reach of the voting power: that power does not extend to the composition of the executive bureaus in which the actual work of governing, in the sense of applying, interpreting, and enforcing law, is done. "The people vote; but they neither make the laws nor apply them"; the bureaucracies, with their swarming officialdom, appointive and beyond popular control, owe no duty to the people, but only to the top members of each hierarchy. It is only necessary, thought Marx, that these top members be capitalist or in the pay of capitalists, to keep the fruits of legislation in line with the interests of "the bourgeoisie." It is therefore, he argued, the bureaucracy that must be "smashed" to establish the rule of the proletariat—the conferring of voting power is a fruitless gesture![6] This argument may have been, in its own time, a shrewd bit of insight into the back door of political control. And its guiding thesis, to the effect that even with the ballot, the phrase "government *by* the people" is a euphemism, since the governed can do but a fraction of governing, is, as we noted, an inescapable truth. But in this cynical picture of the voting democracy, Marx, Engels, and Lenin failed to reckon with one trait of the people: *they are keen at detecting fraud.* The vast administrative machinery of a modern state hides many a secret, but its dominant personnel are known; appointments are scrutinized by a public informed and critical; party biases are visible; tendentious bending of nominations to the judiciary is openly denounced. In short, today the operative meaning of the laws can not stray far from the line of good faith with the public—the Marx-pictured bureaucracy can simply not exist.

. . . AND THE PRIMARY STRENGTH

What, then, is the primary strength of the free, the democratic government?

Its strength lies in its development of the electorate, its awakening, encouraging, educating, lifting power, through the gift of responsibility. This gift—though made at large expense of efficiency—develops capacity by assuming it, and thus releases the springs of all efficiency.

Its particular lifting force is this: it calls on a Demos unskilled in political thought to think, and to think in a way which is in itself an exercise of power. For a vote is a unit of power. Of how much power? A vanishing fraction of a small factor of a decision of state, a fraction that grows smaller as the number of voters increases: if it takes a million votes to make a majority, each vote has the power of one one-millionth of a decision. Hardly worth the trouble, do you say? That way lies apathy, and public apathy is the besetting curse of the democratic process. But I suspect our mathematics are at fault. The citizen's vote is his thought; and his thought is sharable—what he can't get rid of is its intentional universality: its power is that of as many millionths *as he can influence or persuade!* There is all the difference between having a vote and having none: the sum of zeros is zero; the sum of small fractions, infinitesimals if you like, is *something*—possibly a unit, an election. With the vote, political power is "out there," among the people: passion can turn into act; and the mental advance is that of crossing the immeasurable gulf between futility—the enemy of all human dignity and happiness—and effect. When freedom of thought and expresion become freedom to act, to budge the nation, then for the first time we make every man a whole man, a being whose thinking has power.

THE CHRYSALIS OF DEMOCRACY: THE SUPINE PSYCHOLOGY

Since the democratic machinery is called on to create what it presupposes—the Demos as politically stirred, intelligent, alive, responsible—its beginnings must always be handicapped, its assumption contrary to fact. Though Bryce has grounds for his judgment that the rise of democracy has been chiefly in revolt against abuses of power, the Self-directing Demos has, in the nature of the case, emerged from a relatively Supine Demos.

If democracy begins in revolution, erasing the prior rulership, its first stages will be moments of maximum confusion; not only because revolution never knows how much it destroys, but because the replacements have to explore their unaccustomed roles *de novo*. The French Revolution in eight years called for help, and in four more years lost its life to the Empire. If democracy arises by evolution from a prior régime of autocracy, it emerges from a Demos relatively quiescent, from what we may call the Supine Psychology. Under despotic rule or that of a set of feudal lords, the working masses become mentally localized. Accepting their lot as a decree of Nature (or of Karma), habitually leaving wider issues to traditional authority, the Demos becomes exploitable, helpless in emergency, incapable of revolt. A century ago, there was no more striking contrast between the masses of Asia and those of the West than the simple acceptance of poverty on the part of Asia. The Western idea that poverty could be analyzed, attacked, eventually overcome, an implication of the spirit of science as applied to social facts, went hand in hand with extensions of political power to the public, including the right to organize, in various parts of Europe, and with demands for more, including in spots the demand for revolution. Existing democracy could call for more; non-existing democracy could call for nothing, lacking so much as an ideology, a plan of action. It was the existing liberties of England and Germany and France, incomplete as they were, that made the socialist movements possible, by first defining the problem as a human problem, approachable by human enquiry and resolve.[7]

Since the effective Demos has to be built by imputing to it more understanding than it at first has, the early stages of democracy will be marked by an emphasis on tangible objectives. The supine psychology knows what it wants, in terms of material good; its ballot reports wishes, not judgments on public questions. If, as Carlyle thought, Bobus will elect Bobissimus, it is also true that Porcus will elect Porcissimus. Where each person, each group, plans and acts in self-interest, and measures the worth of government in terms of benefits received, there can be only a pseudo-democracy. The actual government has to maintain a mental separation from the Demos, in order to avert shipwreck. Democracy, so far a partial failure, excites a call for more radical measures.

This primitive stage of democracy still lingers with us. Our multiplicity of small groups, whose vital power springs in part from the fact that we need, in addition to the national premise, the fellowship bond to make us fully "at home" within the vast total which is the USA, have for their cumulative effect the relegation of the nation to the psychological fringe, relatively shadowy and unrealized. In the colonies there was still, with all the advancing divergence and complexity, a surveyable totality with a common character and spirit: in the struggle for independence, having a common foe, we were further welded in feeling, resolve, destiny. That almost-tangible unity is now difficult to capture in imagination. Even the attack on Pearl Harbor, stirring instant response, left us as a people somewhat dazed by the question, "Who is this 'We' that is called into action by nerve-lines from such remote quarters of the world?" As a spiritual entity, dedicated to purposes built into our native *telos*, we know the answer. As realized in myriads of near-by persons and groups, we tend to serve the USA by serving *them*. And when local needs and clamors produce a Rivers and Harbors Bill loaded with strictly local favors in the name of the nation, we fall easily victim to the sophism that the general welfare can be nothing more than a composite of multitudes of private welfares. We are indisposed to the knowledge that "favors" are the reverse of "welfare," and the inner ruin of national life. As a result, this nation exhibits, in a moment of crisis, a radical weakness, an incapacity for sacrifice and

self-restraint in the pursuit of that good-of-the-whole which,
through defect of habit, has lost its place as first premise of
our action. And our directing heads, mindful of party
necessities, hesitate to apply the curb. We lack capacity for
that seriousness which characterizes the temper of the
USSR. Must we acquire it through national suffering?

DIALECTIC OF THE DEMOS

Revolution in Russia, coming to a people rendered partly
supine by recurrent repression and national defeat, yet capable of anger—symptom of latent power—proposed to leap
over the stages of democracy visible in Western Europe, as
well as the "Liberal" movements coming forward in middle
Europe. It saw, in the partial achievements of people's power
here and there, not convincing signs that the will to oppress
and the answering supine psychology were becoming obsolete,
but mere placebo—ineffective, tangled in parliamentary
wrangling, class egoisms, party sophistries—a deceptive
front for entrenched capital power, successful only in industrial production. Russia had its liberals, but no Liberal
movement.[8]

Revolution was to be thorough, and also prompt. It proposed immediate redress of social injustice, liquidating the
exploiters, putting the exploited at once in control of the
productive apparatus. But, of course, under guidance. The
Supine stage is no preparation for economic—still less for
political—responsibility. Anger may supply energy and
endurance; it does not by itself insure competence.

Whose guidance, then? The only mentally active guidance
available—that of the same surgeons who had beheaded the
existing order. Compelled to replace the functions of the
severed head, including the control of the economy, these
surgeons, heads of party, set up by necessity a dictatorship.
(The phrase "Dictatorship of the Proletariat" in its Eng-
lish garb is accidentally precise: it is not *by* the proletariat,
but *of* the proletariat *by* heads of party. Not quite what

Marx had in mind, but inevitable.) Revolution, child of democracy and science, must destroy extant germs of democracy—as in halfway Kerensky revolutions—in order to survive. To annihilate the supine psychology of Acceptance it requires a supine psychology of Conformity, attempting at first to enforce conformity in the very inmost thought and emotions of the people. Revolution not only never knows how much it puts to death; it seldom knows how much it *cannot* kill, even by the searching pressures of Pavlov's conditioned reflexes.

But the decisive fact is this: that *revolution also —and necessarily—learns*. It is compelled to learn by the exigencies it creates. It cannot survive without Production. And it learns that Production, whether bourgeois or socialist, requires motivation, incentive, morale—the morale of the worker and, first of all, the morale of the farmer. Then the morale of the technician and the morale of the scientist. With this step, the concerns of the revolution fall into unison with the concerns of democracy; for the scientist can survive, *as scientist*, only if he is a whole man, and free.

We come in sight of the dominating principle of social order: whatever the form of government, the ultimately ruling power, the motive force of this on-pushing dialectic within history, is the *drive of human nature for full humanity*—akin to the biological drive for type-maturity—present in every people. The people as Supine must give way—is everywhere giving way—to the people as Productive. Success in production requires more than the economic pressure; it requires liberation of thought and expansion of hope. Man as Productive is far more real, more complete, more human, than man Supine by dint of his necessities-controlled-by-masters. But man Productive is still incomplete.

We and the Soviet Union at the moment alike enjoying the conscious power of technique in production, are destined,

I believe, to find alike a subtle shame in preoccupation with productivity, implying a certain subservience to commodity wants. For man-Productive is bound to seek an escape—not alone from the prison of want but from the prison of wanting —to become man-Creative. As Productive, man uses the world of nature: but to master nature, he must still *obey*. As Creative, man adds to the world what nature alone would never contain. Man is only fully free and fully himself when he becomes man the Creator—let us say, as symbol, man the artist, remaking the world from within the world.

Art has the miraculous capacity of reuniting the nations without blurring the uniqueness of nationhood. The graphic art of Japan is universal, yet utterly Japanese; and it is part of its universality that no one in the world would want it other than Japanese. When Van Cliburn wins the Tschaikowsky Prize, it is for playing Russian music; and when the USA wishes to join in the joy, it is that same Russian music it wishes to hear him play. *To develop an art is to develop a nation*, and *in the same stroke*—not in a separate and additional stroke—the *Internation*. When art thus reunites the nations, the ultimate confession of human identity is made. And with it—not peace, for the nations remain separate— but the beginning of peace, for there is a common sky that transcends difference.

To recover the vitality of art requires recovering the spirit of the nation, within the universal. The ideology of the USSR must get beyond its abstraction, and welcome a *revived national sense*, as concrete and racy of the soil as custom and dialect and folklore. For these, Marx could have no feeling, and Lenin could keep none, absorbed in the countermyth of an impersonal economic necessity, under whose material pressure all peoples were to march to a common destiny. It is noteworthy—I will not say surprising— how empty of national feeling is the entire literature of the Communist Movement, beginning with "Workers *of the*

world, unite." Not surprising, since economic determinism
can make place in theory no more for the soul of a nation
than for the soul of a man. In presence of the great split,
capital versus the exploited masses, a split held to be running
through all nations, all other splits, it was felt, become insignificant—they must be forgotten! This fallacious judgment of relative importance was tested in 1914 when the
workers of Britain and France declined to join the workers
of Germany in their threat against the wills of the British
and French nations. And again in 1917, when German
soldiers verging toward defeat rejected the overtures of
Russian soldiers ordered by Bolsheviks to fraternize with the
Germans in the hope of stimulating a revolution on both
fronts.

It is a radical weakness of revolution on Marxian lines
that the "exploiting classes" in regions dominantly agricultural rather than industrial—that means China as well as
Russia—are likely, as landed aristocracy, to be the bearers
of the *historic culture* of the nation; and with their liquidation
—not the national spirit itself, but the voice of that spirit,
is muted. The national premise lives on in the land-and-
family customs of the people, their folklore and folk-art; but
its vitality *needs the conscious care of the vocal element*—
the "intelligentsia"—of the community. Attack on family
coherence in China constitutes a double blow to the nation,
and a further weakness to the regime. No state can thrive
on economic fodder alone, nor even remain economically
strong, as Mao is presently discovering.

To point out the universal tendency to a class-divergence
of economic interest has been an important service of the
Marx-Engels philosophy to human self-understanding; but
that divergence itself takes on radically different forms in
Europe and Asia, in France and England: it cannot be made
a world issue to be dealt with *en bloc*. The nation remains the
fundamental political community. What the "International"
would obliterate, the arising sense of a composite world will

restore—a world of nations as varied experiments in law-making, unitable not by an indifferent economic pressure but by reciprocal cultural regard—as of Slav for West Europe and of West Europe for Slav—and thereby recover the democratic world solidarity in which the strength of separate nations is most deeply rooted.

Democracy itself, we know, was in its early day a revolution. First a revolution in thought—government not master but servant—a revolution which could be pleasantly emblazoned on the standards of despotic Hapsburgs in the proud words "*Ich dien*," I serve. But then came a revolution in blood—one which put monarchs underground and confirmed the bonds of government's duty to people, spelled them out in written law. The *soi-disant* democratic monarchy must necessarily give way to the democratic republic, because rulership by the individual had to become more than a sentiment, had to become a literal power, almost nothing in amount but infinitely expansible in hours of public passion.

Given the democratic republic, no other social revolution is either needful or tolerable. When this point is reached, revolution, becoming unnecessary, becomes a crime. The Russian Revolution had an idle monarchy to replace: it was two revolutions in one. It took on the extremest load; it was therefore obliged to resume monarchical functions in dictatorship. It has now, for its own growth, freely to restore its own democratic principle: *initiatives to this end are discernible and indeed numerous.*

What that democratic principle is, we have now traced to its mental and moral roots. We recognize its character as indestructible, based as it is on the central maturing-impulse of human nature, the same in all men: its dialectic is in the long run irresistible.

At the same time, we recognize that, just because its principle is inward, its translation into institutions is *always ex-*

perimental and revisable. We are freed from the fallacy of identifying "democracy" with the specific mechanisms of the American republic, a fallacy which to some extent misled our efforts to recommend democracy to a Germany under military occupation.[9] We are prepared to acknowledge that —just as we still stumble over what Liberty includes, what Equality requires, what Fraternity commands and allows— so we *still enquire the full meaning of Democracy.* We still fall into its counterfeits.

We are prone to the democracy of *dependence*—looking to the State as caterer. To the democracy of *relaxation*— flattering our incompetence, scornful of paying the price for excellence, at ease in mediocrity or less. We have still to learn that the fundamental equality among men and citizens is the *equality of standard*, unrelenting, unbribable.

But especially today, through party zeal-to-please, through duty to listen to every voice, every fellowship-group as claimant or combatant, our democracy becomes a democracy of *blurred view-merging*, devoid of clarity and force. Its groping, synthetic direction risks a fatal surrender— surrender of the leadership required by the exigency in world affairs. This leadership calls for a powerful unification of national purpose which can only arise from a grasp of the world situation far beyond national limits—the international realities, mental and tangible, of the present world scene.

What are these realities?

VII

REALITIES OF THE
INTERNATIONAL SCENE

NEW DEPTHS AND NEW HEIGHTS

IF THE words "communism" and "capitalism" fail to touch
the central problem of our time, the words "socialism" and
"individualism" also fall short. To discuss matters of economic system or degrees of democracy in government as if
these were the primary issues confronting humanity today is
to hide our heads from the facts of life—from realities which
are equally facts of death. It has become the fate of this
moment of world history to confront the Worst, the blank
end of things. To see the Worst as actual possibility, to see
it steadily and not retreat—this is our particular call to
adequacy, perhaps to greatness.

We in our local and mounting—and perhaps dangerous—
ease are at a certain disadvantage in our attempts to grasp
the situation; for Progress is itself a reality, is it not?—and
Progress should bring us nearer the Best. Instead, we find
ourselves called on to plunge, from a height of civilization
and security, into the primitive cockpit of struggle for survival. The extreme gamut—from the summit of civilized
living to the depth of uncivilized chaos—is ours to span, to
feel, perhaps to experience.

This "Worst" is not simply the specter of abrupt racial
extinction. This common enemy, which forces the USA and
the USSR into the minimal fraternity of mutual dependence

in the will-to-live, confers, so far, a paradoxical benefit. The Worst is the union of this dead end with a moral reversion to prebarbarism: the extinction would take place at a moment of rejected human dignity, as if the meaning of all human history were, to date, a cipher. For it is the appalling fact of our time that man—not alone under Hitler and Stalin—has so far slipped away from civilization as to resort again to torture to compel a political result or extort a falsehood convenient to the occasion, and to reject all morality—including truth, good faith, justice, mercy—for the sake of a supreme end. The triumph of reason has become a triumph of something called "objectivity," in which humanity itself is to be held at arm's distance to determine its engineering qualities, its durability, elasticity, its response to temperatures and pressures, the "strength of materials." Morality must submit to this same test. The summit of rationality has proved itself capable of reaching the summit of what was once called criminality but is criminality no more: for if Nihil is our creed and Annihilation our ultimate outlook, morality becomes an irrelevant weakness in carrying out the Great Resolve. To be in command of the technical means for the total destruction of humanity would not in itself be a peril, if this were not at the same time an era in which mass murder is accepted as a possible factor of progress, a perhaps-necessary means to the social consummation. (We dare not forget that the event at Hiroshima, and the prior event at Dresden, in which the USA took part, were mass murders of civilian populations.) The hard-won sanctities of human life which since Grotius have limited the ferocities of war have lost much of their deterring force with the arrival of total war, for human death in vast numbers benumbs the sense of personal tragedy. Humanity has claim only where life has meaning; and how, in view of the mass reckonings pressed on us by events and by the spirit of history, can human life retain individual dignity, not to speak of "sacredness"?

It is experience that presses this question, and calls on

each of us to refuse the mental shelter of circumstance, under
the moral penalty of disqualification in our right to judge.

It was Norman Hall, speaking of his initiation in
France with the Lafayette Flying Squadron, in early
1917 when aerial warfare was in infancy, and experiment
and accident were the order of the day, who said to me "I
am not sure this is doing me any good. We have to clean
up so many messes, and then go on as if nothing had happened. What we need is time to think." Yet he was at the
moment shortening his own furlough, after having been
shot down, in order to get back into the fighting over
Verdun. There is something in us that rebels against
shelteredness.

To men whose experience has brought direct knowledge
of the newer refinements of purposive torment, whether in
war or in police control, or of the inhuman strains of underground resistance, these dimensions of inflicted suffering
tend to combine with the apparent indifference of High
Heaven to recommend a posture toward the Whole far different from "accepting the universe." We too-weakly call it
Atheism; and to call it Nihilism leaves out its positive core
of refusal to pay reverence. Call it perhaps a blunted surface,
a metallic skin, an acquired toughness of outlook in which
many of the lost, or angry, or "beat," or act-for-act's-sake
youth of the Continent, England, America, Japan, end their
questioning. They mingle with their inability to accept traditional faiths and philosophies a temper of cosmic wrath
(which contains a latent moral demand for justice) such as
could conceivably touch off a contemporary version of the
crowd-crushing suicide of Samson. After all, the "pillars of
the house" have now reduced themselves to subatomic al-
mighty invisibles.

Security, once a first-rank treasure for men and nations,
no longer exists. But why worry over security? If meaning
has vanished, death is no longer a calamity. Death merely

closes the account books of bankruptcy—blacks out the worthless remembrance of *temps perdu*. Better not to survive: for willingness to survive in Hell would be a proof of deserving it.

This temper which cancels insight into the possible meaning of historical suffering, and rejects as myth the traditional consolations of groping mankind, may still understandably cling with desperation to a material Utopia born of revolutionary excess, consonant with a political scheme apparently anesthetic to moral appeal, yet in subconsciousness hoping for recognition and some shred of fraternity—wanting to *belong*! It is a weakness of the USA in this juncture that its relative normality gives it so little sympathy with the temper that has begotten the wars and revolutions of our time. For nearly three years from August, 1914, war in Europe was solely Europe's business—not possibly ours! We have been insulated from the Worst; now it becomes part of our foreground reality. We are righteously indignant, we denounce in fury—and we remain impotent, because we cannot understand.

It is evident that the situation cannot be met by reiterating the pieties of Christendom or the Geneva Conventions or Woodrow Wilson's principles of international order. We cannot abandon them; we cannot compromise; we cannot appease. But we *cannot persuade*. We may, however, by an immense effort achieve an understanding, and a course that creates a new footing. Let us try.

THE THREAT OF WORLD REVOLUTION

The most hopeful fact among present realities is that, as of today, neither America nor the Soviet Union has the will either to suicide or to vast human destruction: the *minimal fraternity* implied in this mutual self-restraint—seldom spoken of—is a reality of the first importance.

The most ominous fact, for the continuance of this fraternity, is that the USSR has an inherited mandate, with the compelling force of an ideological goal, for *world revolution.*

And to all appearances, the pressure to move toward that goal, to expand the area of political sway, remains unabated: Russia seems prepared in favorable circumstances—adjacency, etc.—to impose this mandate on regions indisposed to the revolution. The word "coexistence" is invoked to lull apprehension; but each side has reason to doubt its final validity in the mind of the other: the USA because of the continuing symptoms of the will to expand—in the Far East, the Mid-East, in Latin America . . . ; the USSR because of a sense that the "capitalist" system, committed to regard a "socialist" regime as pernicious, is in its nature a threat to its own existence. Capitalism *delenda est* because, for capitalism, socialism *delenda est.* The appropriate stance being one of mutual fear—mother of suspicion, deceit, intrigue— each must reserve from the other the healing act of trust. For trust involves risk. And risk, for those who still hug the phantom of a vanished security, is felt as treason to those who still value life. An act of trust committed with conscious acceptance of risk, based on the valid judgment that a life hagridden by fear and suspicion "is not worth living by a man," and which carries the bare *chance of eliciting an answering trust*—such an act could be the ultimate greatness; and for it *individuals* may indeed be ready: but individuals—even governing individuals—cannot assume to commit a nation, not even to a creative risk.[1]

This tense situation can be held for a time in the unstable equilibrium of the tightrope walker. But not forever. And while the time holds out, it is the part of wisdom to ask whether the mutual fears are themselves realities, or whether they are dependent on judgments partly fallacious and therefore alterable.

VICIOUS CIRCLES OF MUTUAL FEAR

The situation is intrinsically absurd: socialism must be destroyed because, for socialism, capitalism must be destroyed; and, vice versa, capitalism must be destroyed because, for capitalism, socialism must be destroyed! The most vicious of vicious circles. Shall we simply dismiss it as the reverse of reality—a nightmare? But there it is!

Yet, to accept it as reality renders the practical problem insoluble, a fact of which we have also daily proof. Nothing is more fruitless than the continued confrontation of diplomats each of whom believes the other a disguised blackguard committed to his destruction—all-black against all-white. There are such diplomats, on both sides: their middle name is Futility.

Ostensibly they are the true Defenders of the Faith, the loyal expounders of the hidden reality. Citing facts and scriptures, they remind us that the USSR is, under whatever mask, out for world conquest; and that nothing but our superior force checks its persistent advance. What we have to deal with, we are told, is "a long-range struggle to destroy the way of life of the free countries of the world." And if it is true, as a very on-the-spot book authoritatively assures us, that "The Soviet Union is at war with the West right now,"[2] we can do no less—and little more—than stand on guard and keep our nuclear press-buttons handy. These voices are not to be discounted.

But could it be possible that the USSR is of *divided mind*, speculating on our intent, while we speculate on theirs? Blowing hot and blowing cold, because (a) the circle is there; and because (b) the circle is palpably irrational and hopeless, and must—by some inconsistency—be broken? For us, the relieving reflection is that *the aims and fears of nations are not Solid Fixtures, but living growths*. No firm reality is on the surface. No one but Mr. Khrushchev is final authority on what Mr. Khrushchev really intends, and perhaps he himself is somewhat in doubt, allowing a factor of adjustment to opening experience.

THE ROLE OF MYTH IN NATIONAL FEAR

It may be of use to remember that fear, in the political world, is engendered by ideas. And great fears have their sources, together with great aims, in ideas wrapped in imagination—the hope or apprehension of things to come. The Marx-Engels Apocalypse with its suggestion of world overturn in violence has, in its aspect of hope, the advantage to its believers of bringing a spirit of moral warfare into the grim historical process, even while that process is deemed materialist and inevitable, clothing the horror with a shimmer of justice and achieved Fraternity. It is this dream, alluring to one side, that terrifies the other. And while few things are so difficult to uproot as a dream enshrined in dogma and upheld by a nation's passion, nothing so evades proof of error. A dream cannot be refuted!

All dreams, political and religious dreams included, are indeed subject to the re-interpretations of maturing thought and experience. Leaders seldom have the courage to correct them. And while they live on, unrevised, in the public tradition and in the hearts of their followers, the fear they evoke in their potential victims will persist.

It is not so much actual Israel as the prophetic vision of Zion that maintains Arab distrust. And what continues to haunt the Israeli imagination is less actual Arab unifying than the empire of Nasser's dream. The fanatical devotion of fighting men and their equally fanatical cruelties are less products of a barbaric disposition than of dreams of destiny. Lord Russell of Liverpool has recently reminded us of the ferocities of Japanese fighting and treatment of prisoners in World War II; but he omits the mental roots of the intensity of suffering inflicted and accepted. Those roots lie in the traditional vision of Japan, emphasized by Bushido, as the one nation commissioned by Deity to world rule and governed by the living presence of the Sun Goddess in her lineal descendant, The Em-

peror. Professor MacIver had not exaggerated the role
of myth in government, and hence in history. There was
wisdom in the treatment of the Japanese situation by the
USA after the surrender—not, as some wished, to bring
the Emperor to trial, but to persuade him to a public
denial of his divinity, as a free act on his part. No other
act could so finally have dissipated the myth: the Emperor
earned his right.

HISTORIC SOURCES OF RUSSIAN DISTRUST

World revolution, as an article of scriptural USSR faith
—enlarged by Western fears to the quite different vision of
world conquest—begets an answering fear of the West on
the part of Russia. This fear, not eased by our original
policy of containment, reaching a morbid intensity akin to
claustrophobia, accounts for a considerable part of the forcible imposing of the Soviet system upon unwilling neighbors.
The resolve with which the USSR now holds a buffer belt
across mid-Europe, including East Germany and Czechoslovakia, is in part pure economic brigandage—a milking of
the neighbor's resource and energy for the imperative nour-
ishment of a needy USSR. But it is also—and I think chiefly
—an expression of fear, a fear of the continuing hostility of
the West, a hostility promptly announced in the original
anti-Bolshevik crusade of 1917-22.

Of this crusade, Professor William Yale writes that
"our intervention in the Russian Revolution . . . caused
untold suffering to the people of Russia, without accom-
plishing its purpose"; it accomplished just the opposite,
as with the intervention in 1792 of other European powers
in the French Revolution; it "strengthened the revolutionary government, aroused mass-support, stimulated an
intense feeling of nationalism."[3]

Memory of that anti-Bolshevik campaign, still living,
serves as concrete evidence of the spontaneous, perhaps natural, and therefore persistent Western attitude, to be pru-

dently guarded against as long as the tension lasts. The buffer region will serve.

This judgment is confirmed by M. Arthur Wauters, former Belgian ambassador to Moscow, in an article on "Four Constants of Stalinism,"[4] the first of which is "capitalist encirclement." Wauters speaks of this obsession as a psychosis which accounts for the numerous annexations, beginning with the Baltic states, the western Ukraine and White Russia, Bessarabia and Bukovina, together with the new frontiers imposed on Finland and Poland. From these to the mid-Europe security zone, the steps were consistent. And for the future, M. Wauters says that "This consideration will from now on dominate the diplomatic actions of the Soviet Union, including its German policy— as illustrated by the Rapacki Plan." My comment is that, given the fear as a permanence, this forecast is foregone: but precisely because it is a "psychosis," the alleged "constant" is subject to revision.

Quite apart from the anti-Bolshevik campaign, fear, as a sense of being on the defensive, lies *in the very nature of revolution*. As an outbreak of violence, no purely observing nation can sanction it. As social decapitation, much of the most precious to all men is alienated or destroyed. Among the émigrés of 1917 I count some of the noblest souls I know. To the revolting masses, indeed, revolution replaces the intolerable—anything is better than the slavery, tyranny, arrogance, misery that has gone before. But no one else could judge it necessary, no one who had not been co-sufferer of that special evil, and sustained by the special vision that, to the doers, justified the fearful deed. In short, revolution in its nature *expects* the condemnation due from sympathizers with, or apologists for, the decapitated régime: this expectation is its own bad conscience—and every conscientious revolution will have a bad conscience. If its revolt is against, not solely a particular tyranny, but against an ism—say capitalism—it will further expect the hostility of all who incor-

porate that ism; it will even court that hostility through the
mission involved in its act—that of the world-spread of its
principle, if not of its rule; and indeed no revolution can be
justified *unless for a cause thought to be in principle universal.* To this extent, for the USSR, a fear of the West, including the USA, lies in the nature of the case.

IS THERE AN ELEMENT OF HONEST CONVICTION?

This fear is further justified by a certain incapacity on
the part of the USA to credit the original dream of the
USSR—say the dream of a classless society—as a genuine
ideal, entertained by sincere and devoted human beings. We
are far away from the scene of crisis; we see chiefly the
angry sparks struck out by the continuing frictions. Seeing
little more in the notion of a classless society than a perverse
version of equality-and-fraternity, and largely ignorant of
East European history, we are impressed chiefly by the continued inhumanities of the USSR's struggle for stability—
its fear of freedom, repressing salutary dissent, capable of
starving kulaks by the million, imputing false motives to our
acts of defense, riddling various nations with subversive
agents, refusing to implement agreed clauses of the Peace
Treaty, misusing membership in UN to thwart action fa-
vored by all but itself. All this indisposes us to see integrity in
the original fire of revolt: we cannot believe that the Soviet
Union has a genuine faith. Yet—and I speak to my own
skepticism—we must know that an unrelieved picture is a
false picture.

An unrelieved picture must be a false picture—not because
the leaders of a revolution, whether American or French or
Russian, must necessarily be men of lofty principle and
patriotic mould, free from the conspiratorial and sadistic
tempers, but because we are dealing not with leaders and
theories alone but with the slowly focused response of a great
people to an altered direction of their living. Our question is
not whether Marx and Lenin were men of pure intentions, and

honest thinkers rather than constitutional crooks: our question is whether the people of the USSR have a genuine ideal, one with which men of good will can be in sympathy, if not accord. Our situation is such that the offenses I have mentioned fill the foreground, and we can easily forget that there is a background, an immense up-driving effort with defective implements, among them a provisional repression of freedom for unity in the task, yet sustained by respect-worthy hope and purpose. Listen to the words of a man well known as a severe critic of Communist principles: Dr. Charles Malik, then UN representative of Lebanon, knowing whereof he speaks, said very simply, "The Soviets have a belief that they are willing to die for." This statement implies no unanimity of Soviet people in regard to Marxian tenets, but a general co-ordination of purpose, and an earnestness of striving toward national objectives which impresses itself on visitors. Can we say as much of our own national seriousness?

In any case, this is one of the realities we face: the Soviet phenomenon derives much of its force from an honest conviction at the center, able in some degree to transmit itself —not solely by false promises—to peoples formerly supine. To give the Soviets credit in our own minds, not for having "the right answers" to anything, but for "a belief they are willing to die for," may well be a step toward making "co-existence" a realizable stage in which competition and persuasion—wholly free of compromise—may relieve the disastrous pressure toward an unattainable military security.

And with this degree of understanding, it becomes possible also to dispose of a fatal postulate, which seems to poison much of our foreign policy, that all steps toward this stage of peaceful rivalry proposed by the USSR are covers for sinister designs; and that the most admirable triumph of our intelligence is to detect and expose the cheat. The vanity of the sleuth destroys the statesman. A failure of due caution would indeed be inexcusable; caution has a role even when security has vanished. But how much more deadly a failure to be so far "dupe of our own distrust" as to refuse an open mind to possibly honest tentatives toward breaking the vicious circle!

Have there been any such possibly honest tentatives?

In a statement before the Supreme Soviet, December 21, 1957, Mr. Khrushchev declared (I use a free translation):

"The victory of a social order will be achieved, not by jet missiles, nor by atomic and hydrogen bombs, but by developing that social order which best provides material and moral good for mankind."

Whatever the difficulties may be of making these words valid, whatever inconsistencies the speaker may show, the fact that they have been publicly and responsibly spoken marks an epoch. They are in themselves a departure from a Marx-Lenin orthodoxy which, for its own good, the USSR must someday find full liberty to reconceive. The Twentieth and Twenty-first Party Congresses had already begun the work by declaring overt war an avoidable event.

Since that time, with the announcement of the seven-year plan, the conception of peaceful competition has become a staple of the professed outlook of the Soviet government. The sagacious American observer now inclines to accept the profession as essentially sincere: Mr. Adlai Stevenson reports from his visit of August, 1958, without qualifying phrases, "Mr. Khrushchev envisages the further expansion of Communism as a peaceful process."

These words, and certain minor deeds of similar trend,[5] do not of themselves dispose of the orthodox Marx-Lenin dream of world revolution. They suggest that a familiar process is taking place of transposing that dream from the realm of literal program to the realm of symbol, from a call to war to the guiding spirit of experimental challenge. We should like to believe in their sincerity; would we be right to do so? What are the real aims of the USSR?

We face the riddle that has been before us throughout: motives are invisible. What evidence can there be for those whose conscience and responsibility forbid indulgence in credulity? What we have to note is that for an answer we are *not dependent on guesswork,* nor on mind-reading. For there are objective realities which create necessities for thinking men everywhere. Chief of these is the dread of all peoples, not of statesmen alone, of the suicidal character of war; and next, the incompatibility of war with any economic planning.

But further, the immediate outlook for world change lies chiefly in that half of mankind still tormented by poverty, the merest beginning of whose relief from whatever source calls for elaborate capital investment, inconsistent not only with war itself, but with the continued and mounting costs of war preparation. In brief, any considerable passage of underprivileged peoples from the Supine to the Productive stage presupposes a dominant peace. And if we suppose with Mr. Lippmann that the Soviet eye is directed chiefly to Asia and Africa, its responsibilities there and at home would forbid preliminary conflict with the USA.

It is conceivable, is it not, that the USSR may have seen this bit of objective logic earlier than we, and that its talk of peaceful competition may be governed at least as much by realism as by sentiment?

With this suggestion we pass from the mental realities of the international scene to the political and historical realities.

VIII

TANGIBLE REALITIES:
The Power and Up-push of the Peoples

IT IS NOT the governments, as "powers" great or small, that we have first and always to consider. It is first of all the *peoples* of the world, as realities bearing and shaping all the other reals we have to deal with.

For the governments themselves have first to consider the people as the reality without which the governments are nothing. The folk of any state are its substance, not only as raw material, nor as working energy, nor as combat force, but as minds and wills having a bent of their own, a remembering, feeling, custom-holding, purposing vitality. Wholly without technical "representation," simply as living agents with their own prejudice and momentum, they lend, as we have seen, a factor of democracy to the most autocratic rulership. The human nature of this living substance is never on vacation. Its tolerance—as at least a negative good will—is a *sine qua non* of every ruler's lease of life.

Intelligent tyrants discover this reality, and bend to it in time to escape "the deluge"; Machiavelli has shown them how. Unintelligent tyrants undertake to ignore it, and with an ideally supine public, disposed to take their political environment in one piece with the physical as Fate or the will of God, may long maintain a society in which, as Hegel put it, "One is free"—one only. Given that one, showing to

the masses the single fully rounded specimen of human am-
plitude—one man a whole man—the rest may take a certain
pride and release in his majesty and magnificence. (Though
it weighs heavy on our democratic conscience, we must agree
that a capacity for vicarious fulfillment is a genuine human
resource. A human hive with one Queen Bee [or King] has a
far ampler imaginative reach than the same mass with unrelieved equality. The glory of the topmost is the visualized
fairy tale of all.)

But the position of the unintelligent tyrant is safe only so
long as no breeze of new hope blows through his realm. The
situation today is that *the breeze cannot be kept out*. And
because of this, the logic of experience is at work, the dialectic. Autocracy everywhere is made aware of the drive to
maturity within the living substance it governs. If an untrammeled Freedom must discover, through anarchy, the
need of Authority for its own existence, so equally, untrammeled Authority must discover, whether through rebellion or
through mass decay, the necessity, for its own existence, of
Freedom—some step toward the scope-to-be-fully-human on
the part of the people—*every man* a whole man. The newer
dictatorships, simultaneously with the older empires, are
today rehearsing both discoveries.

THE PEOPLE'S VOICE VERSUS THE OFFICIAL VOICE

But if the people are a prior reality to which their own
government has to bend, they are also a prior reality *for all
other governments*. It follows that in our own relations with
other states, we dare not forget that it is the people of those
states, not the officials, with whom we are chiefly concerned.
The foreign government may be, and usually is, the only
available voice—at least the only available official voice—for
its people. Yet it is seldom—I will venture to say never—a
perfect voice. It is an experimental interpretation of the
people's sense, with an unspoken reservation: "I speak subject to revision." The real voice of the USSR need not be

identical with the words of its rulers, nor the real voice of China with the proposals of Peking. Nor, we must add, is the real voice of the USA identical with the dicta of any Administration. These voices are all meritorious attempts; as official, they may carry binding decisions: but we who seek realities must listen for the interpreting echo behind the words.

It follows, further, that a diplomacy addressed—by an easy official illusion—solely to governing persons, documents, or ideologies in books is addressed to façades, not to realities. And if ignorant of the people behind the façade, or devoid of the interpreting intuition—devoid, that is, of human sympathy and understanding—it risks being a diplomacy of blinders, groping in the dark for the living sense of the formal issues.

Shall China be admitted to the UN? Look at certain deeds and words of its leaders, and say no. Look at the Chinese people, and say yes: they are China.

It is indeed necessary to deal with these official persons and ideas. The body of Leviathan cannot speak except through its head. But also, the head of Leviathan cannot feel or act except through its body. And if the head propounds intolerable policies, it is precisely at such a point that well-argued legal answers are not enough. One must first consider whether this intolerable proposal is in truth the will of that people. If the voice of the spokesman were the only source of judgment as to the people's will, there could be no recourse; but that is seldom the case.

It is certainly not the case with the USSR. The fortunately growing access of people to people affords a relieving comment on official language which, with its ever-present concern for ideological correctness, contains here and there echoes of the "imperialist plot" and kindred ghost-chatter, as part of a propaganda pose difficult to dismiss. There can be no doubt that the people of the USSR, like our own people, *do not want war*; the announcements of "peaceful competition" as motive—and of peace as the necessary condition—for the succeeding five- and seven-year plans, have won almost unanimous response: there is no popular demand for the violent overthrow of our "capitalist" system. The evidence we have of the people's temper constitutes a tangible reassurance that Khrushchev's program of competitive coexistence is a genuine USSR aim, on which we may build.

But there is still firmer ground.

THE RUSSIAN PEOPLE AS A SOURCE OF CHANGE IN MARXISM

That further ground lies in a world situation which we may approach by dwelling for a moment on the people of the USSR in their early interaction with the revolution-ideology.

These people, over the vast expanse of the land, are still chiefly the villagers and the workers. There has been until recently only a thin layer of mercantile and industrial enterprise outside of the cities, very little that could be called a "middle class" or "bourgeoisie." Like all peoples, they bear the mark of soil and climate, they have their own ways and lore, their own ideas and metaphors for the total universe and human fate. The *mir*, as name for the age-old village community, is also, significantly, a name for the wide world: the cosmos is a well-ordered, large-scale *mir*—as with the Chinese and Plato and the Stoics, the order of human society echoes the order of nature-heaven. It is these people to whom the revolution came with its denunciation of the other-world-compensation-prospect as opiate and its calls for immense worldly effort for a worldly correction of fortune.

Under these circumstances a people no longer supinely accepting became a people expecting. The leadership itself, exploring an unbeaten path, guided only by a doctrine now given its first tryout, must be hypersensitive to experience, responsive to public sentiment, alert to blind spots in that doctrine. In dealing with these expectant people, revolutionary theory *has already undergone change*, radical change.

First, in the time-prospect of the withering away of the State. Marx regarded the proletarian revolution as the moment for beginning the relaxation of state force. Lenin found this out of order. The State cannot begin to relax, must even increase in power, until every vestige of exploitation shall have been banished from the earth.

Second, in the conception of the State itself. If there are no more exploiters, the State continuing in existence can no longer be defined as "the instrument whereby the exploiting class keeps its hold on the exploited." Since the Lenin-Stalin intensified state control could never be justified on that theory, the Marxian state idea breaks down completely.

Third, in respect to the very core of Marxian philosophy, the economic determination of history. The call of Lenin for "activism," the demand for a purposive leadership, and for something more than assent on the part of party members—affirmative disposition to spread the gospel—implies that Economic Determinism *will not of itself do the work*. The masses are not self-directing; what we have called the "supine psychology" is precisely not prepared for initiative. Economic need, pressing on the masses, makes no proposal for its own relief—is itself headless. Hence an ideologically active core of workers must assume directive functions—a Party. Thus the theory that economic conditions determine the political structure becomes at this point the reverse of the truth: it is the activated political organ that must shape and develop the economy.

Marxism thus loses its clue to history, the most disastrous of all deviations.[1] Lenin and Stalin have been too politic to put the matter in just this light; later thinkers may do it for them, though at the usual perils of an amended orthodoxy. For our purposes, there is no need to press particular points of departure from doctrine: the important consideration is that the basic theory does change; that it changes in response to experience; and that the experience is a tacit interaction between the dictators and the people, the people exerting a silent force of character, at once universally human and of distinctive quality among the nations.

The fact of change is not in itself a matter to be hidden or disavowed: it is the contrary, a sign of life, and especially of a living interaction between rulers and people. The changes I mention are radical, from the standpoint of the original theory; but they leave intact the fundamental contrast between the centralized economic system of the Soviets and the free enterprise of the USA: they are changes within the opposition.

At the same time they carry definite admonition regarding our diplomacy. Any diplomacy which addresses itself to a static entity called "Communist Doctrine" risks aiming at a target no longer there. Political life tends to acquire a vested interest in preserving hostilities, under familiar slogans. (The two-party system is in perpetual grief over this necessity.) This tendency becomes a menace to peace in the international field: both the USA and the USSR have to learn that a diplomacy based on stereotypes is in principle addressed to unrealities.

We have now to look beyond the simple fact of change in our immediate context, to certain necessary changes in the world context.

THE TIDE OF MASS AWAKENING

Looking to the peoples of the world as our primary reality, we are prepared to see as the most significant event of the present century something that is happening to peoples— and because of them to governments—in Asia, Indonesia, Africa, Latin America. One uses the word "revolution" with hesitation, for the change is not so much explosive as tidelike, an almost wordless, irresistible heave. Its force is capable of dissolving empires, and it is doing just that, but it is first of all mental, a profound awakening and a lifting of ambition and resolve. It carries with it a quiet evanescence of the supine psychology, with special regard to poverty and ruler-neglect.

My first encounter with this new force was during the first World War. Behind the Allied lines in France there were some 300,000 Chinese, a large labor-force to carry out the engineering work of the new trench and aerial warfare. The morale of these coolies, far from home, cut off from communication by their own illiteracy, went from bad to worse. A graduate student at Yale, Y. C. James Yen, wangled an assignment to the French front, saw the difficulty, opened a night school for reading and writing Chinese, using a limited set of characters—some 1300 instead of a scholar's 5000-10,000—and printed a weekly paper in Paris using these same characters. He found that these plain workmen could in four months master that degree of literacy. The problem of morale was solved. From this beginning sprang the "Mass-education Movement" which in postwar China reached many millions of the people, prior to the Japanese invasion and the Communist flood.

But in China, "Jimmy" Yen had enlarged his program. He found that his people, the peasantry and the incipient industrial population, needed more than literacy: they had four enemies—ignorance, poverty, disease, political passivity—and his mass movement had, accordingly, to adopt four objectives—literacy, improved technique, santitation, "citizenship." As the movement spread, interest was aroused in other lands—India, Cuba, Central and South America; an international office was opened in New York. Yen has recently done impressive work in the Philippines, with the strong support of the late President Magsaysay. For us, the interest of this remarkable movement is in its diagnosis of the conditions which, in substance, are the incentives of the silent revolution we speak of. Our impulse is to light on poverty as the prime mover in a people's revolt. Yen's lighting on illiteracy as the main evil was to some extent an accident of his original problem. But it truly indicates that *poverty never acts as the sole spur:* the propulsive force of the revolution before us is—on an economic text—a spreading awareness of *incomplete human maturity*, the will to be whole men in economic status, health, knowledge, political valency.

Let us say, then, that our silent revolution is a pressure wave for a human status *commensurate with the achieved stage of nature-mastery* of the world we live in. Its stimulus is chiefly the penetrating power of our agencies of communication, whereby no part of the planet is sheltered from the bombardment of ideas—ideas at once of the material possibilities opening to mankind and of the sciences, laws, rights, which form the thin spiderweb network underlying the "Coming World Civilization."

The vanishing of secluded areas carries with it a distinct loss for humanity's ripening of long-term cultural fruits— for it is still true that great arts and great ideas are "prepared in secret"—but its result now in hand, both a gain and a formidable problem, is that the peoples we used to describe as "backward"[2] are now insistently pressing forward. Turkish Foreign Minister Zorlu has accurately expressed the broad impulse: "The present disparity between the more and the less advanced areas of the world should be considered as inadmissible in an age in which we are so readily inclined to boast of man's unparalleled technological achievements." The term "backwardness" is now generally discarded in favor of such gentler phrases as "underdeveloped" peoples. But under whatever label, no statesman of mark ignores the sweeping character of the event. Prime Minister Nehru, noting that the real division of the world is not between communists and anti-communists, but between Haves and Have-nots, sees "an explosive ferment of change working throughout Asia [among] the hungry and illiterate peasants who make up the great bulk" of the population. The "explosive ferment" is indeed there, and not throughout Asia alone.

COSTS AND MOTIVES OF AIDING THE UP-PUSH

It is important to observe that this radical discontent with a lot hitherto accepted as man's condition is *not at first revolutionary* in the sense of being directed against any culprit. It calls for aid; but for no other aid than Jimmy Yen's educational and technical proposals could afford to the self-effort of newly hopeful peasants and working classes. It became, only by degrees, pointedly critical of complacent political authorities. Its ideology, as a people's stirring, was nonexistent, except in the improvised form which directed wrath against the *zemindar* as tax collector, or the foreigner as alien dominator.

In this nondoctrinaire form—though for that reason subject to leading by theorists of various stripes—it has become a factor in the phenomenal "Passing of Colonialism" which, within a half-century, has seen the melting of great empires, beginning perhaps with the Chinese dismissal of the Manchus (1911 and following) and the liquidation of the Ottoman Empire during the first World War. The transformation of the British Empire into a commonwealth is peculiarly instructive, indicating as it does that the imperial relationship has not been wholly insensitive to the motives of this pressure wave, but in some degree an aid to its development and definition. Britain, to some extent, has supplied India with the equipment wherewith to put off the British yoke, together with some initiation into the techniques of modern living involving a heavy economic investment in the development of the colony. One explanation for the swift passing of the empires has been the realization of *cost* by the imperial power—its increasing relative weight with growth of population, not to mention the costs of famine, flood, pestilence. The position of the underdeveloped regions, thus set "on their own," is one of awakened consciousness of need, which

by its very advances in intelligence, in health, and therewith
in explosive human numbers, calls for progressively more,
not less, economic aid in the struggle for self-sufficiency: the
gap between high standards and mass standards of living
tends to widen.

Granted a degree of autonomy within the Empire, such
regions most plausibly turn for aid to the ex-imperial
source. Within the Commonwealth this aid is usually forth-
coming, though as one British editor once put the case,
England finds it "much harder to continue in the thank-
less and humble role of assistance [to peoples who] often
behave as independent and headstrong nations."[3] It is
because of this realization of continued dependency that
Guinea alone, among African colonies of France, has undertaken to stand outside the newly defined Metropolitan
family, and may yet be overtaken by prudence.

The flight from colonialism thus uncovers a growing need,
fostered by colonialism itself, which marks the passing of
the supine half-life, without solving the problems of that
passing. For these, together with other underdeveloped lands,
offers of assistance are in order. The question is open: Who
has the means to help? Who has the will? *And for what
motive?* Any one may answer.

RIGHT OF NEUTRALITY; RESPONSIBILITY OF THE UN

I have dwelt on the formidable economic cost of bringing
forward an underdeveloped region—partly because the observer often light-heartedly assumes the undertaking a much-
sought prize; partly because those romantic misleaders
called "idealists"[4] tend to overlook the financial burden (as
did the mandate theorists); but chiefly because to realize
that burden gives point to our presently essential question
of "What motive?" While specific contract jobs, or loans for
a region's own doings, can quite well be undertaken on a
business basis, the actual administration of such a region
can seldom promise foreseeable reimbursement, unless under

renewed driver-and-driven conditions. It involves in general a long-term financial outlay such as embarrassed a war-impoverished France in its mandate over Syria—making full allowance for preference in trade and hence in access to certain raw materials.

The fact that the USSR has been prompt to see these needs as opportunities, and to proffer its services, need not be taken as proof positive either of pure benevolence or of a drive for world conquest. There are other conceivable interests—more security, more kudos, a more diversified economy with control of raw materials, or discomfiture of competitors, or simply more power as a step toward winning the "peaceful competition." There have indeed been occasions, apart from the buffer zones, of enforced acceptance of the Soviet system. But there are also indications, as in the pact of 1954, that the USSR sees the tactical blunder of thus renewing the worst feature of departing imperialism, compulsory dependency. We see an immense effort for persuasion—in Latin America 250 newspapers, 100 book publishing houses, efforts to place spokesmen in trade unions, even in universities! What is the mastering idea?

The Kremlin has, at least on one occasion, let fall its own interpretation of the silent revolution we have in mind. In view of the Fourth Centennial of the University of Jena, Moscow sent a message which included its official judgment that "the peoples of the world are turning from capitalism to communism," presumably as a factual generalization, with the corollary that *qualified* professors would, of course, so instruct their students.

This corollary, it appears, won from professors and the Rector less than unanimous assent; there were certain decisions, the Rector's among others, to leave the University and the Zone. The incident has its instructions. But our concern is with the proposition about the turning of the peoples.

As an observation of fact, we can endorse the main clause
of the proposition: "The peoples of the world (at least some
of them) are turning"—the precise phenomenon that now
concerns us. If we then ask, "From what are they turning,
and to what?" our first point of doubt might be whether the
peoples in question have sufficient ideological sophistication
to understand that Capitalism-Communism issue, let alone
to have made a choice. Their plastic condition is one inviting
a nice political stroke of predetermination by fiat—it might
easily "work" and thus become pragmatically true, but for
a fair competition this would be definitely not playing the
game!

For them, the turning is simply from their half-life toward
full life, by way of noncommitting aid. They are shrewd
enough to recognize covert angling for adherence, and to
identify it as a subtle bribery. The USA has in times past
tried to supply aid under a definite condition of some *quid pro
quo:* it has earned resentment and aversion. The USSR has at
times tried to barter aid for adherence if not alliance, and has
observed similar reaction, most recently from Egypt. The
inference is becoming clear to all parties. The needy lands
seek an aid, only *as blest with the privilege of their neutrality* toward any doctrines of the aider. An aid, however,
which is not pure charity but a fair business venture.[5]

If the matter were purely one of business, we would be
inclined to deal with it on the principle of free enterprise,
and let the jobs go to the highest bidder. But since the considerations are not purely financial or engineering, we might
look on from outside the present motive-mixture and indicate
the fact that the matter is *definitely a world problem,* toward
which every nation in the well-favored areas has a certain
responsibility. It is no empire's burden, no white man's
burden, no capitalist's burden, no communist's burden—it
is a world concern. And by rights, the *existing world union
should assume it and guide its administration.*

This is precisely the idea underlying the conception of the mandate under the defunct League of Nations. The idea of "tutelage" was right; the idea of "advanced nations" as mandatory powers was right; the idea of reports to the League, and of established ways to complain through a Permanent Mandates Commission was right. The idea of leading through tutelage to independence was right—and three of the A-mandates, Iraq, Syria, and Lebanon, after certain tribulations reached the proposed status. But the *costs of the mandate to the mandatory* were not provided for; and political interest took the place of the presumed humane motive of helping the "backward" peoples, not yet "ready to stand alone under the strenuous conditions of the modern world." There were secret agreements recognizing political motives, and the USA, having no tangible interest in the case, refused all share in the mandatory burden. The USA was as worldly in its refusal as the others were in their acceptance. The League itself had no capital to invest in the wide-spreading mandate enterprise, and had therefore to leave it to the older imperial interests to find their compensation in customary ways. In spite of all this, the history of the mandates is a long step in the advance from irresponsible imperial administration.[6]

And the central principle—that of world responsibility —is *still valid and available* for a simplified use in the present wholly comparable situation.

But we are not looking on from outside the world; nor yet from the standpoint of a conceivable UN taking responsible care.[7] We are looking through the actual eyes of the USA and the USSR—also world-minded—but chiefly considering the silent revolution as affecting their relative standing in the next stage of world history. And what we seem to observe is a certain preliminary competition for the expensive privilege of administering substantial long-term aid. However paradoxical such a competition may be for nations whose budgets are chronically strained to the breaking point, it carries this not-unwelcome consequence: that the motive to spend for bringing forward the underdeveloped regions comes into direct conflict with the motive to spend for superior striking force in nuclear missiles.

This clash is not accidental, but intrinsic and inescapable. It constitutes an additional ground for the judgment that, without canceling existing issues of enforced control, the will to coexistence in peaceful competition, as announced by Khrushchev, is for him realistic and genuine.

ANALYSIS OF THE PRACTICAL SITUATION

The practical situation, as I see it, is somewhat as follows:

1. That the total need, or capacity to use, is greater than the combined margins-for-aid of all potential lender lands, taking into account private as well as public contributions. On this count, neither the USA nor the USSR has an interest in excluding the other.

In 1955, *private* investment in underdeveloped lands from the USA alone amounted to over one and three-fourths billion dollars, an amount exceeding the total USA federal assistance during that year to these same countries. This federal aid, partly military, presumably created the conditions of stability and peace which made the private investment attractive or possible under cold-war conditions—an additional motive for eliminating these conditions.

2. The initiative for such aid normally comes from the recipients, and is governed by free contractual relations between the parties, in no case being imposed by force.

Propinquity and mutual interest will naturally play a part in decisions to enter into these relations. But there is nothing in the nature of these relations to constitute a claim by the aiding party upon raw materials, oil, metals, etc., still less to political or ideological control. It should be wholly consistent with their *neutrality* as between the USA and the USSR.

Nor is there anything in the nature of these relations to forbid co-operation between the USA and the USSR in the total task, or in any part of it. In point of fact, both are presently involved in aid to Egypt; the USA in roads, and the USSR in the Aswan Dam, and the way is still open for USA co-operation in the Aswan Dam project—not a bad idea!

3. With these understandings, the "peaceful competition" for building the social order best serving the material and moral good of mankind becomes wholly dissociated from the comparative areas of aid to the underdeveloped lands.

This ideal dissociation is not to be anticipated as an early achievement. The regions to be aided will choose their sources of aid with some eye to the type of polity they most admire, unless their choice is implied in their history. Such a group as the "Colombo Plan" countries, having its origin as an inter-Commonwealth group, will naturally hold a selective attitude toward its sources as reciprocating members of the group. Hence President Eisenhower, recalling some four billion dollars spent in that connection since 1951, could refer to it as "a valuable instrument in the winning of the cold war."

This could hardly imply that if the cold war were transformed into a peaceful competition, one motive for aid would cease. It remains true that just so long as the acceptance of aid becomes an irrelevant political alliance, neither the aid nor the competition can appear in its true character. For the competition is qualitative, not a matter of area or strategy. And the aid, to be honest, must be adjusted to capacity and promise, not a bribe for support.

4. The difficulty of maintaining the integrity of the aid motive indicates the need of a world-regulative touch on the whole picture of programs and processes of aid and competition, such as the UN might give.

A tense self-interested strife for the privilege of aid-giving could involve serious consequences for the world, namely, an illicit stimulus to increase of population, an increase which, without artificial spur, is one cause of the poverty of the underdeveloped regions.

THE RELATIVE ADVANTAGES OF THE USA AND THE USSR

In a fair competition, on grounds of free choice, the USA has certain initial advantages due to the incentives to steadily improved production involved in free enterprise, the ample rewards of invention, the incomparable ingenuity of our people, the equipment of our research laboratories, our adequate capital at the disposal of experiment. It would be fatal to assume that we have all the advantages; perhaps we have not even the most important, as our comparative performances in the satellite field and the field of nuclear energy have amply suggested. Russia has initial advantages in another dimension: one of which is that it comes *to* the under-privileged, not from the far-along prosperous, but *from* the recently underprivileged, hence with an easier fraternity; and—as a not unimportant detail—it has an adept command of languages.

But it has a further advantage: it is able to develop a differentiated economic world-pattern, for mutual benefit.

The several underdeveloped regions are vastly different in resource, situation, and capacity. It would be a radical error to assume that they must become uniformly industrial—every nation its own factory-town, thus undercutting the volume of export-import trade with other industrial centers.

It was one complaint regarding imperialism that it discouraged colonial manufacture in the interest of the mills of, say, Great Britain. When Gandhi in 1931 visited England he took occasion to address Lancashire workers; he began with a candid confession that the home-spinning he had promoted in India was one cause of the unemployment in Lancashire; he asked them simply to consider the far worse condition of the Indian weaver, and received with the notable sportsmanship of the British an ovation of approval! But world problems will not be solved by the opposite error—an attempt to impose identical remedies on diverse situations.

There must be functional differentiation—manufacturing centers of special types in free contractual relation with other regions supplying raw material and perhaps contributory part-products. Specializations could conceivably be regulated by the mutual interest, each region doing what it is best fitted to do, whether on a free-trade basis or on the basis of an intelligent management.

Here the USSR has the advantage of a dictatorship's central control, which in some instances it has exercised without trying to monopolize the total economic advance: it has shown a capacity to share the gain, no doubt for diplomatic purposes of its own. If others have something to sell, something which they must offer in trade, while Russia in already producing the same thing, it can cut down its production at that point, do something else with its acreage, and buy from the other source: it may import Chinese silk or Egyptian cotton, and limit its own production to maintain a working balance of exchange. Contrast our own policies of limiting imports, say of lead and zinc, to the detriment of our relations—perhaps even of our agreements—with Canada, Australia, Peru, Mexico, suggesting a moral as well as political weakness of our government in face of local lead-zinc interests.

The notion of a regional economic pattern, actual or potential, does a great deal toward relieving our minds of the postulate that any impulse of the USSR to assume charge of a given underdeveloped region is *prima facie* evidence of the world-revolution complex. That there is self-interest in the design there is no doubt. The uneasy relations of Moscow with Tito and Peking indicate an internal rivalry in precisely this pattern-making. Moscow aspires to be the center, economic as well as ideological. If China becomes a co-ordinate steel center, something will be drawn away from the USSR as *the* steel center. But if both enter the world market for steel, the USA will have to move over even farther in the export field. In this and other export markets, American inflation, our own private shot of heroin, restricting foreign trade, promotes isolation. It insures in advance a handicap in the proposed competition with the elastically controlled planning of the socialist complex.

I submit these reflections in no dogmatic spirit. In economics the tracing of cause-and-effect is no simple matter— otherwise our economists would agree more substantially than they do. But I speak in the assurance that today there are neither economic nor political solutions if the new patterns of relationship due to the upsurge of peoples are misprized or misinterpreted. And in the further assurance that their due recognition lends realism to the view that Moscow and Peking, more nearly neighbors to the upsurge itself, in proposing a competition with the USA terminating the race for nuclear arms, are following their own judgments as to their interests—in this case common interests—and their own visions of necessity. To doubt their sincerity in this particular is to doubt their sanity.

Let me now turn to the realities within the present course of history which undergird these judgments and provide an outlook toward the future.

IX

TANGIBLE REALITIES:

The Process of History

As CONTRASTED with governments and governmental voices, the peoples of the world, I have said, have a primary reality: it is they who lend to their *states*, which express their will to permanence, a durability greater than that of governments. But all such structures are subject to necessities suggested in the saying that "the mills of the gods grind slow": there is an underlying reality, a Process of History, which has to be reckoned with.

The prophets of Marxism have appealed to it, in the shape of economic determinism, as certifying their goal; the critics of Marxism have appealed to it, in the shape of moral necessity, as certifying the inner collapse of that system.

I fully agree with the premise that there is an element, not only of necessity but of Judgment, incessantly at work in the process of history. Economic necessities are there, precisely as necessary conditions, never as sufficient conditions, for human existence. Ideas and Rectitudes are at work as well; and the process of history is—with an apparent strong mixture of blind fatality—also a slow, inexorable Judgment.

If radical wrongness of any kind is built into a social system, that system is doomed to ultimate collapse—assuming that it persists in its wrongness. To infer at once from the inherent perversity of Marx-Leninism the impending dis-

integration of existing Marxian states is, however, a wishful
thought that overlooks the most pertinent reality now speaking through the Process of History—the relentless impact
of experience on wrong systems.

Let me set up a few propositions in regard to pertinent
phases of that Process:

1. *The USSR (and socialist China) are here to stay for
some time.*

Those who assume that intrinsic errors in ideology and
behavior presage an eventual crumbling of the structure are
entirely reasonable, in case the errors are rigid fixtures. But
what if those errors are *the very points on which experience
is bringing about revision?*

We had during 1958 several expressions from responsible
sources of an anticipated "inner collapse of Sovietism," one
by Prime Minister Nehru of India, and one—less categorical
—by our then Secretary of State, Mr. Dulles. Their grounds
are similar and substantial. For Pandit Nehru, because Communism "ignores certain essential needs of human nature,"
individual and national freedom. The world, he observed,
"has now come to the point where any attempt to impose
ideas by force is bound to end in failure."[1] For Secretary
Dulles, because, in sum, the demand for normal human freedoms will make for the Soviets "grave and, in the long run,
insoluble problems."[2]

In my judgment, the valid principle here relied on may
be given an even stronger statement: the "attempt to impose
ideas by force" is not only "bound to end in failure"—it is a
failure from the start. A posture can be imposed by force, but
no power on earth can "impose ideas." And when an external
uniformity of speech and act is achieved by terror, the inwardly protesting ideas are stung into intenser life. After
a power seizure, all dictators in peril, from the Emperor Wu
to Hitler, Franco, and Stalin, have tried to make speech

and discussion perilous; and all are faced in one way or another with the fact that violent suppression of reasoned opposition, while it may stop mouths, is not an aid but an enemy to public morale, a self-defeating confession of fear of truth. As the government's status is stabilized, terrorizing tactics diminish, as an inherent outrage to human nature.

In the present case, the degree of censorship that remains is less an expression of a dictator's fear than of his disapproval, and dispenses with the more violent measures for conformity. With the proposal of peaceful competition the Soviet ideology submits itself to experimental support or nonsupport: the Doctrine has ceased to be Dogma, and has become Hypothesis.

The way to a full freedom of expression is still a long one. But the fact that Pasternak's great novel cannot yet be published in Moscow, and that Pasternak himself has suffered public humiliation, is less significant than that outspoken reporters like John Gunther are welcomed, that scientists from the USSR can sit down with scientists from all other lands and confer with approximate freedom on world scientific problems, that our respective farmers and students and steel-makers can swap notes, and that a dyed-in-the-wool capitalist can confer quietly with Mr. Khrushchev in Moscow. The important observation here is not simply the fact of change but the direction of change, and the motive force directing that change, namely, the never-resting postulate of democracy, Every man a whole man, in thought, speech, deed.

2. *Necessities of Ideas Become Necessities of Historic Fact: the Dialectic.*

That the motive force thus identified with the fundamental democratic principle is not an abstraction, but a working factor in the rudest phases of the mélée of public affairs in our time, is the central thesis of this book. It implies that the

"Dialectic" which Hegel and Marx alike attempted to apply to the total movement of history is first of all a power operating beneath the surface, in the logic of day-by-day experience.

We have encountered it in earlier passages, as in pointing out the inescapable association whereby private property ties itself in with common property, and common property with private (p. 55). Let me now give this necessity a more concrete setting in the case that chiefly concerns us, the dialectic of Authority and Liberty—autocracy and democracy.

If with the Weimar Republic we resolve to be thorough with democracy, we incline to make liberty so far absolute as to call for liberty for the enemies of liberty, liberty for plotters and subverters of public order. We may find to our cost (as Weimar did, to the sorrow of Europe and the world) that the subverters take over liberty: that liberty without inbred authority loses its life, and perhaps its soul, first to a Hindenburg, and then to a Hitler.[3]

If, from the opposite pole, we attempt to make authority absolute, what we shall be obliged to learn is no matter of historic accident. *Any* authority attempting to substitute itself *in toto* for the wide-range thought and will of its people must find itself in futile command, if not of a nation of rebels, then of a nation of ciphers, and hence devoid of strength economic, cultural, or political. The most extreme test of this thesis might be in the military sphere:

It is precisely in the military sphere that experience has compelled the reversal of the Scharnhorst ideal of implicit, mindless obedience. The freer formations implied in the trench warfare beginning in World War I have required each private to be able within limits to direct himself during action, and hence to be informed of the objective and the general plan. "Theirs not to reason why" has disappeared from the school of the soldier. Marshal Foch's principles of land warfare (making some use of American conceptions of the private's initiative) completely displaced the Prussian model, and inaugurated a new era in tactics.

And if in the military field, then in all fields of lesser tension: for its own sanity, as well as for its strength, authority is obliged to incorporate liberty. To perceive this necessity adds force to our judgment that the forecast of the inevitable collapse of the USSR must become something quite different—a forecast of its *inevitable self-revision.*

3. *There is a Transitional Role for Authoritative Government.*

Full scope for human development is a necessary goal for all peoples; full freedom is not a valid ideal for every stage of development.

The issue between the dictatorial system of the USSR and the free, individualistic order of the USA is in part an issue of ultimate ideals, but in part an issue of the stage of public development. In the worldwide effort to meet the needs of underdeveloped regions, it must be recognized that a degree of dictatorship is inescapable for the first steps out of the supine psychology. A people uneducated and uninformed, devoid of the habit of thinking out their own destiny, must proceed toward self-government under responsible guidance.

How are the first-stage efforts of the underprivileged regions to be guided?

Is the USA, having done a first-rate job in the Philippines, proudly bringing that region through to autonomy, disposed to extend that type of responsibility? Or does there still remain in our temperament something of that aversion to tutelary functions which rejected the invitation to assume a mandate? If so, do we concede in advance to the USSR—by its present habit and disposition, not averse to imperialism of its own—the advantage in picking up helpfully the first-stage efforts of the have-not lands? This would imply that, having welcomed the "peaceful competition," we would decline to compete, except in terms of financial aid and of the

excellence of our domestic way of life. It would also mean
that we would cease to object to the extension of USSR
influence in the first stages of the progress of the silent
revolution. For it is guidance that is essential in most of
these regions, and not simply aid and advice.

Our recent touch on these situations of emergence has been
less than entirely happy. We have learned that the ideal of
"self-determination" of peoples is not a simple matter: escape
from colonial bonds—"out with the foreigner"—does not at
once make democracy possible. Release from the imperial
power is not, as a rule, release directly to the people, but to
some politically minded élite, interested and available—perhaps a feudal lordship or a sheikhdom not less self-centered
than the ousted imperial power.

> Indonesia, through a rebellion at least partly home-
> made, first throws off Dutch control, then throws off Dutch
> collaboration on liberal terms, and finally confiscates the
> Dutch capital assets which were the Islands' best resource
> for their own upgrading. Its own policy, apparently popu-
> lar but with uneasy saddle, gives way to a "guided de-
> mocracy"—guided from Jakarta by aid of arms and
> presumably of some external advice. Revolution does not
> insure a valid autonomy.

The assumption that ex-imperial regions are *ipso facto*
democratic—with the corollary that the USA as democratic
should support the new government against all comers—is
clearly naïve. It is not even an axiom that ex-imperial regions
are ready for democracy: a good case could be made for the
proposition that independence is always premature, if only
because the arts of governing have to be learned by governing. The political independence of Egypt, declared by
England in 1922, with the four reservations that made it
seem a pseudo-independence,[5] something like a continuing
protectorate with resident British forces, may indicate fairly
well that the transition from paternal to fraternal relations

commonly finds use for an interim of uncle-relationship!
Who, then, will serve as uncle? Uncle Sam?

The crucial question, from the standpoint of the budding
community, is not whether the power offering the needed
guidance is itself an autocracy or a democracy, but whether
it *aims to release its hand.* The way from the supine psychology to a working democracy can be kept open only if the
provisionally authoritative regime is minded to guide things
that way. If the USA enters such a situation, the question
would be whether we are as well qualified for the initially
authoritarian steps of the long journey as for the later steps
and the release. Are we indeed willing at this moment of world
history to bear a considerable share of the total guidance
effort?

And are we willing, to that end, to join the USSR in
securing some of the capital for that effort by terminating
the morally and economically monstrous contest for superiority in nuclear arms—arms destined, if we can trust the
residual human integrity on both sides—never to be used?

4. *World Control is an Illusion, Whether as a Hope or
as a Dread.*

In fact, world conquest is the aim of no government
today; and world revolution—a quite different matter—
is tacitly dropped from the actual objectives of the USSR,
though verbally retained in its mythology.

For consider: while world destruction is quite possible,
there is no possibility of world administration. Abstract
world interests can be administered—world commerce, postal
service, banking, agriculture, law—but world living never!
Imagine the USSR trying to administer the USA; imagine
the USA attempting, directly or indirectly, the administration of China! No person, no government, could seriously
contemplate a conquest of what he or it could never administer. Great Alexander's small world was bounded by an
ignorance we can no longer enjoy: we confront the invincible

plurality of the cultural groundworks of the great experiments in living. The coming world civilization will respect this plurality.

One reason for the unreality of the world-control concept is that individuality of peoples which leads each to value the idiosyncrasies of the other. Not only the customs and laws, but the actual economies, so far as they are in contact with soil and climate, are as diverse as habitations, costumes, manners, folk songs and dances. This is why economy alone can neither explain nor produce culture and history: economy is a measurable generality; value lies in the particular, the personal, the national. If we compete in productivity, there will be a presumable winner; but win-or-lose in that contest leaves untouched the spirit of American or of Russian labor and life. The diversity of quality that comes not from ledger accounts but from firesides, family tables, music corners, the privacies of the world—this is what makes each people indispensable to all others. I have said, "Without freedom, no authority": let me now say, "*Without intimacy, no creativity.*" The privacy of the home is the vitality of the nation; the wider privacy, which is the nation's spirit, is the vitality of the society of nations (and incidentally, the only permanent inducement to travel; for who would care to pass from hotel to hotel in a metropolitanized planet?).

There are clear indications that the USSR for its part begins to realize that it must not only accept the continued existence of the USA, with its unharnessed vitality, its diffuse, wasteful, and often fruitful experimentation, its strange mixtures of self-seeking and expansive good will, but also *wish for* its welfare, hoping to share in its respect and fellowship, as well as to make use of its power and capital resource. If this surmise is valid, the load of terror we are widely invited to feel in view of the approaching superiority of the Soviet intercontinental-missile program in 1960-64 is measurably relieved. Fear is the worst counselor for a constructive foreign policy: though security has become a cheat, the fear which may take its place is a chronic liar, and an assured source of weakness to the nation admitting it.

In view of these things, I take the liberty, not to psychoanalyze but to semanticize the language of our suspicions. Let me say that the talk of world control, world conquest, world revolution is devoid of sense: driven to the concrete filling of its terms, there can be no such thing as a "contest for world supremacy," on the part of any nation or group of nations.

As I write these words, I find the report of Walter Lippmann's recent conversation with Khrushchev, reaching this judgment:

> "the most stubborn obstacle to that mutual toleration" (which he considers our best available outlook) "is the failure to recognize that there are many worlds, not merely one."[6]

This states very precisely that inescapable pluralism of control, on the world scale, I am here asserting. In Lippmann's view, the Soviet leadership is more concerned with winning the uncommitted peoples of Asia and Africa to its side than with any direct contest with the USA, which, if it took military form, would involve destruction of its primary programs: it neither wishes no contemplates war.

Accepting this outlook, we visualize an increasingly important role for the UN in umpiring the colossal task of lifting the backward regions into self-support and solvency, while preserving their right to such neutrality, or such affiliation, as they themselves may choose. It would thus check in advance any tendency of the professedly peaceful competition to outrun its legitimate aims.

THE CRUX OF THE WORLD SITUATION

If these four judgments regarding the realities of our present world situation are valid, we are measurably relieved of our reasonable doubts of the sincerity of Soviet proposals for peaceful competition. They are sincere. They are dictated by the necessities of the case: they are "realistic" as seeing realities.

No one can doubt the co-existence of another psychology in the leadership of the USSR—a determined hostility subtle and amoral, a wealth of overt and covert schemes for political control in various troubled regions, an unconcealed will to outdo the USA in the implements of aggressive war. Our prevailing official and editorial attitude takes this determined and unscrupulous enmity as the sole Soviet psychology to be considered.

Commenting on the British Labour Party's current proposal that Britain join with others of NATO in renouncing nuclear arms and testing, *The New York Times* sees it as promoting "that one-sided disarmament which the Soviets seek." When the Advisory Committee of one of our Parties proposes to "banish military aggression as a Soviet policy" by building up conventional and long-range ballistic resources to the point of a "double stalemate" (since the Soviets can now neutralize any Western nuclear advantage), this same paper puts the critical query, "What of the enduring military advantage of a nation free to attack without notice?"[7] This editor seems unaware that his query invites another: "Since that free-to-attack situation has long existed, and will continue to exist, what are we to make of the fact that the attack does not occur?"

The hard fact is that without further effort we have already made aggression too costly an enterprise to be ventured on by the USSR. But there is a further fact, namely, that the Soviet will-to-aggress is but a half-mind, and *no longer the ruling half.* The dogmatic long-distance psychologists are ignoring that half of the Soviet mentality which has in it the promise of becoming dominant. Let me call this auspicious half-mind the *evocable will* of Soviet Russia.

What I point out is, that in the USSR as in most intelligent entities under stress, there is an unresolved *doubleness of psychology*. There is, in the evocable will of the Soviet leadership, a realism on which we can count. On the ground of this evocable will, the USA and the USSR are *already in tacit agreement* on one presently crucial point—that nuclear energy shall be used only for the common good, never for world war.

The essential unlocking of world-tetanus waits upon a stroke of our third type of diplomacy, able to recognize, evoke, and implement this tacit agreement.

Could this agreement be given concrete form, the thaw would begin, and would duly penetrate not only the peripheral zones now marked by military outposts, outdated in effect by intercontinental missiles, but also the buffer zones in Europe. The continued domination of these unwilling neighbors is the most flagrant contradiction of the democratic profession of the Soviets, and the worst strain on the world-repute of its system. Maintained, as I have held, by the "encirclement" complex, a release of anxiety on this score would promote the inevitable spring-back toward autonomy, without necessarily re-Balkanizing East Europe.

But what first step can be taken?

PROPOSAL OF A CREATIVE RISK

No first step toward checking an armament race can be taken without risk. There is no such thing as a perfect balance of strategic or tactical potentials. Even a perfect balance could not constitute security: at any moment, any one of three powers can now begin the destruction of any other. Shall we then continue to live as under threat, with loss of perspective toward those long-range goods that most make life worth living?

Or shall we refuse fear, and with a clear eye take a risk that may be a *creative risk*, i.e., a risk tending to bring the

evocable will of Soviet Russia to dominance. A risk based
on certitude, because the evocable will is there. But a *risk*
in so far as we deliberately forgo—not defense—but the
futile effort for the next pennyworth of security now that the
trillions-worth have already gone over the dam.

In view of the all-but-chronic impasse in all types of
negotiation with Soviet Russia, there are few who today
conceive such a step as possible. Yet, there are few who would
not greet with pride the notion that, for our own country,
such an act, as a *risk from strength*, could be conceived and
executed. There must be a break-through, and such break-
through must have its risk, as all life-giving has its risk.

The conditions for the success of such a deed are severe.
They are chiefly of a moral, as well as psychological, order,
and demand a type of strength which few governments can
claim. It would be wholly futile if done as a routine decision
of political strategy; and if a statesman doubts its wisdom,
his hesitation is probable proof of his incompetence to achieve
it. Nevertheless, I believe that precisely because the statecraft of the USA, in contrast to that of the USSR, is built
upon a tradition of faith in the moral factor of the Process
of History, it is this nation that is called upon to take the
step.

But it can be responsibly proposed or undertaken only
with full grasp of the ultimate foundations of national
strength, and of the conditions of a justified risk. To these
enquiries we now proceed.

X

FOUNDATIONS OF
NATIONAL STRENGTH

STRENGTH, as we are using the word, includes power, but is something more and other than power. By the "strength" of a nation we mean its ability to affect the course of history, not simply to exist and hold its own but to do things—to bring about durable changes in the world. Strength in this sense is the *pull-together of powers under direction* toward a proposed end. As we noted at the outset, a nation with great power may be low in strength; it is also true that many a nation not conspicuous in power, like ancient Greece or modern Netherlands, has shown prodigious strength in periods of marked unity of purpose.

Strength, like power, is not a solitary trait: national strength exists only within a society of nations. It may be exhibited *against* others, as a capacity to impose its own will on the course of events. But it culminates in what we call *leadership*, a strength *with* others—a mental-moral relation implying some community of goal: in this relation, the more strength the less need to bring into play power or the threat of power. An old Anglo-Saxon phrase may illustrate the point. One requisite quality for a chieftain was that he must "be able to speak, and be listened to." Listened to, because he was aware not only of his own interests but of the interests of all concerned; and because he was credited with wit enough to devise plans serving the general need. This primitive

167

axiom is still valid: leadership cannot exist without something more than intelligent self-interest—let us call it *mental
inclusiveness*.

This bit of logic should dispose of a current superstition
among the politically wise to the effect that "national self-
interest" is the sufficient—perhaps the only legitimate—
basis for foreign policy. Cordell Hull sometimes spoke in
this vein; and obviously no responsible Secretary of State
would propose a policy contrary to the nation's interests.
But the term "self-interest" suggests a limitation of concern wholly incompatible with leadership. If leadership is
desirable, and we seem to prize it, then self-interest must
include it, and therewith a wide reach of interest beyond
self—the suggested limitation is cancelled. The term "self-
interest" then becomes either false or else too ambiguous
for use except in soothing apprehension.

For us, the important point is that the strength of a nation
implies a sphere of concern and activity reaching far beyond
the borders of its technical sovereignty. The entire basis of
political philosophy is involved. How far beyond the domain
of sovereignty this active sphere of influence must extend,
the USA is only now beginning to realize.

FACTORS OF NATIONAL STRENGTH

We are not drawing an invidious contrast between moral
strength and physical power. As in the human body, the
musculature is a necessary condition of any action whatso-
ever. Moral strength lies in the capacity for decision; decision
is the passage of idea into deed: no muscles, no morality.
The body is the miracle of organization whereby physical and chemical energies are subordinated to purposive control. It is the hierarchy of forces, not their absence, that
constitutes concrete freedom—the capacity to make ideas
actualities.

Nor are the arithmetical factors of national power to be
discounted—magnitude of geophysical domain, manpower,

resources, economic and strategic potential. But the directing of action must be independent of the powers involved in action: to direct power is to stand *outside the power-system*. This is the insight (metaphysical, if you like) on which men normally act: it is also the insight without which there are, and can be, no free men and no free nations.

In material Nature, considered as a closed or "conservative" system of energies and events, action directs itself: present action flows continuously from previous action. So considered, the whole story of the cosmos is but one unceasing process, a patterned but seamless fabric: there is no point of new-beginning, no initiative, no "spontaneity," no "decision"—for decision is a "cision," a cut. Classical Materialism, taken literally, makes human history an integral part of physical Nature, reduces human initiative to a subtler obedience, and has for that reason been tacitly repudiated by Lenin and later activists of Moscow. In the real world, the world of real wills as we instantly know it, new action enters the physical process through decisions in control of an organism of powers—physical, chemical, electrodynamic—meshing into the processes of Nature.

So far as these organized power systems reach, free decision shakes off determination by material causes, and also by all psychological "conditioning."[1] Decision rules events not arbitrarily but by its *goals or ends*—chosen, discovered, imagined, created. From an ever-renewed, ever-growing vision of value-achievable, new vitality incessantly enters history. In any case, the powers take their position as means. Where—reversing nature—power is allowed to dominate decision the means are allowed to sway the ends; and man becomes the servant of his own natural servitors.

Here we stand. The first business of all statecraft defines itself. It must be this: to maintain in the world this hierarchical *dominance of end-seeking will*, as against every abdication in the name of power politics.

We shall always have in a world of many nations the clash

of wills—the arbitrary I-will versus another arbitrary I-will.
The major history-making rule has been hitherto to let
superior power decide, not as a pure abdication of right and
reason but on a plausible assumption—not wholly false—
that superior power implies superior organizing capacity,
therefore superior mind-and-will validity. This assumption
lay behind Hegel's much-condemned hypothesis of the role
of war in promoting the "march of the Idea through the
world": the right of the new vision—he thought—*deposits
itself* in more powerful weapons and tactical devices—the
phalanx against the heavy line, the gunpowder against the
bow. As across wide cultural gaps, it has been the prevalent
apology for compulsion, the common ground, for example, of
the European invaders of the Western Hemisphere as against
the aborigines; and while few would be disposed to reverse the
achievement of conquest, the semisavagery of the process
remains a burden on the record of "civilization." As of today,
the "right of conquest" remains on the books as a lingering
anachronism *faute de mieux*, a companion piece of the *fait
accompli* no matter *how* the *fait* were *accompli*. In the present
situation, we stand before the necessity of its repudiation:
even with the valid faith that right promotes might, the
superior-power rule of thumb is no longer tolerable, if only
because the testing of that superiority is now suicidal.

But if we repudiate the "right of conquest" and its paper-
money substitute, power politics, what have we to put into
their places?

What we are actually doing is to substitute nuclear tests
and stockpiles for deeds. We continue the race in power accumulation, permitting our current world status as commanding or obedient to be determined—not by using these powers,
God forbid—but simply by figuring their amounts, differentials, probabilities, congratulating ourselves that we are
wealthy enough to allocate further billions for arms never to
be used! In effect, we make the humiliating admission that
for major non-justiciable issues we lack competence to lift

the conflict out of the force-area into the area of humanly intelligible grounds of decision: we can find *no mental equivalent* for war.

That equivalent we must find. But not by a false contempt for power. Rather, by understanding the significance of the all-human will to power and the conditions under which this will may become a source of union rather than of hostility.

THE WILL TO POWER IN MEN AND NATIONS

Of power the old saying holds good that the corruption of the best is the worst. The phrase "will to power" has a bad name, and with good reason, but the normal will to power, for men and also for nations, is the necessary drive toward effectiveness in action. It is the rejection of the major curse of any purposeful being—futility. It is the determined refusal of involuntary servitude, whether to man, or to Nature, or to Fate.

Deepest of the instincts, the will to power is the integrating force in human nature, in some sense an auxiliary instinct of all instincts.[2] Kant was right in saying that the clause "I think" is prefixable to every item of knowledge: it is equally true that the clause "I can" is prefixable to every item of action, and to each unfolding of instinct from infancy upward, "I can walk, I can talk,"—the rightful pride and joy of the growing person, the rightful hope of the mature human being. Since, as thus understood, the will to power is the man, that will is *ultimately invincible*. It is the latent defiance of all tyranny, the nemesis of all top-monopoly in government.

But the will to power in the citizen is no subtraction from the strength of government: on the contrary, the strength of government depends on it, for the sources of power in the human individual are the original sources of strength in the nation: from power-starved citizens, no national strength. And the converse is equally true and important: the power of the state is normally the power of each citizen and a necessary condition of the fulfillment of the citizen's individual will to power.

In fact, the entire purpose of the state can be understood as creating the historical structure whereby, for each citizen, the will for durable effectiveness can be assured. *The state exists to confer upon individuals a perpetuity of effect* and a range of effect which as persons or as tribesmen they could never have.

The normal state has indeed power *over* its citizens, in order that it may have this indispensable power *for* them, making achievable the essentially democratic impulse, every man a whole man. Prior to any external leadership, the State exercises an internal leadership which interprets to the several members their wills to power, with the authority of insight: "This is what *we* want (not what I alone want); this is *our* path."

In no state can the effective freedom of the citizen be greater than the accuracy of that authoritative leadership. The difference between leadership and tyranny does not consist in the circumstance that tyranny commands while leadership leaves everyone to his own bent. It consists in this: that tyranny makes its I-will dominant over the We-will, whereas leadership makes the We-will the essence of each I-will. Tyranny is exercised by the egoist mind, leadership by the mentally inclusive mind, recognized and accepted as such by those to whom it speaks with authority. Both command.

THE EXTENT OF NATIONAL STRENGTH

This conception of the State's function has, in its logic, certain formidable implications which we must now face.

I believe it was Bagehot who said that the State exists to provide for its members "a calculable future," *i.e.*, one that would encourage long-term enterprises. That is one form of the normal will to power, at least of the human male: he cares to contemplate an achievement that will last. If the state is immortal—and few states intend to die—there is some chance for a citizen's durable effect. Little as men ordinarily worry over the perpetuity of their own achievements, they feel themselves looking forward into a continuing social order maintained without end by political will: ask a citizen when he expects this order to terminate, his answer might well be, "It doesn't."

But ask the corresponding question about spatial extent: "Where does the state's responsible control end?" The answer may be, "At the boundary of its territorial domain." I submit that this answer is in error: it should be, as with time, *"It doesn't end."*

For in order to offer durability in time, the State cannot renounce its involvement with the remainder of the planet: if it has no rightful concern there, what security can it fairly offer on its own soil? Since we are entering contentious ground, let us steady our steps by aid of the past master of sobriety, Immanuel Kant. In his essay on *Perpetual Peace*, Kant suggested not a world State but a group of republics of such character that a traveler would everywhere find, certainly not his own state, but *statehood*. He would be accorded certain minimal rights of civilized treatment, including the right to do business with anyone disposed to trade with him. Writing some half-century before Admiral Perry blasted a trade-way into Japan, Kant proposed the notion of world citizenship, implying a thin, common fabric of legality pervading all nations, a *Weltbürgerrecht* needing no support of over-all sovereignty. He anticipated what in the succeeding century became a general tendency among nation-states to support what each considered the rightful interests of its traveling or trading citizens in other lands, and to assume responsibility for their crimes, whether under extraterritorial treaty rights or under the laws of the country visited. It was in view of such considerations that I ventured in 1926 to write as follows:

It is not alone *the state* that is everywhere: it is *each state* that is everywhere. As state-interests and domains

interpenetrate on the high seas, so their destiny is to interpenetrate throughout.[3]

This risqué proposal was not challenged at that time. It
had some support from a highly questionable quarter,
namely, the extending intrusions of imperial powers in the
domestic affairs of other nations—the widening claims for
right of intervention, such as we tried to stave off in South
America by our Monroe Doctrine, and yet, as an anti-im-
perial power, fell into ourselves, in relation to the Open
Door in China, to natural resources in Mexico, to order-
keeping with our gunboats on the Yangtse in 1924.

Let us extend our historic range for a moment: consider
the empire builders of all time. Was their common dream of
worldwide sovereignty all wrong? As monopoly, yes. As
world State, yes. As administered world order, *no!* If we add
the principle of *interpenetrating sovereignties,* limited in
scope to an identical minimal legality, consistent with the
complete separate integrity of national characters, properties, laws, populations—with this revision, I say, we reach
a new conception of the function of nations, not only right
but imperative. Put it this way: no nation has a right to complete nationhood, to "self-determination," until it is prepared not alone to keep order at home, but to co-operate in
world-obligation and to exercise world-strength. I submit
that this is precisely what the concept of the State requires
—nothing less.

And by this measure, it will be agreed that in the case of
the USA vis-à-vis the USSR, we who are but gradually and
with reluctance opening our eyes to world responsibilities,
exhibit a comparative weakness in principle. We have not
yet taken the measure of the function of leadership. Mind-
ing our own business is a great merit: not knowing the extent of our own business, leaving much of it undone, is a
great defect. Let us re-examine the factual picture with this
standard in mind.

GROWTH OF THE USA TOWARD WORLD MISSION

Leadership in world affairs is a role for which we have been disinclined, and accordingly have hardly begun to pay the price.

Britain, France, Germany, Russia have been accustomed to think of themselves in world-shaping efforts. America, shaking off colonial status for itself and in principle abhorring imperialism, dedicated not alone to domestic liberty but first of all to the liberty of national independence, has long been satisfied with enlightening the world by demonstrating the good life within its own domain. To "raise a standard" worthy of respect and imitation has been regarded as a great—and sufficient—world service.

By dint of the logic of events—the Spanish-American War, the first World War, the Versailles settlement—we have reluctantly accepted the necessity of functioning beyond our borders. The discovery that we could fight, and fight well, on European soil was to some extent a surprise to ourselves as well as to Europe. But the experience aroused no ambition to continue the exercise of power, though it was President Lowell of Harvard who chiefly promoted (as against General Smuts) the cause of a "League to *Enforce* Peace." And if today we are asked to define the national purpose of the USA in the wider world, we are likely to answer simply, it is "pushing forward the frontiers of freedom," *i.e.*, extending the area in which our domestic ideals prevail.

What we have had first to learn, and are learning, is that an ideal, even a universally valid ideal, is not enough to constitute a purpose. A purpose is a plan for embodying an ideal—something specific now to do about it, in a world perspective: and in that process, learning more exactly what the ideal means. Our political ideals are indeed stated in universal terms—it is "all men" who are declared to be created equal, with political consequences for all "govern-

ments instituted among men." But until 1945, we had never
tried to apply these ideals to a highly developed nation with
widely different culture and historical background. In the
years of the German Occupation, we had to think out what
liberty and democracy could mean in an environment of
which we knew too little, and in which we were obliged by
the situation to maintain an undemocratic military control:
we could give but a hamstrung demonstration of our meaning. Nevertheless, we were there, as we believed, to educate;
and to educate in terms of our national ideals. Nothing could
have offered a clearer test of our understanding of them.

And nothing is so instructive to a teacher as his own discovery of his imperfect preparation for the task of instruc-
tion. We have still to gather the rich fruits of that brave
experiment.

Our effort to help the new Germany to the beginning of
more liberal institutions was far from a failure. There was
a manifest good will in the Occupation which duly replaced
the punitive beginnings and begot its own natural response:
we helped the new, though divided, Germany to its feet; and
Germany joined us in shaking off the Hitler obsession. But
Germany also remains clear that *the Load-lifting Idea was
not imparted, because we did not have it.* That Load-lifting
Idea had to do with "the mission of a man and of a people."
A "mission"? What is that? A purpose is more concrete than
an ideal; a mission is more concrete than a purpose: it is a
specific task in world history, a unique insight, to be made—
through leadership and concrete action—a universal possession. Have we a national mission?

Our main deficiency as instructor of Germany was the
faulty diagnosis that attributed the Hitler outburst to defective domestic institutions which admitted a dictatorship.
Hence we tried to teach democracy; whereas the essential
German wrong lay in the field of external politics, adopting
as goal of the Third Reich the domination of Europe as a
step leading to world hegemony. The Nuremberg Court

undertook (with what was essentially new law) to punish crimes that attended the methods of the campaign. The dream itself, the ambition, was rebuked only by defeat, and by "denazification," the purge of those who dreamed it.

This diagnosis and prescription *evades the entire issue* of the Hitler program, whether a status quo (as of a shackled and cooped-in Germany) can be intrinsically wrong, and if so, what to do about it. The baleful allure of Nazism had at its core a sense of world history, and of a nation's role in history, which can become a noble passion, or else a demonic passion. Did we intend to denounce the idea itself of a nation's mission? Or, specifically, the "über Alles" element and the unscrupulous and inhuman means of reaching it? We failed to make this clear. We seemed to be condemning in blindness the mission because we condemned the means.

And is this perhaps because we ourselves still lack a sense of history and any vital knowledge of history—even our own —and hence wholly fail to catch the pulse of the argument of historic growth and our place in it? Of course, we learn a lot of "history," but where do we catch the firm emphases that recognize our own mental and moral origins in Palestine, Greece, Rome, the Medieval synthesis, as well as in the Renaissance, the beginnings of Modernity, and the Revolutions? Without this feeling for the unfolding of the European spirit, we can achieve no sense of membership in its destiny; no power of inclusive mentality toward other history-rooted peoples, such as India and China, and Russia poised between; and hence no ability to lead with understanding strength.

It was in one respect fortunate that we concentrated our efforts at tutelage on the concept of democracy, namely, that the actual obstacles we met in trying to instruct on this topic a nation that had given to the world the works of Pufendorf and Kant, of Bluntschli and von Gierke, and had given the Weimar Republic a serious trial, had obliged us to recognize the relativity of our own ideas of democracy (on

which point I must speak further, p. 192). But for the main
gleaning of the experience, the duty upon us of assuming a
continuous responsible world-role, it has shown us the necessity for our due national strength of a far firmer foundation
throughout our public in the interested knowledge of world
history and world need. We require nothing less than a
breaking-out of self-absorption in the whole scheme of our
education, especially in regard to historical understanding,
in order to achieve general support for a diplomacy of
genuine strength.

Who that has been abroad in recent years and in the
neighborhood of American military posts, has not been
startled at the spectacle of American boys in uniform
drifting in groups through the streets, bored and devoid of
interest in the lives, ideas, problems of the people among
whom they are stationed? It is not alone that the only-some-
times-"Ugly," more commonly indifferent, American is sure
he has the answers; it is also that his Public Philosophy has
not taught him that no answers are exportable like so
much grain—they cannot become human food until grown
in each local soil.

Of the necessity of such a world-role I believe we are now
well persuaded. Our strong concern with the building and
development of the UN indicates as much. We have contri-
buted materially to its general framework of principles and
have helped to give it effect as an organ of decision in pre-
legal issues, the nonjuridical problems in which the residual
sources of war abide.

That is a good beginning; and we have now the additional
duty of preserving it from the common fate of well-thought-
out institutions, that of embodying a mass of excellent general resolutions, not precisely applicable to particulars, to
the unique individual cases which still require tough and new
thinking. We cannot dismiss our world responsibility as
already provided for in an accepted set of general rules.

The strength of the USA will be exhibited when we take seriously the idea that with our national maturity we must recognize and accept a world role, individual to this country, deserving the name of a national mission. Only thus can we hold leadership.

Suggestion of such a role may grow directly from our experience with Germany, whose strong sense of mission was inflamed by a perverse leadership. We learned that our own task was *not to destroy that sense, but to sublimate it.* After first undertaking to crush the nation, in the name of just punishment and in the spirit of the Morgenthau Plan, we discovered the radical error of that aim: the power of a great nation as a potential for world good must be conserved and re-directed. Is it not conceivable that the Soviet dream of world-domination, pernicious in its possibilities, calls equally for reinterpretation rather than for blank repudiation of its limitless capacity for world-benefit? There could be no greater challenge to the latent moral strength of America.

And certainly no other nation is similarly called to this task, either in terms of power-engagement or in terms of position as direct *vis-à-vis*. Nor, in my view, *is any other nation so fully qualified* in terms of the moral resource demanded by this formidable task—I point again to the achievement in our sector of occupied Germany under our great High Commissioners, Clay, McCloy, Conant, the achievement of comradeship with the renewed German nation, comradeship in the denunciation of the evil of Hitlerism, marking nothing less than a national rebirth.[4] (The difficult belief in this re-birth is indeed a part of our task with Russia, in its attitude to the issue of Berlin and the divided Germany.)

What we require is nothing less than the mental as well as moral effort of translating the actual issues of conflict into terms which can be arbitrated by a total-human-good affirmed by the united wills of the contestants. We have now to analyze the conditions for such a deed.

XI

CONDITIONS OF
JUSTIFIED RISK

WE HAVE, I say, to translate the issues between the USA and the USSR into terms which do not imply mutual destruction—terms which preserve the invaluable energy of national ambition, though that value may be concealed under the repellent and senseless phantasy of world domination.

In point of fact, this translation is already under weigh. In abstract sketch it is already begun by the co-membership of the two powers in the UN. That co-membership implies acceptance by both of the aims of the organization, an identical will-to-peace and co-responsibility for peace. To this extent the world-missions of the two powers professedly interpenetrate.

The profession is indeed belied by the armament race which this co-membership nominally makes impossible. Nevertheless, the formal commitments stand, and in view of the capacity of political entities for two-mindedness, a sort of schizophrenia peculiar to nations in conflict, must be considered as working factors in the actual situation. To translate the issues of that conflict into terms that could be arbitrated would at once release these agreement-complexes into conscious control, and hence to sincerity!

I speak of arbitration, not of law. Appeal to Law as the

normal clue to peace is at present being urged with exceptional vigor and pertinence. To arrive at a Law and a Court
whose jurisdiction is acceptable to all honestly disposed
nations, and whose decisions are binding upon them, is an
end deserving every effort. But even if there were a finished
code of international law, that law *could not be the first* source
of relief. For the acceptance of a common law is a consequence
of living together, reaching empirical adjustments which become first custom, and then law. Usable law grows from two
ends—from the grass roots and from the Ideas: apart from
the grass roots, the Ideas cannot be trusted. And the chronic
inadequacy of international law is that there is as yet *no international custom* except in such fragments as maritime law.

For strife between nations, the analogy of domestic law
as the secret of peaceful settlement is not entirely pertinent,
for several reasons:

The subjects of domestic law, typically human individuals,
are *supplied by nature* whereas the subjects of international
law, typically the nations, are shaped and altered, made and
unmade, combined and divided, by processes in which human
will has a part.

Again, the cases arising in the international field are *highly
unique*, seldom fitting any ready scheme of classes, whereas
law must deal with classified situations for which general
rules can be framed. Nations are individual; their quandaries
are unique: the law can seldom define an exact precedent.
The diplomat must make history as the attorney-at-law cannot do. Diplomacy must be a perpetual improvisation, and
international disputes must accordingly bear a political character, raising ever anew the question, "Do we—humanity at
large—will this new state of affairs to last, no matter how it
has come to pass?", a question strictly pre-legal.[1]

Then again, domestic law can proceed on an assumption of
equality-for-legal-purposes of its natural subjects, whereas
when the subjects are as diverse as are nations—not only in

size and power and stage of advance, but in actual need and moral temper and experimental programs—this assumption becomes treacherous even when logically valid. For this reason, no nation can safely put its vital interests in the hands of a judge or group of judges, however impartial, unaware *through direct experience* of its unique requirements.

I cite the case of Iceland. Iceland, poor in natural resources, declares a twelve-mile limit for its fisheries. Britain, relying on the traditional uniformity of the principle of coastal waters, proposes to ignore the demand of Iceland. The case for Iceland could hardly stand before the International Court of Justice, under present rules of law. But no decision could be truly just, unless the Court were willing to adjourn and live in Iceland for a few months before rendering its judgment! In my view, Britain's legal rectitude is, in this case, wrong.

With this situation in mind, we may understand why both the USSR and the USA are reluctant to throw themselves bodily into the arms of a Court decision by judges unfamiliar-by-immersion with their specific life problems. Their stand-out definitely lames the influence of the Court. For that reason, if for no other, we must look first to the bases of law, not to the law itself.

In the present case, there is also a deeper reason. Willingness to be bound by the decisions of any Court, finding judgments under any law, assumes the full consent of each client state to *the existence and normal development* of the other. When each client state retains a lurking doubt lest the other half-contemplates its destruction, the barest minimum of identical purpose, necessary to make any joint enterprise viable, is lacking.

Hence our first step must consider the very bases of international order. We must re-examine that elemental mutual distrust expressed in the vicious circle we have previously defined (p. 127) : Communism must be destroyed because for Communism Capitalism must be destroyed, and vice versa.

THE VICIOUS CIRCLE REVISITED

The mutual distrust is not superfluous: it exists for good and sufficient reasons, *on both sides.*

We need no persuasion regarding the good reasons for our own distrust of the USSR. They rest not only on our lengthy experience of the cold war, for whose inception each side holds the other responsible—a matter which history could conceivably clear up—but quite as much on the openly professed amoralism of the founding saints of the revolution. Did not Lenin counsel the hesitant Trotzky, "*Succeed!* You prefer Napoleon to Kerensky, don't you?"? The Great End justifies the means, inhuman or otherwise, necessary to promote it: the crime is to fail.

But we remain candidly mystified by the counterdistrust professed by the USSR for the USA. Have we not, on the whole, kept our promises? Have we not been of large material aid to the Russian people? We certainly reject the Communist ideology; but we have long ago accepted a version of coexistence which renounces any will to destroy the system by attacking the Soviet state complex itself? Why, then, this persistent distrust? Or is it a dramatized attitude, for purposes of maintaining domestic morale and discipline?

Walter Lippmann has recently written to the effect that the fear is real; that there exists in the background of the Soviet psyche a lurking fear-belief to the effect that when (as the Russians assume certain) the USA finds itself losing the competition for leadership, it will feel bound to attack. My own judgment is that it is quite possible that there is such a factor of Soviet subconsciousness, an unintended tribute to the resistless working of incompatible philosophic convictions. (I shall examine this issue explicitly in our final chapter). I doubt, however, that this is the main working source of distrust. Coexistence without conquest was originally a USA proposal. The active springs of suspicion are elsewhere.

First of all, in the Marxist psychoanalysis of the capitalist mentality. Noting the powerful mental momentum of economic privilege, Marx sees the attaint of hypocrisy as built into the system itself. The lay figure of the *bourgeois* is erected, as an enjoyer of profitable injustice who defends his prerogatives as "sacred rights" of property and contract. This despised trait is the reverse of a professed immoralism —it is a professed moralism covering a crass self-interest.

But chiefly, the USSR's distrust is based on specific passes of history in which judgment falls, not on the USA separately, but on the "Western powers" in the rise and fall of economically motivated empire. Anti-Western sentiment in the USSR uses the pejorative "imperialist" today, far more than "bourgeois." As involved in two world wars generated in Europe, the Soviets have had an intimate view of European diplomacy. One would like to believe their interpretations unduly cynical; but it is in order for us to recall that it was the Russian archives that brought to light the secret Sykes-Picot Agreements which so bedeviled the principles of peace on whose proclamation Woodrow Wilson had brought the USA into the war.

This is not the place to develop the indictment in detail. Let me only say in broad lines that Russia, old or new, has had all too little reason to respect the authors of the Versailles Treaty or of the Munich Pact in which its interests were specifically involved; for the beginnings of World War II were laid in that Treaty and that Pact, as I have above suggested. Allowing this to be the case, the version of this crucial pass of history which has become an almost orthodox Western official interpretation, throwing the onus of starting the Second World War upon the USSR, on the score of the subsequent (August 1939) Hitler-Stalin agreement, must be characterized as an evasion of strict truth. And when our own State Department passively accept this version—as in the publication of January 1959 referred to above (p. 83) —the effect can only be to confirm Soviet suspicion of our will-to-truth, and invite continuance of their own indirections, which are many.

Let this suffice to indicate that the mutual distrust is not gratuitous *on either side,* especially when we of the USA accept the heritage of West-European diplomacy since 1917, however little we may have been responsible for it. We must allow the Russian tendency to cynicism regarding Western foreign policy a certain basis, which their own ideology leads them to project as the "realism" of all statecraft. To this extent we can understand, without excusing, their practical response: the chess-play of "outwitting Western gamesters at their own tricks."

The temper of mutual distrust thus tends to confirm itself, and establish in diplomatic motives that vicious circle in world aims we have already defined. Each move for defense on the part of the USA is interpretable by the USSR as a covert scheme for aggression. Each call on the part of the USSR for dismantling the encircling posts, as threats to its security, is interpretable by the USA as a play for extending Communist tyranny. And the two publics, not specifically informed, feel the pressure of loyalty to accept the official denunciation as truth, and accordingly to steel their minds against any step toward common ground. The rational line will be the tough line; and *each must keep ahead of the other* in respect to armament.

The task of genuine statesmanship is thus indicated.

It is not first of all the task of canceling world peril from nuclear arms: fixing attention on this essential result may distract our immediate aim.

The armament race is a creature of the distrust, not the distrust a creature of the armament race, though the race tends to confirm the distrust.

To dismantle or hold in check the armament program without first dismatling the distrust must be—as experience is showing—an all but hopeless task. The entanglement of nations seeking security in measures for adequate mutual

inspection was foreseen with uncanny prescience by Secretary
of War Henry Stimson in 1945, before the atomic bomb had
been produced.[2] The logical first step is an attack on the
distrust; but how can it be attacked or dismantled?

There are, I conceive, two necessary steps, of which the
first could be quite simple. It need be nothing more than *defining the vicious circle* in terms both sides must recognize,
avowing our own part in it, and showing that it *no longer
describes the actual issue.*

For the anti-Bolshevist powers, the mental stance of
1917-22 might have been fairly expressed in the terms of
the circle: Communism must be destroyed, because for Communism Capitalism must be destroyed.

The situation now emerging after forty-odd years is:

(i)   that neither Capitalism nor Communism in the sense
      of 1917 exists;
(ii) that the changes involving principle taking place dur-
      ing this period have been not fortuitous but necessary;
(iii) that these changes, without obliterating the opposition
      of principle, have been convergent.

In view of these three facts—largely the burden of the
present book—the present stance may take this form:

The Soviet system may (and perhaps should) co-exist,
because for the Soviets the American system may (and perhaps should) co-exist; and *vice versa.*

Assuming that there is here a possibly-honest experiment
in whose outcome mankind could have a concern, the destruction of either competitor would destroy the competition, and
thereby all would lose its demonstration. Without asserting
that this general interest has much force in a situation in
which each side is convinced that the other is in principle
wrong, both are in full accord that war is excluded as court
of appeal. And each is ready, without treason to its own faith,
to tolerate the existence of the other in an honest rivalry for

achieving the highest "material and moral good for mankind."

This simple step could have an immediate and considerable effect in the release of tension. For us, the difficulty in "avowing our part" might consist in the always painful admission that we have learned something. But the act of acknowledgment of the new situation, if it could become mutual, would set both parties at once *outside the vicious circle*, in the field of common human objectives underlying the area of contest.

The ground is thus prepared for the second step.

Once the circle has been seen for what it is and the mood of suspicion deprived of veto power, the next and decisive task is to break the circle, *not by thought alone, but by an act*—an act whose meaning cannot be misunderstood, an act releasing the tetanus which once broken is everywhere broken, like the soap bubble punctured in one spot! No "strategy" is necessarily involved—the act must be one expressing good faith and tending to elicit good faith, presumably an act of confidence where confidence has had no prior rights. We face the final issue of a justified creative risk.

RISK FROM STRENGTH VERSUS NEGOTIATION FROM POWER

It is easy to propose an act of creative statesmanship, hard to define such an act. There are no recipes for a creative diplomacy; if there were, it would not be creative.

We may point out that distrust is infertile, the most barren of all chronic tempers. This does not make it rational to trust the unworthy, nor does it make trustfulness fertile in proposals for acts moving an opponent to accept them as interpreting his own will.

The logician is always on firm ground in showing that, since assured understanding of invisible motives cannot exist, diplomacy, in honor bound to avoid pure gamble, must judge any circle-breaking deed unjustified. But the logician is assuming, with most of current psychology in his support,

that there are *no certitudes* about human mentality. I am
prepared to reject this unproved and unjustified assumption. The steps that can be taken are, if you like, based on
realism, that is to say, on a perception of realities in human
nature *about which certitude is possible.*

SOME AVAILABLE CERTITUDES

The only possible basis for proposing an act daring to
interpret the will of another is an assurance regarding his
total will; and the only certitude one can have regarding
the will of another human being is—the element of *universality in one's own will.*

This, however, is *the central certitude* of our lives, the
instinctive assurance with which human beings initiate communication with one another. Beneath every diversity of
taste, sentiment, conscience, purpose, there is the universal
will-to-live, the will-to-power, some version of humanity,
some horror of inflicting arbitrary suffering and wholesale
death.

Whatever the mystery of Soviet motivation, however alien
the Slavonic temperament and capacity for wile may be felt
to be, there can be no shadow of doubt that they who share
with us an official willingness to prepare weapons for the
collective extinction of populations entertain not alone a
fear of retaliation but an inward revulsion to their use.

If we find it in our national world mission to translate
the apparent will of Soviet Russia to impose an unwilling
yoke of ideology on peoples incapable of physical resistance
—if, I say, we find it within our mission to translate this into
terms of honest competition-in-human-fulfillment, my confident assertion is that the answering humanity is already
there. And with the authoritative proposal, "This is what on
the whole you want; and this is the route to its achievement
—a goal and a path in which our two world missions may
interpenetrate," there arises the possibility of an act of de-

liberate risk, refusing any longer to shelter one's national purpose behind the continued threat of mass annihilation, an act whose specific implementation need not here be defined, but whose initial stages would involve an announced abandonment of the pursuit of an infinitely retreating security.

Such an act would be based on certitude, not on hypothesis: it would constitute a clear instance of our third type of diplomacy.

It would, indeed, be futile if done from fear; equally futile if done as an attempt to purchase good will by appeasement. The conditions are simple, but severe and absolute. If the statesman has no assurance of a common human reality, and no inclusiveness in his understanding, he may as well quit the stage. These qualities cannot be put on as a gesture; they are well within the reach of the normal spirit of this great land.

But even with that assurance, and that inclusiveness, would any statesman be justified—we recur to this ultimate issue— in involving the nation in his own creative risk?

He could have no such right were it not for two further considerations: First, that risk-taking cannot be escaped. Second, that only through individual decision can any nation fulfill its own will. Attend, then, to these two judgments:

THERE IS NO ALTERNATIVE TO RISK

Wherever will meets will, there is some formative action of each on the other, for better or for worse. To dodge an affirmative is commonly to risk a negation. Let me illustrate:

In Geneva, at the September, 1928, meeting of the Assembly of the League of Nations, German disarmament was the issue. By the Versailles Treaty Germany had been essentially disarmed, with the allowance of a force of 100,000 men, chiefly for policing purposes. Also, as by Treaty, the Allies were to carry out by stages a comparable disarmament.

France, however, with an understandable reluctance to assume a defeated Germany reconciled to its limitations, was not alone in failing to follow suit: it was involved in certain rearmament enterprises, especially in Poland. Yet when Germany had been admitted to the League in 1926, France had been prompt to welcome the event, so full of promise for the recovery of Europe. Stresemann, who as Minister of Germany had been loyally co-operative, was to have spoken at the 1928 League Assembly, but he was ill and Chancellor Mueller spoke in his stead.

Mueller spoke effectively of Germany's desire to co-operate in the rebuilding of Europe. He recognized without complaint the natural apprehension of the Allies toward a Germany so recently a war-maker. He requested for Germany, as a gesture of encouragement and good will, a limited token step toward the promised Allied disarmament.

The plea, made in a temper of conciliation, seemed to have made a favorable impression. Then Briand, who had made the cordial speech of welcome on Germany's admission to the League and had actuated the Lausanne agreement, rose to speak for France. But instead of meeting the German request at least halfway he vehemently denounced the proposal. "Germany disarmed?" he cried. "Germany is *not disarmed!*" Was she not increasing her heavy industry? Were not her factories, new-built and with large aid of foreign capital (largely American), ready to be turned to munitions? Were there not secret plans for military recovery? Germany must expect no step toward disarmament, so far as France was concerned.

Was Briand right? What were the facts? There were indeed officers harboring hopes for revenge. There was much feeling against the grievous terms of the Versailles Treaty, some impossible terms unless relief were to come. There were furtive plans for work with Russia, training Russian units while maintaining something of the German military structure forbidden at home. German engineers went to Russia to advise in building munitions factories. There were grounds for the feeling, not confined to Germany, that while the

Allies were defaulting on their part of the Treaty Germany could not be strictly held to hers. The circle of mutual suspicion was being established in mid-Europe.

But the point for us is this: In 1928, the dominant party in Germany, as represented by the Weimar Republic and Stresemann, was for loyal co-operation under the Treaty. The attitude of Briand, who now seemed to adopt the rooted suspicions of Poincaré, was a decisive blow to the co-operative spirit. The moment had come when the ex-enemy had to be trusted, or else maimed. At that moment, if I am not mistaken, Briand, for France, sealed the fate of the Weimar Republic and bent Germany toward Hitler and the second World War.[3]

Briand felt that he had no right to risk the security of France; he felt no inner certitude of power to shape the plastic will of Germany; he did not see that he was risking what he had even less right to risk—the recovery of Europe. The statesman must know, I say, that he cannot act without risk, for better or for worse.

THE NEED FOR INDIVIDUAL DECISION

It is only as an individual, alone in his private conviction, that any man becomes effectively universal. Just as the exploring scientist, alone with his devised experiment, knows that he is seeking a truth not for himself alone but for mankind, so in the field of political decision it is the individual vision that must be the guide for an act of state having universal validity. It was when young Lincoln was present at a slave auction that something arose in him that, unforgotten, made history.

I will go farther and say that in confused public situations it is only the individual, with his private perception, that can offer the releasing idea—not to dictate, but to convince. It is the corporate officialdoms that are helpless and barren —the parties, bureaus, departments, cabinets, commissions —barren because of the inner cancellation of each other's certitudes. The composite program, prudentially polished, has every virtue in it but *life*. "Where there is no (personal) vision, the people perish."

Particularly in a deadlocked situation such as the present one, in which an inability to take the affirmative risk of unilateral action involves the continuing negative risk of headless energy unbound, the resource of inner assurance in a nation's spokesmen will play the decisive role. Here is the final test of national strength, the availability of that moral virility which, with mental inclusiveness and certitude, can break through vicious circles by acts of creative risk.

REVISION OF THE CONCEPT OF DEMOCRACY

I realize that the position here taken involves a revision of our current notions of democracy. In point of fact, I regard this revision as perhaps the chief necessity, in the recovery of the normal strength of this great nation.

There is a view of democracy that is inconsistent with cherishing any certitude whatever, since all ideas have an equal right to be heard, and the prior probability of the truth of any one of them is precisely zero. Each must take its chance in the general tussle, and submit to the results of majority vote. The idea that any one can achieve an absolute is a form of arrogance that must be rejected—with absolute arrogance. What we are sure of is that we can be sure of nothing. As I noted above, we have deeply invested in this type of amiable relativity, which has its own type of aristocratic superiority, superior to convictions and standards—since there are no decencies, there are no indecencies. Disbelief in an absolute can make an absolute of disbelief, or reach a point of nihilism that seeks fulfillment in what common folk call crime. But as a people, while on principle tolerant of guidelessness, we shy away from extremes, and limit our relativity to a cult of moral and intellectual ease, evading the full manhood of responsible judgment. Compasses tell approximate truth, but after all, they wobble and deviate, and is it not folly to be overprecise with imprecision? A philosophy of Genial Drift can readily content itself with a democracy that relies for guidance on the mutual supplementation, or mutual cancellation, of guideless individuals in unwieldy representative bodies.

It becomes also easy to distrust one's own more specific convictions as prejudices, and yield in friendly deference to the judgments of our fellowship groups. We suffer the less from the double morality we were considering, because the solitary voice tends to become mute. In the midst of our wealth of intersecting groups we become estranged from ourselves, forgetting the accent of our own consciences: after all, the modest whisper from inside may always be suspected of a false absoluteness, like that of the Natural Law theorists taken so overliterally by our founding fathers! If what we call conscience is simply "the group voice represented in symbolic recall," we can get at the right view more directly by taking the actual group as the sufficient authority in matters we call "right and wrong."

I am prepared to set myself in clear-cut opposition to any concept of democracy growing—as I fear much of the supposedly democratic sentiment of the USA grows—out of this miasma of sophisticated, pedantic, self-distrust, a complete rejection of the birthright of our liberties.

The point is of the utmost simplicity—it calls for no reliance on axioms or a priori propositions—it demands nothing more than a firm statement of what everyone knows. The foundation of all national strength lies in the conviction of the individual thinker. The value of that conviction comes from the normal universality of private judgment: the truth for the solitary thinker is the truth for all—a principle on which every man acts without a second thought. What our practical democracies most need is a definite provision for every official to get away from the noise of all groups and be alone with himself. This normal universality at once defines a democracy underlying all more specific democracies, a democracy of mankind.

For what we call "solitude"—being alone with the world and our thoughts—is filled with the possibilities of companionship without specification of person. The underlying democracy is best realized precisely in the seclusion of the hermit or of a Robinson Crusoe startled by the sight of a footprint. Here attempting to escape intrusion, we confront tokens of the all-important fact that the very Nature that clothes and secures our solitude is common property, known to be such —every spot in it accessible, not actually but by line, from every other. By the very nature of the things and objects we contemplate, it is *impossible to be absolutely alone* in the world, impossible to grasp truths which are not truths also for others. In whatever corner the solitary "I" seeks escape, there the print of the "thou" as co-owner is stamped on every object.

And since *My world* is thus everywhere *Our world*, and my geometry and physics are everyman's geometry and physics, so is my caring for things everyman's caring; the possible co-viewer is also the possible co-user, with co-will-to-live and co-will-to-power, possible competitor, possible helper. The moral first rudiments—the community of truth, of hope, of freedom, of regard—are embedded in the situation, not as extraneous commands or tables of the law, but as factors of the elemental human existence. This aboriginal democracy— with its identity of generic traits, for which the word "equality" could be used without any quantitative significance, is prior to any special relations that may arise between us as friend or foe or fellow citizen. It is not a matter of choice— we might call it an ontological necessity. He who denies it denies his own being, for the world is not "mine" unless it is also "ours."

And the fundamental mental trait of this aboriginal democracy, simpler and more primitive than any actual society, is *certitude*: the indubitable identity of the world common to all, the indubitable community of the problems of existence, the indubitable freedoms and duties imposed by the common lot.

It is the absolute and final repudiation of that conception of democracy, festering to death, whereby, since no one has any certitude, the majorities of the ballot box or the market place or the publicity-whipped fashion-drift are the truly liberal ways to determine what is true, just, or beautiful.

As always latent, this radical democracy establishes a norm for all human intercourse. Its most spontaneous expression is the *will to converse*. In fact, democracy might be defined as the application in all relations of the norms implied in ordinary conversation. This is suggested in Thoreau's remark that "all the abuses that are the objects of reform are unconsciously amended in the intercourse of friends." But the democracy is there even in the accosting of entire strangers, assuming their willingness to exchange ideas on a footing of mutual understandings: to open conversation is to postulate democracy.

This being the original form, we may fairly say that all the technical embodiments of the "conference"—from primitive village communes, Indian powwows, Anglo-Saxon witenagemots, Russian mirs, Hindu ashrams, to the intricate functional balance of a modern state—are derivative. The derivatives struggle against odds to preserve the primitive brotherhood, some with major success, some with forbidding complexity, or counterfeit, or even caricature. In these straits, the man who presumes to speak from his own certitude, who takes the creative risk—often at great peril—of leadership, calling not for obedience but for corroboration from the certitudes of his own neighbors—that man is the true democrat. He evinces, through his own peril, the fundamental respect for human nature which marks genuine fraternity.

Note then that all life is attended with risk, and ought to be. The difference between the valid risk and the gamble is that the valid risk is based on a certitude. The inalienable vector quality of all life, its quest for meaning, is the basis of the legitimate risk of all action.

The opening of conversation is a risk—a creative risk, as expecting a reply in kind—based on nothing more than the certitude of the aboriginal democracy. Conventions that shield the polite privacies of the far-civilized or the seclusions of the proper hermit may well limit its indiscriminate application. But love, war, and emergency uncover the basic situation, and reveal the elemental obligations. Enmity itself, as we have seen, has its presuppositions of agreement; and these presuppositions may be made dominant in the demand to converse.

It follows that the simple existence of conversation, personal or official, gives grounds for pressing the human postulates of the ultimate fraternity-in-democracy to the point of creative risk, given but a clear head in the initiator and the moral power that goes with certitude.[4] Here lies the incomparable advantage of man-to-man diplomacy. It is the near-solitude of each that most readily speaks from the underlying realities to the other and—without canceling concrete issues —sets them in valid perspective.

We could make good use of an extension of our concept of freedom, a freedom in statecraft corresponding to the freedom of the artist. Let us believe in a freedom that rises to the power to create, even in the unpromising world of international rivalry.

But to clear the way for that freedom, we must now take note of the moral dilemmas that may confront its use.

XII

MORAL DILEMMAS
OF PEACE

WAR is an implicit denial of the aboriginal democracy we
have spoken of. It is the breakoff of conversation. It is a decision to treat one's opponent as a thing-among-things, to be
dealt with by physical force. This decision implies a judgment that his will is a bad will, thoroughly bad, hence no
longer human and therefore blastable without compunction.

On the other hand, to continue conversation is to convey
tacitly the presuppositions of conversation; the convictions
regarding agreement, fraternity, and elementary morality
implied in all competition and hostility. It is to convey and
confirm the aboriginal democracy, as it were inductively,
without insisting on its terms.

This is the great value of trade and intercourse, the exchange of delegates, merchants, industrialists, columnists,
artists—especially artists—and plain visitors. Whatever
they see or say, their simple presence bespeaks the irresistible
common human nature, and refutes without words the doubts
and denials of our tough philosophies as to the meaning of
human life. Instead of minimizing this conversation, surrounding it with barriers, and measuring it out in cautious
spoonfuls, *maximize it*: open wide the channels of travel,
trade, exchange of technique, science, and the temper of inquiry. In due time, the implications of this widened mutuality
will make themselves felt.

CONVERSATION IMPLIES AN ATMOSPHERE OF SETTLEMENT

We know what these implications are, but their reach, as silent arguments, is astonishing. The nucleus of experience, making its way into common speech, is as wealthy as the nucleus of the atom.

All living, for example, implies the forward look. The sense of the present includes futurity, a continuous real-izing of idea, without terminus. To assert a terminus, cutting off the remote future, lames the *élan* toward tomorrow. If human history runs to a blank end in racial death, the personal fragment of that total-zero of meaning has just the worth its conscious moment can contain. It loses nothing, one might say, nothing but its infinitude, and that "call of the whole to the part" which gives the human *telos* the dignity of a cosmic destiny, and the daily duty of transcending what tangibly appears in the measurable objectives of farm, commune, workshop, office. Strange how eloquently the intangible is always speaking to the tangible. Imagination is alike appalled by the final zero, and by endlessness. But when the sense of morality shrinks to the area of party loyalty and the amenities of mutual aid, while the total obligation of rulers falls within the circle of promoting one's system and caring for one's own by whatever means, human or inhuman, one feels without argument that something significant is missing; that the vague infinite-remainder thus trimmed off contained some weighty factor in the morale of persons or peoples confronted with the tragic hostilities of our time.

Such a reminder-without-argument of the instinctive drive of the human self toward wholeness of outlook is peculiarly potent in our present context, because it is involved not in the theory but in the appeal of the revolution itself. The goal of revolution is indeed set in history, with nothing beyond; but it defines no terminus, and regards its cause as ruling the historic process. It has its heroes, its prophets, its martyrs. It calls on its followers to accept hardship, privation, iron discipline, perhaps death, for its sake. And revolution finds that willingness, for the spirit of man is better than its theories, and spirit contributes its own meaningful outlook to the supposed necessities of matter. A revolution made for the establishment of a materialist dialectic is a contradiction in terms, though revolutionists have shown singular capacity to live with it. But whatever the lapses of consistency, or the artificial boundaries of sympathy implied in its ideology and polemic, they are silently answered and dismissed by the universal standards of judgment implied in the simple process of conversation across lines of conflict. Nothing is settled; but the temper of settlement is being fortified, and some of its premises are being built.

I say "*some* of its premises": certainly I do not suggest that the temper of settlement is sufficient to produce a settlement—though it has happened. I merely urge its importance, and point out that when, as now, we are dealing not merely with competing interests but with strong currents of feeling, the "collective passions" of which Camus speaks, the factor of temper may make all the difference between a hearing for reason and stopped ears.

Camus himself, whose analysis of these collective passions is superb, proposes two modes of taming them: the risk of the revolter and the spell of art. His Rebel does not at first converse; but he acts to break through the insulation that prevents conference: he asserts the right to be heard, and thus establishes the solidarity in which conversation takes place. But the less imperative sway of art is Camus' final reliance, especially for the conversation of peoples: partly because of the priority of feeling over conceptual thought, but chiefly because art creates its mood. And "when the passions of the times put the fate of the whole world at stake," it is only creation that can command the turn of destiny.

This great call touches us near home: for our public art —finding its way to the masses through drama, cinema, tele-

vision—is heavily drawn upon for mood-changing, surely a
creative task, but dominantly a change from sobriety to
gaiety. Where is the art that can make the reverse change of
temper from levity to resolve, or from resentment, even just
resentment, to a resolute fraternity?

But if the concrete and specific issues between the USA
and the USSR remain outstanding, is it important to create
an atmosphere of settlement *in advance?* Will the atmosphere
not naturally follow items of settlement, through tough un-
ravelings of rights and interests, as in the problem of re-
unifying Germany?

Most postwar settlements in history have had this piece-
meal character. No previous settlement has had the advantage of so much prior systematic reflection and agreement
as to the methods of reaching agreement on "peaceful
change," together with a working UN in which the main
contestants are already members, and therefore signatories
to the procedures which, with good will, could lead to settlement. Very few of these refractory problems are within the
reach of international law: as problems of status, they belong
chiefly to the nonjusticiable region. For law has, as yet,
neither rules nor principles to guide decisions in respect to
the birth or death of states, or their definitive area and
identity. The assumptions of our fundamental democracy
propose no solutions: they might however propose what is
not yet in evidence—a willingness to accept the offices of UN,
or some *ad hoc* tribunal, or still better a direct confrontation
of the principals, with some new vista of a *world order that
could be tolerable to both.*

In a talk with Walter Lippmann, Mr. Khrushchev put
his finger on this issue of the order of events in achieving
concrete solutions. Confidence, he said, must come first; arrangements for inspection and control will naturally follow.
The USA, he said, insists on the reverse order. As a matter
of psychology, Khrushchev is undoubtedly right. Confidence

is necessary, even for the willingness to refer a dispute to a mediating body.

The old League of Nations lost its life precisely on this issue. Its crucial case was the Japanese *démarche* in Manchuria in September, 1931, in which the mediation proposals of the Lytton Commission were rejected by Japan; and on the ground that the issues were uniquely a matter of vital interest to Japan, to an extent that precedents and analogies became irrelevant. Stimson's note, applying the USA's doctrine of the nonrecognition of regimes established by force, became an impertinence, from this point of view (an impertinence recognized later by a distinguished Hepburn Professor of American Constitutional Law at the University of Tokyo, Dr. Yasaka Takagi, in *Toward International Understanding*, ch. viii, "America's War Aims," esp. pp. 86-87; Tokyo, 1954).

During the early years of the League's life, I had occasion to bring to the attention of its Secretary the case of certain minority groups pleading "self-determination." His answer was that such problems belonged definitely to the League's functions as arbiter, but that it was at that time unable to assume them: "Even your Supreme Court had first to build its prestige; give us ten years and we can deal with these matters."

"Prestige" is a mediated form of "confidence"—a confidence between the contending parties, by way of a mutual confidence in the arbitrating body. And confidence, for mediation, must come first.

The fundamental difficulty with mediation is the uniqueness of issues we have spoken of. Every mediator casts about for analogies and precedents as a guide to principles, the raw material of "law," which is always a generality. Generalities neglect precisely the elements that make particular cases refractory. And it requires no subtle observation to sustain the judgment that for the present set of issues between the USA and the USSR there are no analogies. Our problem, for specific settlements, is to *create a world map, not to deduce one.*

In creating it, however, we must be guided by certain broad general principles, such as (1) the right of clearly marked national entities to existence as undivided individuals, (2) the right of existing federal unions to continue in peace their experiment in social order, so long as the peoples involved freely co-operate in that experiment, and (3) the right of unfederated nations to free neutrality and free alliance, unprejudiced by contractual agreements for economic aid and guidance.

Such an undertaking does indeed presuppose a prior element of "confidence," at least confidence in basic humanity, whether or not it could yet take the form of a "treaty of friendship." But even for this beginning, we confront the formidable issue which, unmet, tends to maintain the hostile alignment of armed boundaries—*the issue of plain right and wrong*, which for many men of good will comes first instead of last, and eliminates useless discussion.

DOES DÉTENTE IMPLY DISLOYALTY?

I am entirely convinced that there can be no *détente* until there is first of all a change of temper; that in this change of temper the USA owes the initiative; and that an essential part of this change is, not a weakening of the right-and-wrong issue, but a truer perspective of it, an element of humility to accompany our a priori certitude that the right-and-wrong issue is drawn where we incline to put it.

I believe that the steps of maximizing intercourse and the act of creative risk on our part can be taken without compromise of any pending issues: such steps do not constitute a deed of acceptance of any wrongful *status quo*.

Nevertheless, any such prior *rapprochement* does suggest that our protest against such wrong is reduced, and that meeting halfway will be entertained. In any agreement to peaceful competition, in any acceptance of coexistence, some acquiescence in accomplished fact is involved, among others the fact of Communist state-building we have vainly tried on principle to prevent. Can we escape the suggestion of our own consciences that the attempt to establish friendly relations in this situation has a moral quality of compounding a felony?

For myself, I cannot shake off a haunting sense of near-disloyalty in easing—if only for a moment—the pressure on issues that are clearly issues of right and wrong, even for the sake of a peace without which human life everywhere must become a persistent abnormal suspense. I find myself in the moral attitude of those who, in presence of a clear call to cancel principle, prefer extinction to surrender—at least one's own extinction: if we must go out, let it be with clean hands.

Even more keenly, I suffer the inner reproach of seeming —in calling for an end to nuclear arming—to forget the cause of persons wronged, whether alive or dead: persons who have fought or are still fighting the good fight—the Lithuanians, Ukranians, Hungarians—the Russian refugees in Dubrovnik, Milan, Paris, everywhere: Berdyaev, the Homyakoffs, the exiles on Taiwan, the dispersed elite of the noble culture of eternal China.

The churnings of history recur to the lawless plea of "accomplished fact," accomplice of the corrupting "right of conquest." I have expressed my revulsion against this plea, which hastens to declare the crimes of the "accomplishment" expunged by the laudable result. For that unscrupulous planning which deliberately aims at effecting a meretricious *fait accompli* with the intent to raise at once the cry of "Peace," when there is no peace, I have proposed the maxim "No fact is 'accomplished' until it is accomplished right": what is done with violence and fraud must not with our consent be built permanently into history. I hold to that.

But I have also to remember our own history: our dealings with the Indians, our Mexican War with all the devious procedure of 1846, the history of other revolutions—none free from crime.

And especially I must bear in mind the principle of judgment we have arrived at: that the people are the primary reality in any historic event, the people and not the statesmen with hands bloody through their own incompetence. Deeds which do bring about a renewal of the life of peoples, deeds done in blind passion through a dim sense of neglected good, deeds whose affirmative germ has been mutilated by superfluous negations, and brought to birth by cruelties of frightened despots unable to stand without the support of terror—such deeds may be built into achievements we must accept, *unless we are prepared to go to war to undo them!* And such war, though Holy War, must once again tear open the wounds of a suffering people.

The hope of mankind is to rescue the fabric of human history from this desperate wrenching of hoped-for goods by entailed evils, which constitutes the tragedy of our time. The realization of that hope can be definitely promoted by a perceptive analysis which can disentangle the evil from its involvement in the unique global *strategy of national existence*, and achieves agreement on the principle which condemns that evil. For example, the USSR, which respects to some extent the independence of Finland and Sweden, continues for a mixture of reasons the forced incorporation of the European buffer states into its federal area. Apart from that mixture, not yet fully analyzed, the USSR is clearly aware of the folly—to us the wrong—of compelling the Sovietization of well-developed nations committed to an independent version of the economic-political order. It learns that its ideology has no prospects in the USA nor in most of western Europe: it retains hopes in regions still more or less plastic; it believes in the principle of learning by doing, even in the form of learning by being compelled to do, and still hopes for reluctant conversion through manifest fruits with intervals of drastic discipline. It envisions a line drawn across Europe—farther west than it belongs—not ignoring the principle of the self-determination of peoples, but subordinating the dubious spirit of chauvinist nationalism to the larger outlines of the great competition. And in that process, it hopes, among other things, to obliterate the longstanding aspersion of Slavic dignity, the ancient Germanic assumption that the Slavs are an inferior breed. Wounded vanity plays no part in our decorous legal concepts governing the outlining of sovereign states. But it plays a very definite part in national ambitions.

And we of the USA, who for love of liberty formulated the great principle of "self-determination"—and then sanctioned its demolition in the breakup of ex-Ottoman Asia into the A-mandates, and the later breakup of Palestine, have still to recognize that "self-determination" is the vaguest of vague formulas, unless we are prepared to identify the entity which can rightly claim that power.

The situation faced by the USSR and the USA is that nationhood is a reality not to be smothered under an economic-political formula, a reality which the future world will value more and more highly as it suffers under the bulldozers of leveling abstractions and becomes hungry for a domesticity *within* federal totalities. No empire such as the USSR is in practice can gain by suppressing it. It will learn that fact, and learn to identify the real nations. But we of the USA have also to see that nationalism, which has long made a quarreling nest of the Balkans, is a menace to the necessary world unity; its disintegrating passion leads many a serious thinker to propose its death. It is today mangling the outlook for international economic balance—and in this dangerous game the USA is one of the worst players.[1] We have much to learn.

Holding as we must to the conviction that it is *never right*, even for experimental purposes, to compel an unwilling nation to live under an imposed ideology, we must recognize (i) that the outlining and equipment of nations is an unfinished problem of world order, and (ii) that on the economic-

political plane, since the peaceful competition is in principle
accepted, none of the competing ideologies in their present
and growing forms can be denounced as pure evil. The element of evil lies in the compulsion, which a change in world
temper may hope to remove.

THE ULTIMATE ISSUE OF RELIGION

But why halt at the level of the social system, the economic
and political aspect of Communist ideology? The most radical issue remains untouched. Unrelenting opposition to Communism remains for many of our citizens a matter of principle, and of more than principle—a moral third dimension,
a holy war. An absolute enters the international field, and
calls a plague on all temporizing, all fine weighing of social
goods and ills.

Whatever the valid incentives of the revolution, in terms of
justice and brotherhood for the toiling and oppressed masses
of its own region—yes, of vast world regions still in want—
must not a system be rejected out of hand for which there
is nothing beyond physical nature and the material furnish-
ings of life? Any kindness toward Communism by the tender-
hearted—does it not lack precisely that moral virility we
have spoken of, an element of *righteous hatred toward evil*,
a hatred not alone of the original and continuing crimes of
revolution, but beyond that, a relentless hatred of the atheist-
materialist degradation, not of the earth and its fruits, but
of the spirit of man in its cosmic insertion? How can we
make peace with a system that destroys the light that lifts the
whole mixed tangle of history into partnership with infinitude—the infinitude of time unclosed by racial death, and
the infinitude of the whole spectrum of value, touched and
untouched—a limitless glory of potential being which we
can believe to be at the source of things because we have been
touched by its remotest shimmer? The word infinite means
the rejection of boundary: and a world view that closes the
prospect of humanity within a value-wall, however it prepares

the conquest of space, does daily hurt to the human sense of life, both in its tragedy and in its joy.

This deepest of issues pertains to the ultimate passions of mankind—the passionate hatred of evil and also the passionate love of the infinite. It is the passion commonly called "religion"—a word which may be hurt in its nobility by doctrinal measuring sticks and symbols, but which we may simply identify as "world passion"—a reach of kinship toward the totality in which at rare moments we not only feel but know ourselves to be immersed. It is that inner passion for what is beyond the evident that glorifies the man-animal and spurs him to build into history, through art and faith, a fraction of his cosmic love—which is, in fact, his love of life. What, then, can we feel but horror toward a regime that would stamp out this aspiring flame, which is the soul of humanity?

There can be no dissent from a protest against making peace with radical evil. There is but one thing to do with radical evil—that is, to fight it, even if we and our world go out in doing so.

The questions which this attitude puts to the facts of Soviet ideology and policy are inescapable: they are my questions. I have also a few others: whether the antireligion of the Soviets is identical with that of Marx and Engels; whether it is the same as it was in the 1920s; whether the religion they are against is honest religion or a partial travesty; and if the latter, whether their hatred of it has to some extent the flavor of a crusade in which we could sympathize.

Undoubtedly the revolution had, and has, its passion. It has its hatreds which it embeds in its favorite words of objurgation—the "bourgeois," calculating, self-centered, exploiting, and crawling with churchly credentials to the steps of his Heaven; the "idealist," proclaiming a rational deductive scheme of abstract law and virtue, supporting bourgeois rights, and a world picture based on a self-idea puffed up to cosmic dimensions. Revulsions of this sort are not confined to the Communist persuasion. We dare not forget that we live in an era in which the naturalist and secular dispositions are dominant and "idealism" has become a current term of reproach. In the hatreds I have mentioned, our "angry" and "beat" generations are in full agreement with the Soviet outlook, puking at respectability, and consulting their inner volcanic rumblings for some source of earth-shaking fire. An antireligious passion, as part of a world passion in search of a credo, can sometimes be a disguised religious quest whose hidden power plant shakes the man until his power lines can train its forces to rational ends. Violence is commonly a bedeviled quest for an absolute, through a will to annihilate an absolute touched with decay.

There was a time when the USSR would stamp religion out; it is far from clear that they would do so today. I have indicated that in points of economics and politics, revolution *learns,* not from external insistence but from the logic of its own experience. May this not be true also in its attitude toward metaphysical normality?

CHANGING ATTITUDES IN RUSSIA

No one who was near the scene when Bolshevism took over can forget the disturbing effect of its successive measures on stable Europe. Switzerland, as the center of stillness in the eye of all political hurricanes, spoke through the staid columns of the *Journal de Genève* of Bolshevism's iconoclastic strokes, its scornful rejection of Kerensky's halfway overturn of bourgeois conventions, its blows at family order as well as private ownership, its radical surgery upon its mortal foe, the religion of Russia. It attacked the Russian Church through its properties, confiscating its lands in the general nationalization, refusing its customary subsidies, making marriage a legal contract, making unlawful the church's teaching to "more than three at a time." Between 1917 and 1941 there was literal decimation in the number of priests and churches.[2]

In these and other expressions of "thorough," revolution alienated many of its own natural allies in western Europe, sowing the seeds of that defiance and fear with which it still faces westward, and stirring revulsion in many who, feeling the same need of radical reform, rejected the cultural dismantling, thus influencing the turn toward Fascism, toward Mussolini and Hitler, begetting in its environment a tide toward what it most zealously wished to destroy. It earned by right the sweeping denunciation of the Pope, not only of its ideology but also of persons kindly disposed thereto, to the point of excommunication of priests and laity.

Revolution finds it hard to confess an error; but if one asks whether the Bolshevik revolution has learned, there are definite affirmative answers:

Stalin's Constitution of 1936, with its lip service to human rights, indicates a positive public step, widely affecting Soviet law, on the part of the leading exponent of Communist terrorism. In 1943, having already admitted through a party publication that it was proving difficult to uproot religion, and having allowed the election of a Metropolitan of Moscow, Stalin announced that the party "could no longer deprive the Russian people of their Church and freedom of worship."[3] The concurrent—seemingly purely political—*rapprochements* with Western powers, among them the exchange of ambassadors with the USA (1933) and participation (1945) in founding the UN organization of "peace-loving states" (though with cautious insistence on a veto power that could cancel any action of the Security Council), carry an assumption of having learned at least the untenable nature of cultural isolation, and of strident negativity toward the sources of Western civilization. Of the USSR also we must say, "*E pur si muove!*"—"And yet it does move!"

THE DESCENT INTO HADES

The USSR, I believe, has still much to learn in regard to the world passion upon which the health of every state de-

pends: the state that cuts off its citizens' free communication
with the totality of purpose in the world, in emotion and ob-
servance as well as in art, robs its people of an enzyme needed
to sustain its own cohesion.[4] Unless the human spirit is free
for its farthest reaches, not even the glorious advance of production and technical prowess can permanently hold the
public morale. And so long as fear remains the last whip—
fear the costliest of state adhesives and the most ephemeral—
it becomes murderous to that free loyalty that must maintain the strength of a nation.

But what we of the USA almost totally fail to see is that
the USSR, in its experiment in antifaith, has been doing
something *for the West.* Its effort to make thorough with the
materialist conception of man and the world is in some degree
a vicarious effort. For that effort is our duty as well!

It is necessary for us also to follow through with all consistency the world picture of human life as a phenomenon of
the lifeless. The premises of that philosophy are present in
our own tradition: it is Feuerbach who hands them on to
Marx. We can refute them, and have refuted them. But
what we know today is that it is never sufficient to refute,
especially not in regard to the deepest persuasions of the
human mind. We must carry the argument to the one ultimate authority, experience: and in this case to experience on
the community scale. Many have done it as a personal experiment in atheism; men like Camus have done it heroically
under the tensions of underground defiance; but Camus
himself has said that "in order to dominate collective passions, they must in fact be lived through and experienced."[5]

The experiment is that of probing the entire depth of
world-alienation, of living consciously and aspiring in a
world devoid of sense and of sensitivity. It is necessary to
see not only that human life and history are tinged with
Absurdity, leading perceptive individuals to nihilism, anti-
moralism, wallowism, damn-the-rules-ism—the pathetic courage of private defiance which secretly hopes for comradeship

in one's violently captured solitude. It is *necessary to find the bottom* of the meaninglessness and accidentality of the physical biological universe—the senseless Fact that environs and unknowingly begets the transitory spark of human reason.

It requires a certain moral strength to explore that depth: the pertinent symbol for the task is that of the Descent into Hades. And the weakness—I must say the failure—of contemporary religion is the fumbling of this task through hesitance to recognize its necessity or the blind courage of those who, under apparently hostile flags, have essayed it.

It shares this weakness with prevalent current philosophy, which—twiddling its thumbs over the analysis of words and sentences—shrinks from the task of meeting the factual world head-on, the fact-world for whose threat to man's destiny every language has unambiguous words—"life" and "death"—and for which science offers whatever precise definitions are available. In fact, it is science itself rather than philosophy which today offers the clearest statement of the Sphinx riddle for which this Hades-descent is the experimental path of inquiry. Together with drastic human experience, science today is writing—not explicitly but on its margins—the best philosophy of our time. A moment's glance that way:

SCIENCE LOOKING BEYOND ITS BORDERS

Taking together the explorings of astrophysics and biology, we see the human episode as a transitory passage in cosmic history. As W. T. Stace has fairly pictured the situation, it is Man Before Darkness, or let us say Man Between Darknesses, a moment of consciousness suspended in the midst of boundless nescience. Conscious life itself a biological accident facing the clear promise of annihilation, leaving the self-sufficient field-play of the ultimate particles wholly unmoved by its coming or going.

The arrival of awareness, or "consciousness," remains un-

explained. For biological science, it is simpler to ignore its
presence: the electrodynamic functions of the organism proceed in their directing of growth and behavior without reference to "mind." Philosophy inclines to agree, and to pro-
nounce the ancient mind-and-body problem passé. Mentality
is unmeasurable and incalculable: energy is calculable. As
Sir Charles Sherrington has most clearly put the matter,
"The mental is not examinable as a form of energy. . . . If
you say thoughts are an outcome of the brain, we [physiolo-
gists] as students of the energy concept know nothing of
it."[6] How thought and energy are connected—since science
can ignore thought—is for science simply no problem at all.
And philosophy is naturally relieved of a bothersome topic.

But for us plain human beings, is it perhaps *the* problem?

What we see is that man is obviously a bit of Nature. He
does, somehow come out of Nature. And if his mental being—
his consciousness, his purpose, his reason—is negligible for
science, an accident in the course of evolution, it is for us
a marvelous accident, somehow important. It is this accident
that builds for itself a Nature-*picture*—something that Nature without mind's presence has never had—a picture everywhere touched with "quality" and "feeling," with notes here
and there of an unscientific character called "beauty," and
stirring in man a scientifically unnecessary *impulse to make
"science,"* intending to surprise the secrets of Nature itself,
which Nature never knew to be secrets! Among them, at a
very late stage of inquiry, a method of tapping certain inter-
atomic energies seeming to achieve results biologically important, for better or for worse. But, of course, "importance"
means nothing to Nature, only to man.

At this point we pause to reflect. For Nature, we begin to
realize, *nothing is important or unimportant:* it simply *is.*
For man, however, everything has its degree of importance.
It is man, we may say, who imports "importance" into the
factual. Falsely?

But "importance" is another name for "value" or "meaning": shall we agree that these are purely subjective accidents of the world, nonexistent in reality? The flowering of quality and value in Nature, the attunement of man's powers to the secrecies of Nature's codes, the timeliness of discovery to human need—all these unnecessary suitabilities of fact-history to man's changing engagement in Nature's world are, for science, fortuitous, meaningless, and, so far as importance is concerned, unreal. And if man, or rather, *when* man someday vanishes, together with his mentality, then again in the whole universe nothing will be of the slightest importance.

In this conclusion, there is something revolting to our common sense, and here I hold absolutely with my revered colleague Whitehead that "the ultimate appeal is to naïve experience"[7] and its intuitions. What I find common sense proposing at this point is that "importance" is not merely a private projection of accidentally mental beings, but that a world without it would be incompletely real. There is no world of pure fact, devoid of all meaning, and no world of pure meaning, apart from fact: the two realms appear to us to belong together. It is as though the world of Nature needs its appreciator as much as the appreciator needs the world of Nature's fact. To speak of "need" is, of course, a reversion to the subjective mode of thinking, and without other evidence can be repudiated as an intrusion of unjustified tools of judgment equivalent to superstition, unworthy of a sturdy materialist, or of a church which has a more explicit answer, or of a noble atheist like Camus who finds his Titantic morale in simply "what he knows."

THE ARRIVING ANSWER OF PHILOSOPHY

Beyond this point pure science cannot take us. It has won in our time a clear sight of its own incompleteness: the men who have shouldered the main advances of science—Planck,

Einstein, Bohr, Schrödinger, Heisenberg—unanimously reject claim to total truth by this route. And science makes no pretense of providing the supplement.

Some seek that supplement in "intuition;" and the proposal is valid as looking away from all techniques to something more at hand. But that something remains indefinite: we can hardly permit the main weight of our world view to rest on so vague a basis. We require a *new step in philosophy;* and with this step our century, beginning with Bergson, is indeed engaged. It begins to be recognized that the task is co-operative: that the search for a total truth must accept, with science, the aid of feeling, of *disciplined* feeling; joining with a religion, conscious of its continuing duty to reconceive its message; and with an art, conscious—through its purposeful play with symbol—of a gravity of mission commensurate with that of science and religion. As interpreters of the human lot, all three—science, religion, art—are necessary: but their several voices must be brought to unison. Philosophy is the responsible listener and unifier, seeking for every man the single truth under which he may live, under the two rigorous demands—consistency, and completeness of survey.

Completeness of survey includes, for our time, a newly resolute and unshrinking exposure to the irrational and evil aspects of fact, openness to growing impressions of the absurd and meaningless in the cosmos and in history; of the silence and apparent indifference of God, if there be a God; of the lurking ferocities of human nature; of the collective passions of men, tearing through well-wrought social fabrics and wrecking the most precious historical continuities. An adequate philosophy for this era thus assumes, with its widened empirical conscience, an unprecedented burden. Using whatever light it may inherit from philosophical or religious tradition, or may derive from poetic imagination or speculative ingenuity, it will perforce read the facts in the light of *its own ongoing experience*, sharing the all-human movement at once toward new triumph and new dismay.

For each thinker, the ultimate authority must be his own vision, through his own encounter with the reality at work in the facts—*and he must find it there!* Of my own findings, I hope to be duly able to give a systematic account.[8] So far as they are relevant to the world issues here before us, these findings may be roughly summarized as follows:

1. *The fundamental truths of which man has need are simple and near at hand.*

If it were not so, democracy would be a mockery. For democracy must assume that all men have, not an equal, but an identical standard of truth and right. Socrates was the first to expose this nerve of democracy, in his demonstration that, in education, truth is not inserted but elicited: the all-human standards are *there*.

One main source of weakness in the Western world today is its acquired doubt on this point. This doubt is due in part to the increasing complexity of scientific ultimates and legal principles, but chiefly to one notable advance—the universal acceptance of relativities in place of old absolutes. Euclid's axioms and the "rights of man" must alike bend to the analyses which confirm their relativity. The idea of a "reality" (an absolute of being) within human reach is largely abandoned, forgetting that if there is no such absolute, relativity itself becomes meaningless. For every relative is relative *to something* and the statement of that functional relationship holds good: one could not discover a relativity if he were not beyond it—an absolute in hand.

Thus, wherever there is a network of relativities, there is an absolute-and-real that underlies and gives sense to the network. Just as we have found an "aboriginal democracy" at the core of the various democratic systems relatively valid, so there is an aboriginal faith at the core of the various faiths. There is a central, unformulated confidence-in-being

which is more than an "invincible surmise"; for it has the
character of a perception rather than an hypothesis—what
we believe in is the reality now present. But this central confidence has a trait of activity: to be aware of reality is to
respond to it. This is the ingredient of truth in the Freudian
psychoanalysis, which finds the source of human will in
impulses or "drives" from subconscious caverns. This elemental response I speak of is prior to all specific drives: we
must go beyond Freud, and beyond the mysteries of the
subconscious, by coming nearer to our actual experience, a
verifiable analysis! The elemental response which affirms
being, and brings an active as well as a cognitive element into
"faith," is neither blind nor hidden: it is *our* response—
almost one might say it is *ourself;* at any rate, we may see
it as the nuclear origin of our selfhood as a continuous dealing with the real.

2. *The world process has a meaning.*

This elemental awareness and response is sometimes interpreted as the "will to live." To speak of its affirmation of the
worth of being as a "postulate" (in Kant's sense), a demand
made by us, is to omit the element of perception, making it a
will-attitude without data. We must insist on its nature as a
response to something given: a perception that the world
process (as touched in this miniature encounter) has a direction or trend that can be felt.[9] And within this factual
trend is a *telos* or intention which brings out the answering
inclination on our part. In this response lies the germ of that
sense of personal "task" or "calling" or "destiny"—the
notion of partnership in creativity which can elicit personal
greatness, taking various forms, as in the Puritan sense of
"mission," or the Chinese conception of "Ming" as "Heav-
enly Decree." Thus the trend of the world process is immediately tied in with the sense of an undefined meaning of
individual human life. This primitive rapport makes itself
felt persistently and quietly in two equally wordless and ele-

mental ethical impulses: the impulse to do one's living *well*, and the impulse to find *common ground with others* across all lines of cleavage.

3. *The world process can have no termination in time.*

As this immediate sense of world telos (end-seeking or purpose) becomes a mature conception, it takes the form of cosmologies and philosophies of history, leaving the ground of direct experience, and allowing imagination to shape what scientific prevision cannot define. Most such pictures find their significance in a denouement, an ideal terminus in some state of social perfection, which justifies the long struggle of achievement. Hegel, the idealist, and Marx, the materialist, worlds apart in the traits of their several Utopias, agree on the need of a goal, and of a necessary process, a dialectic, that at each step "means" this consummation. Both face the embarrassment that attends any arrival at the terminal station: shall there be nothing beyond?

The central human impulse knows no terminus: its time span is infinite, both toward the past and toward the future. It can exist, however, only as taking on specific objectives, proximate goals set up as tentative ends, through which an undefined infinitude continues to beckon. These proximate goals—seven-year plans, perhaps, for corporate purposes— have a way of filling the mind without raising ultimate speculations: they substitute themselves for our native and rightful infinitude. World tensions might be relieved by the reflection that no myth can be held as the literal finality it offers; all are dreams subject to revision, serving to reveal to us the growing perfection of our endless sensitivity to value.

In general, we may say that the people of the USSR, highly goal-conscious, feel in partial achievements an eternal meaning which their Marxian theory denies; whereas the people of the USA profess faith in an eternal meaning which their absorption in tangibles denies. The conflict of myths is a mythical conflict—not insignificant, but not incapable of solution on the ground of the all-human ethical impulses.

4. *There are few genuine atheists in the world, even among those who call themselves such.*

The "animal faith" on which men operate and face the future, or come to the aid of fellow men—the natural faith of all life in its forward look—has its own logic. Just as the logic of simple conversation implies an aboriginal democracy, so, digging deeper, the logic of simply experiencing physical objects as valid bits of a physical world common to me and to all men implies awareness of a Thou whose co-presence lends to one's solitary experience the quality of universality. This being the base, no man can be totally alone in the world: in so far as he regards his thought, his science, his art as valid for all men—the Thou-art is there.

5. *The only genuine atheist is the man who believes that there are gulfs between "right" men and "wrong" men so great that no bridge can be thrown across them.*

6. *The depths of darkness, of desperate revolt, of possible disaster now confronting and explored by the human spirit are a measure of the call of this age to greatness.*

What history demands of us is not that we obliterate the refractory will, but that we share its bitter mental and moral adventure, with a will to create, not security, but solidarity. It demands, not that we raze the existing to build the new— which would mean to cure revolution by revolution—but that we make with our obdurate brethren the descent *in profundis,* as we have made with them the commitment to science, and the scientific forecast of death, in order to win with them that right and power to affirm which is the final strength for men and for nations.

APPENDIX I

The International Role
of Art
In Revolutionary Times

IN TIMES of revolutionary change, art has a role of special importance easily overlooked even by the artist himself, a role which calls for a shaking-out of our current views of the nature of art. In broad terms, art is not a copying of the world, nor yet a fantasia on its themes, but a quiet remaking of the world, likely to conceal its proud power under the guise of fancy.

Art is many things at once: labor and play, the element of aspiration built into utility, of form built into function, of infinitude built into the finite, of the beyond-self built into the living selfhood of things—not as extraneous decor but as the fulfillment of their being. Art is the liveliness of life discerned within the mere factuality of life, lending to those facts the assurance of their meaning. Considering the given situation as the taskmaster we are bound to obey, art is the second mile ("go with him twain") we deliberately add to the mile we are compelled to go—the mile freely added not as a boast, but as a promise of a futurity in command of circumstances, not their servant.

It is the glory of man's spirit that in the midst of misery and confusion and revolt, art lifts its head, not to deny the evil but to share it; and not alone to report the misery, nor yet to denounce or escape it, but to transfigure it. An art that merely reports or re-enacts the human load of footlessness, dismay, or despair—as what we call modern art tends to do—may be a loyal art, refusing romantic honors to the headless powers of the time. But stopping at that point, it risks becoming itself *a headless art,* refusing to enter on the uniquely responsible function of creation—that element of world-shaping purpose which silently pervades even the care-free play of human imagination, by virtue of a "depth-psychology" mistraced by Freud.

For the true artist, the world always begins again at the moment of his work. Art is the infinitely recurring rebirth of life through the free man's dream, and of the world, through life.

Art begins in something less than art, perhaps simply in the animal caper that proclaims caprice, the flourish of limb or voice that turns into dance or song—but always the more-than-necessary, and always with a subconscious tribute to life running deeper than the play. From the beginning the steps of civilization have been marked by the signs of joy-in-*form* with which man has lingered over his most compulsory labors, as if to extract from them their tribute to his freedom.

That there is a strand of economic determinism in history no one need doubt: human life is inserted among necessities as tree-roots among stones. But it is the tree, not the stone, that shapes the foliage and the flower: it is humanity, not economy, that dwells on "finishing" its tools and weapons with painstaking ornament, and lends the note of design to its hard-wrought shelters as well as to palace, presidium, temple, and tomb.

Hence it is that the most open book to the soul of a people is the element of "style" in its living quarters, its settlement-planning, its architecture.

Man climbs out of barbarism by way of an accepted dominance signalized in some outstanding structure expressive of "rule" but at the same time of a common desire for unity and joy-in-order. Even underneath the grueling compulsions that built tower and pyramid for the despot, there grew a sense which the despot could neither give nor take away—a sense that "This is ours, not his alone": the finished work became a point of community pride, a tribute not to him but to the human spirit.

When civilization arrives at a nation of free men, the formal centrality in community-planning is not expunged— there is a town hall and a steeple in the New England village. But there is also the homestead. Privacy, as home-right, is built into home-art: not everyone can enter everywhere and always; there is an institution, the "invitation": and this moral factor of controlled association calls on art to embody itself, as in the swinging door, the "yard," the private garden, the hedge or fence, the sidewalk . . . Leaping forward into new East Asia, free Vietnam seeking to embody in property its conception of individual dignity, hopes to secure to every family its "basic economy," its own house and lot! The task of art here becomes formidable, as industrialism looms ahead, and with it, the apartment house: can its advent be postponed, or can the apartment be subdued to the needs of the human spirit? Miss Ehrenfest tried it in Russia.

It is precisely the Industrial Revolution which most clearly illustrates the power of the human will-to-form as lying beyond "function." Feudal and post-feudal Europe, inheriting Classical motifs in architecture and city-design, rewove them into a "Western" visual language for the new-built cities. The Industrial Revolution came as a triumph of mechanism and at the same time as a defeat of human solidarity. Nothing more effectively damned its early character than the "satanic mills," the deadening identity of living quarters in the mill-towns, and the accompanying murder of landscape beauty in Wales, England, Belgium. The industrial economies of today have profited by the lesson. Industry in America has long since begun to exercise a decent concern for human dignity in the homes of its workers, as well as in its sites and factory-design. Not yet a high achievement (though Joseph Pennell found occasional themes for pictorial art in factory scenes), but a distinct step out of the temper of exploit, signalized by a stroke of conscience, as in the ill-fated town of Pullman (1884) intended as an ideal workers' community.

The distinctive spirit of our capitalist civilization, however, expresses (and confesses) itself less in the actual areas of production than in the great office-centers. Something of the dominance of business in America may be gathered from the skyline of New York, not untouched by grace and beauty in its older structures, expressive of a pride-of-power willing at once to outrank and protect the libraries, churches, colleges, the Town Hall, the Metropolitan Museum . . . which cherish a quieter dignity in the shadow of the skyscrapers.

It is a magnificent skyline; and one wonders what would become of it if the varied peaks of those great towers were replaced by squared-off ends like that of the bleak box-housing of the UN Secretariat. The notable thing about present American experiments in architecture under the influence of Functionalism and the *Bauhaus*, is that their "monotonous repetition of cellular façades cloaked with vitreous indifference"—if it expresses any social spirit whatever—is far more symbolic of a *communist* ideal all-alikeness than of a society prizing personality and individual difference!

On the other hand, when the Soviets wish to set up an impressive building, they do not hesitate to borrow architectural themes from classic Europe, as the new university in Moscow may witness. Each pays the other involuntary homage!

The Functionalist commonly forgets the most widely used function of a building. He rightly thinks of the functions of the insiders, the occupants daily users of the internal spaces. If these are numbered by the hundreds, what of those who daily have to see the building, numbered often by the thousands? For them, the structure has a further function which neither it nor they can escape: it must visibly indicate its *raison de'être* in that place and among those surroundings, its role in the community. It must do this by way of the silent speech of form and symbol. It has no right either to the idle luxury of saying nothing (as if like a movable cracker-box it could *be*, without being a member of any specific environment), or by some strident egoism of design crying "Look at me and forget all else."

Hence it is that a competent observer like Sir Albert Richardson, former president of the Royal Academy (whose words I have above quoted), could say that while "fifty years ago America led the world . . . in civic art . . . the present state of architecture in the United States, and indeed throughout the world, reveals soulful despair." Sir Albert believes this guideless period destined to pass.[1]

There are indeed reasons for considering it a temporary phase. Present novelties in skeletal styling and geometrical virtuosity are due in part to developments in engineering and in available materials whose notable capacities have rightly stimulated large-scale experimentation, with natural temptations to extravagance of conception (as in cantilever-projections intended to startle, or spiral ramps expanding skyward). The misfortune is that astonishment is a fading emotion, essentially barren. It is precisely the engineering precocity of these structures, and their admirable durability, that ensures a long toll of public suffering under their defiance of responsible community membership and meaning.

But in this defiance, which is also partly "despair," architecture is not alone. It is but one illustration of a laming common to all contemporary arts, defeating their world-service at a moment of the world's greatest need. We must enlarge our inquiry into the sources of this laming.

I raise the question whether the present phase in all the fine arts—including music, poetry, fiction, and the graphic arts, together with drama and the screen—inclining to assume the label "modern," is not in the main a departure, especially in the USA, from the sound instinct of the nation. And at the same time, whether it is not a *natural* departure, whose motive can be understood and thereby put on the way to remedy.

Is it not due essentially to an impression of failure in the fundamental assumptions of our civilization, a failure so radical as to require shaking off all prepossessions and conventions in order to *renew one's sense of being,* from which alone the work of art can be initiated? The world-turmoil cannot fail to bring with it so wide a loss of order and predictable circumstance that *no art can today bear to speak simply in terms of beauty or affirmation.* Art must find human experience where it is: in an era of hardness, art must speak for the hard. In sympathy for confusion, modern art must echo confusion. It thus assumes the first half of the artist's task, that of knowing the burden, in order to prepare for the second half—that of lifting the burden. Has "modern" art perhaps simply *failed to reach its second half?*

As of today, all human life stands in the shadow of the cruel and the meaningless. The quest for sense in the world-process encounters a blank factuality nowhere better expressed than in the work of Sartre and Camus: it is, they report, "The Absurd" in which human existence is set. Man is subjected to the pressure of a faceless universe, silent as to his Whence or Whither. If he feigns to hear voices from within, they can be the voices only of arbitrary powers, tempting him to equally arbitrary treatment of his fellows, whether through exploit, or war. Whereas for those who hear no voices, believe no gods, and yet refuse exploit, revolution promising violent relief proves deceptive, driven as it is to replace tyranny by tyranny. Camus rejects faith, and equally rejects Nihilism: he rejects revolution and equally rejects exploit; for he has a new answer to the exploiter—a personal revolt, which asserts equality with the tyrant and restores the solidarity of mutual respect. But how can the spirit of personal revolt become a world-force able to curb or dominate the "collective passions" driving mankind to desperate action? Here Camus sees the authentic function of art, the sole available curative agency that can reach the minds of men with a speed and on a scale commensurate with the ills that menace them. In his great work, *The Rebel,* he asserts the mission of art to be addressed to the present world-malady—nothing less. In his words:

When the passions of the time put the fate of the whole world at stake, creation (the function of art) wishes (and is called upon) to dominate the whole of destiny.[2]

This analysis might seem a pure extravagance, were we not witnesses in our own day of the instantaneous uniting force, across the deepest chasms of "collective passion," of a notable musical event in Moscow, or of a ballet, or of a literary masterpiece, or for that matter of the art-element in the near-universal devotion of scientists to the community of truth, as in the Geophysical Year—itself a form of the creative passion invoked by Camus.

To generalize his meaning, let us say that the mission of art is the *Redemption of the Absurd*, overcoming the irrational brute-fact-aspect of existence, not by legality nor by other-worldly hopes, but by the immediate attraction of a vision of human nobility in creating solidarity. The mission of art is to evoke images that universally persuade, and thus create the will to unite.

The power of art in the political arena has never been more highly rated, unless by Plato, who paid the poets of his day the oblique compliment of wishing to exclude them from his ideal Republic, or by Confucius, who declared of the music of his day that there were sounds that dispose men to fair conduct and others that dispose them to disorder: both recognized that there is such a thing as bad art, which can undo the best work of lawmakers. Tolstoi, the artist, would excommunicate art: and the socialists from Saint-Simon onward sought to control art in the interest of social progress. This sense of danger is an admission of its power. But Camus sees clearly that while art, for every reformer, is on trial, it can only exist as free, never as the instrument of a specific polity or diplomacy. As the voice of human hope, art precedes diplomacy, and makes diplomacy possible.

It is Frederich Schiller who most clearly sees art in its historic efficiency. In his *Letters on Aesthetic Education*, he comments on what he considered the failure of the French Revolution.[3] Writing in 1793, all he could see of the out-

come of 1789 was that a great attempt to gain Liberty and
Fraternity had resulted in a new barbarity and terrorism
(as if anticipating Camus' judgment on revolution as fated
to beget a new tyranny). Schiller took definite issue with
Kant's prescription, namely, to "subordinate the senses,"
the natural impulses and passions, to reason and law, as an
ideal Napoleon might have done, and as the actual Napoleon
hoped to do while serving his own ambition. As Schiller saw,
"subordination" is not the word. For civilization is not a
subduing of impulse: it is a *harmonizing of impulse and
reason.* This harmony, he held, is the precise achievement of
art: hence art alone can educate mankind, for only art can
act on feelings directly.

Schiller and Camus see art in its completest scope. To
educate is even more than to cure discord; though the
curing Camus calls for is perhaps the severer task. For
both, the question arises, who or what will educate the artists?

For while this heavy leaning on art for the civilizing and
healing movements of history does not rate art too high it
does make art *unduly self-sufficient.*

It is wholly right in holding cultural advance to be due to
a force of attraction, not solely to compulsion such as
economic necessity: the pull and the push commonly act
together. But the pull, the prefigured goal of the striving intrinsic to human life, is not a creature of the artist's imagination: it is first of all a trait of reality present in experience
to all men, felt by the artist as a member of the race, and
hence incorporated by him in symbols he could know to be
universal.

For the reality we immediately feel is not blank "sensa-
tion": it is also *incentive.* Let me venture—as an essay in
"depth-psychology"—to describe your nuclear awareness of
being: There is a life-pulse, a biological directive like Bergson's *élan vital;* but more than that; more, too, than
Whitehead's primordial "lure" (so akin to that *ewig
Weibliche* of Goethe which "draws us onward"). There is at
once a persuasion and a summons, a promise and a task, a
sense of destiny and a duty: if you like, a female and a male

element, a Yin and a Yang. The Chinese have a remarkable name for it, *Ming*, the "appointment of Heaven." *Art is a response to the incentive* of this reality as directly felt.

What Schiller and Camus alike neglect is the truth that art is derivative—a response rather than pure origination. It is a creative response, because its proposal is clothed in imagery devised by the artist. Art, let us say, is a creative response to a felt purposive factor in the world-process as always present.

If, as I put the matter many years ago, religion is the "Mother of the arts,"[4] we can understand the historical circumstance that the arts are the first language of religion: myth and song, drama and dance, temple and tomb, sculpture and painting, yes, and the primitive laws and sciences as well . . . all appear first as attendants upon the world spirits, and only later fight their way to independence and maturity. And in many ways, the arts remain the most natural, freest, least dogmatic expressions of faith. The poetry of the world not only precedes its philosophy but in many ways remains the most vital expression of our metaphysical sense.

Art must always be free to play, partly because the real demands the widest variety of imagery for its full truth: one might almost venture the paradox that the play of art is too serious for the literalities of analysis. What Rilke said of his early master, Rodin, touches the essential purport of art: "For him, making a portrait meant seeking eternity in a face, that fragment of the eternal with which that person took part in the great process of eternal things . . . an effort at holding the ultimate court of justice!" And, I add, the beginning of *doing* justice, man's creative task adding to the creative work of the world-power.

It may seem at first sight an inversion of the true functions to define the province of art as a type of *justice* ulterior to that of the courts. Yet consider a work like Tolstoi's *Resurrection*, or—to leap into the present moment—like Cozzens' *The Just and the Unjust*. The Greek tragedy was at once play and judgment on the human situation. But come directly to the essential point; consider the words of the ancient story of the woman taken in adultery, "Neither do I con-

demn thee"—the story itself a work of art, whatever its relation to actual happening: the mind of the race continues
to be stirred by it to a deeper justice, because touching a
more germinal level of reality-in-the-moral-life. It is, in
brief, the region in which art and religion refuse separation,
and together carry philosophy nearer to its goal.

And to see this as the great opportunity of fiction, the
drama, the screen, in our day is to groan over the waste,
whether of the writers or the critics, spending themselves on
the trivia of sophisticated psychology. They are misled,
no doubt by the two prevalent learned superstitions of our
time—buzzing close to truth—the Freudian unconscious,
and the Existentialist being-without-essence. The impact of
Dr. Zhivago should open their eyes to the fact that art *is* an
act of attempted justice and in its responsible exercise stirs
the ultimate issues even when it cannot decide them. Stirs the
statesman as well!

It becomes clear that the apparent irrelevance of art to
the fateful decisions in public affairs is deceptive. For policy
must win response from the faiths of a people; and the faiths
rest on what they intuitively trust to, as the ruling powers
of history. If Charles Malik, president of the UN Assembly,
is right in saying that "the Western mind has . . . been
softened and undermined from within and without . . .
losing faith in itself . . . seeking other gods than those which
have so faithfully protected and nurtured it" . . . and that
"the deepest thing at stake is its faith in its values and its
ability to justify and defend them" . . . the fault is not solely
in our thinking: it is in our seeing and our feeling, in the
groping incertitude which, shared by the artist, he, the
artist, is unable to correct.

But let us be clear that the fault is not in his "modernism,"
nor the cure in reversion to an earlier era, whether of style,
or of faith. What is lost in the "modern" is not the certitudes
of yesterday, not the Romantic, nor the Classic, but the
Eternal. It is the peculiar advantage of art, that surrender-
ing the exactitudes of science and the fixities of theology for

the elastic imagery of metaphor and myth, it is able through its localisms and its periods to *mean* the changeless and universal. It is the undefined identity of all the faiths. It is, as Plotinus says of beauty, "recognized by the soul as something long familiar, arresting and beckoning"—a tie to the timeless, a tie without bonds. It is for this reason that "works of art" never lose their speech. It is not yesterday that is better than today; it is vision and truth that are better than blindness and pretense.

However we define it, the world function of art is momentous, and the more fateful, because its power can only be exercised in responsible freedom. A dictated art loses at once the magic of universality. This does not mean that art has no discipline of its own, and that unbridled frivolity can hold the secret of the artist's sway. That secret is lost the moment the artist identifies his whim with his message; it is lost to any public which—as the USA now tends to do —allies its arts primarily with holiday-from-sobriety, escape, loose-ends.

Play indeed it must be, in the sense of passing beyond necessity, doing what no one could compel it to perform, bearing a fruit of superabundance. Like grace and beauty of body, art is the more-than-required, yielded by the human vital-overflow.

But just on this account, it emerges from the secret places of generic piety: the reverse of Riot, Fling, Drip, Abandon. And to grasp even partially the magnitude of the import of art for the human advance, and for the crux of history today, is to see the abysmal treason of an art which reverses the direction of its function, and instead of redeeming the Absurd in human destiny, steeps the soul in Absurdity, as by a deliberate suicide.

There is valid reason for a wide experimentalism in art, and for an abstraction which—like five-finger exercises— plays among the analytical factors of form. There is valid reason also for a subjectivism which turns the thought of the artist—partly—away from the object of the inner impulse, provided that in expressing his feeling he does not forget that art has to be a language intelligible—without excessive puzzledom—to mankind at large.

There is always a valid reason for rebellion against purely conventional limitations of theme and style and symbol, assuming that the rebel is not simply trying to cover, and thus confessing, his own poverty of resource. It has been said, for example, that "in our century, western music has turned to Asia and Africa to save itself from rhythmic and melodic stagnation."[5] When I think of Ravel and Sibelius, yes and even of Elgar and Grieg, I doubt the crisis of impoverishment; but I am sure that there are opening to us wide fields of new resource in the interplay of systems of music long developed in isolation. When Constant Lambert notes the difference between "the modal tunes of European Russia and the chromatic tunes of Eastern Russia," he pays tribute to an Oriental influence which has riches to offer; and such riches are surely more significant than can be found in vacuous tonal drift or non-peaceful competition in cacophony and the "barbaric yawp."

A responsible experimentalism has endless promise—responsible to the world-function of a deeper justice. An irresponsible experimentalism—tolerable in lighter times as exploration of the sportive end of the wide spectrum—may in the present human pass amount to the potential betrayal of a tacit trust. For the peoples—all of them—must look to their artists—not for policies, programs, doctrines—but for their most immediate rapport with the moving energy of the world, the *feel* of its purposive drive and meaning. Through an art adult to its calling, they may sense that hidden glory, beneath the forbidding mask of Fact, wherein the discords of the nations are, in the "anticipated attainments" of the spirit, already resolved.

APPENDIX II

Law and Diplomacy in the International Field

EVERY event in history is continuous with an intricate network of preceding events; and every event is, on its arrival, new and different, if only because it is the only event that has followed just those predecessors. But the humanly willed event has a wholly different kind and degree of novelty—it knows something of its predecessors, selectively, and reacts to them in its own wholly original way. Human history has always to report "It happened"—"once upon a time"—worth recording if it embodies a new idea.

Human institutions are built on recurring needs and situations; by its nature, an institution is a purveyor of generalities. This does not disqualify an institution from dealing with individual cases, for unique cases may still be classifiable. The attorney advises his client how the law fits his unique case; but the diplomat has to advise where law has not yet entered. Nations are personal; their quandaries are personal; their language to each other must bear the personal identity: the diplomat must make history, as the attorney cannot do.

Any critic of statecraft must see the diplomat's position in all its difficulty. It is partly that the diplomat's data for judgment are invisible, not merely the facts, but the emotions, the motives, the whole human insertion of the other diplomat in the history and passions of a people. Not only must he know more than any man can know; he must decide for himself and his nation in the absence of complete evidence; he must resolve into unity an infinitude of detail of diverging indications. The word "impossible" is not too strong; complete rational defense of decisions taken is excluded: must statecraft then be a gamble?

It may be some relief to note that this type of impossibility is the common situation of mankind. No one ever knows enough to bring up a child, or advise a friend, or propose a law. And as to choosing a wife, Socrates indicated—if Xenophon is right—that this portentous decision, exceeding the scope of reason, ought always to be referred to the gods. (So it should, and—believe it or not—usually is.) In brief, an element of *presumption* is inescapable in normal living.[1] Yet decision takes place, and for the most part without the dismaying awareness that the impossible has been accomplished. Partly, no doubt, because we seldom regard a decision as determined by the outer facts alone; we contribute to the situation our own image of what *can be made of it*, and act to the self-willed end. So, as fixed datum for action, the intricate political world is an insoluble complexity for the statesman; but as to some degree plastic to a creative will, it may present a malleable simplicity.

With this understanding, we see that the statesman or diplomat who takes guidance solely from classified situations —that is, from rules and precedents and principles of law— is lost. The uniqueness of every human—and every international—situation can be met only by a continuous stream of creative responses. The "right" outcome is not contained in the data: it will not occur unless we are prepared to make it.

The legal mind has certain advantages in diplomacy because of its command of the condensed experience of civilization in effecting public order. But in the role of statesman, the legal mind has the radical disadvantage of employing these well-classified problems and solutions in meeting a world to which—so far as the present situation is truly unique—history has become irrelevant, and therefore misleading. Today, the very bases of international order must be rethought: there are, we again remind ourselves, no precedents.

And as for the proposals for arbitration, the arrangements for affecting peaceful change, or the now reviving impulse to refer difficult issues to the World Court, to be decided by intuition of justice *ex aequo et bono*—all these resorts stir the minds of well-intentioned citizens in a judicial role to recall analogies or applicable maxims of wisdom in lieu of precise precedents—vaguer forms of the same fallacy. One must indeed postulate that there is a just solution; otherwise there is no way out but to toss coins: and careful thinkers like Lauterpacht can still insist that whether or not specific laws apply, there are really no "gaps in the law" when we consider the widest general principles; there is always *law*. But this is only to say that there must be a defensible solution—a valuable prod to keep us thinking; but no help in finding it! The lost ring must indeed be somewhere.

Lauterpacht is, I believe, on the right track in this respect: the search for a just solution can never be meaningless. Justice is a wider conception than law, and while positive law is always more than justice—elements of history, habit, custom, national temperament, and myth contribute their tangibilities to the abstract picture—the idea of justice is the generating motive from which law is deposited. For example, while the pure concept of law can offer no miracle to transform a *status quo* into a *status juris*, a just consideration of human elements does in particular cases achieve the miracle.

But also the moralizing mind, in its appeal to formulated principles rather than to the living feeling of justice in dealing with particular situations—the moralizing mind is as liable as the legal mind to the irrelevances of classification. The strength required in diplomacy is indeed a moral strength; but the morality involved is prior to general principle: it is the morality of understanding and therefore of mental inclusiveness. Its peculiar psychological equipment is a quality almost totally neglected in the political sciences —emotional depth: the capacity to respond by sympathetic imagination to the full range of human morale and passion, creative and destructive, noble and criminal, and therefore to *understand and evaluate*. In the statesman, a limited emotional depth means a limited sympathy; and a limited sympathy in the evaluation of types of behavior and customs other than one's own is a form of congenital stupidity, fatal for strength: it cancels the first condition for leadership, the mental inclusiveness which must also be inclusiveness of types of motivation.

Such inclusiveness may find the way of justice in the unique situation, through its freedom from formulated generalities, to the creative response which makes justice.

NOTES

Preamble

1. Albert Camus, *The Rebel,* tr. Anthony Bower (New York: Vintage Books, 1954), p. 274.

2. *Failure of a Mission,* (New York: Oxford University Press, 1945), p. 155.

I. *Three Types of Diplomacy*

1. *The Reporter,* Dec. 12, 1957.

II. *The Cold War for Men's Minds*

1. *New York Times* Book Review, March 15, 1959.

2. Cf. Y. C. James Yen's "Mass Education Movement," now international, and presently operative in the Philippines.

3. For more detailed discussion, see *Experiment in Education* (Chicago: Henry Regnery, 1954); "Creating a School," *Atlantic Monthly,* December, 1955; *Varieties of Educational Experience,* Harvard Library.

4. For a fuller discussion of the function of art, and the reasons leading to the "modern," see Appendix.

III. *Our Economic Puzzledom*

1. Edna St. Vincent Millay, Sonnet xlv.

2. There is also an esthetic nose, equally primitive, equally authoritative, equally sensitive to the faintly sweet aroma of corruption. The vital meaning of odors deserves far more respect than it receives. Through the entire evolution of living forms odors are the primitive chemical discriminant in the life-and-death matter of intake. We are only today beginning to appreciate the marvelous *directionality* of submolecular chemical structures, for biological purposes. Perhaps the generalized nose deserves to be—let me say—better listened to!

3. Speech at Harvard University Commencement, June 12, 1958.

4. *The Rebel,* p. 105.

5. *Ibid.,* p. 219.

6. In this subcommittee, of which Mrs. Franklin D. Roosevelt was chairman, and Dr. Charles Malik of Lebanon, *rapporteur,* the ques-

tion of the "right to work" came in for lively discussion. I was present at that session. Mrs. Roosevelt opened the session with a statement of the American proposal, which in substance called for the right of all persons to perform useful labor with due reward, provided the conditions of the total economy permitted. The Soviet delegate indicated that the proviso, which could easily be important in economies subject to the business cycle with periodic unemployment, was a limitation of the right to work which all economies would seek to overcome; and that since the Declaration was to be a statement of aims, not of conditions, the proviso should be dropped. The Soviet view prevailed.

IV. Basic Rights in the Light of Experience

1. "The Legal Norm in Soviet Jurisprudence," Georgiana Melvin, *Proceedings* of American Philosophical Assn., September, 1952, p. 46.
2. *The New York Times,* June 22, 1959.
3. Whiting Williams. Address before The Economic Club of Detroit, Feb. 11, 1957, p. 7, from which also the words of *The Economist* are quoted.

V. Our Double Morality

1. Cf. my *Morale and Its Enemies* (New Haven: Yale University Press, 1918).
2. Indeed, it might be considered that the first five Commandments are devoted to establishing the focus of a fundamental loyalty under another name, that of the object of worship—"no other god"—a loyalty to no human group, but embodied in ritual and in the family and tribal continuities.
3. Reviewing Douglas Edward Leach's book *Flintlock and Tomahawk,* in *Times* (London) *Literary Supplement,* November, 1959.
4. University of California, Berkeley, 1958.
5. Quoted from *Dialogues of Alfred North Whitehead* as recorded by Lucien Price, (New York: New American Library), p. 261.
6. No phase of legal philosophy today is unaffected by the sociological concern, which dominates views as widely different as those of Ehrlich, Timasheff, Roscoe Pound. I have in mind especially Dean Pound's "Legal Postulates" expressed in terms of the demands of civilized society.
7. *The Yale Review,* Summer 1959.
8. *The Rebel,* p. 16.
9. For further comments on that fateful turn, see pp. 190 f.
10. Membership in the UN should be discussed as a matter, not

of righteous intent, which can only be an attribute of passing ruler-
ships, but of a nation's *necessary involvement* in the total purpose
of a unified world order. This concrete involvement has its own logic,
which is the foundation layer of the code both of morals and of law:
the UN's primary function is to keep all members reminded of that
logic. It is precisely the bad actors that should be in, not out; quietly
compelled to think in world terms, and to face the record of fact. This
will require a set of rules which will prevent a separatist will-to-
dictate from canceling the UN's will-to-judge.

VI. The Demos and Democracy

1. For the full letter, see *Experiment in Education*, pp. 145-48.

2. See my *The Spirit of World Politics* (New York: Macmillan,
1932) wholly concerned with this problem, and the general principles
of nationhood and international ethics arising from the Middle East
situations from 1920 onward.

3. Contemporary jurists are inclined to drop insistence on territorial continuity, to raise questions whether the confessional divi-
sions, so important in seventeenth-century Europe and contemporary
India, are significant for the modern state (Gandhi in 1931 was
hoping to get rid of them for India, foreseeing the tragedy of India's
irrational division), and to add the conditions of political independence and jural autonomy. It stands to reason that unless a group
makes its own laws, those laws are not *its* experiment. There could
be no full-fledged USA national premise until the War for Independence was over; but some of the new inductive material was already
present as in Williamsburg and the Massachusetts Bay Colony. See
on this point, *The Spirit of World Politics*, ch. xi, referring the
plurality of nations to the nature of law; "To see that law-making
is experimental is to understand one reason for the failure of ancient
empires—Persian, Alexandrian, Roman—which aspired to universal
scope." Pp. 168 f.

4. *The Beginning and the End* (New York: Harper & Brothers,
1957), p. 149.

5. *Lasting Elements of Individualism* (New Haven: Yale University Press, 1937), p. 133. My first effort to define this postulate, *Law
and Rights*, 1926, p. 74: the "right to become what one is capable
of becoming" or "to develop the powers that are in him."

6. Stanley Moore, *The Critique of Capitalist Democracy* (New
York: Paine-Whitman, 1957), 3.2.2, quoting Marx, Eighteenth
Brumaire, sec. 7, par. 13. The entire context is pertinent.

7. It is noteworthy that the social revolution, when it came, appeared not in the partly democratized societies of West Europe but

in Russia, where the serf-peasantry, who had ineffectively revolted from time to time since 1671 under the leadership of a Don Cossack, had been technically emancipated in 1861 under Alexander II and again repressed, came nearest in Europe to the concept of a supine psychology, incompetent by itself to inaugurate the steps of democratization, and yet mentally ready to accept and use a proffered ideology of revolt.

8. The Kadets, after 1905, might have qualified had they been able to win a following; but a Liberal policy, conserving elements of prior authority, can only acquire strong support in a discriminating public; and this in turn implies a degree of political alertness already present. The Russian temper at that period could be widely stirred only by more radical measures.

9. The topic of my book *Experiment in Education,* discussed further below, p. 191.

10. Cf. *A Portrait of Czechoslovak Democracy* by Ferdinand Peroutka in *At the Cross-roads of Europe* by Karel Čapek and others, Prague, 1938, pp. 247-275.

11. *Alternative to Serfdom,* p. 84.

12. *Economic Review,* New Delhi, quoted by Reuters, Aug. 22, 1958.

VII. Realities of the International Scene

1. At this point the morality of nations must forever remain inferior to the morality of individuals. A Jesus of Nazareth may risk himself, in the strength only of his "truth," and half win over a reluctant Pilate; but he is unable to commit so much as his own disciples, still less his nation. Yet something of this sort—this *Satyagraha*—must exist before a working international law can exist in the absence of world government. Belgium in 1914 approached this level. And in the end, the West did not let Belgium down. The thing is not impossible, even today.

2. General James M. Gavin, *War and Peace in the Space Age* (New York: Harper & Brothers, 1958), as interpreted by Orville Prescott, in *The New York Times.*

3. Letter.

4. *Western World,* August, 1958, p. 20.

5. For example, since 1950 in Rumania the principle of peaceful competition has been in operation to the extent that the collectivizing of farms has not been enforced but has been left to the farmer's choice in view of the actual working of the collectives. Each peasant may hold to his private ownership. Though 51 per cent of the land

has been socialized, the numerical majority of the peasants still prefer the joys and risks of private ownership.

VIII. The Tangible Realities: 1. The Power and Up-push of Peoples

1. Indeed, this deviation is implied in the well-known dictum of Marx himself: "Philosophy meditates upon the world, whereas the task is *to change it.* "The criticism of the usual philosophic habit is pertinent; but changing the world as a *task,* implying a duty, assumes freedom in a sense incompatible with determinism.

An *ex post facto* recognition of this necessary departure is involved in a new doctrine about the *nature of matter,* introduced during the twenties into the teaching of the Institutes of Philosophy of Moscow. Matter is now considered to be "autodynamic," not inert as the atomic theory of the Newtonian era proposed. A materialist on the pattern of the new matter-concept could more readily understand the evolution of self-starting human organisms from primitive matter. Free particles give rise to free animals: determinism is out. (Free vegetables should be possible also?)

2. Cf. *The Spirit of World Politics,* Part I: "Backwardness and Its Measures."

3. *Times* (London) *Literary Supplement,* July 18, 1898.

4. Among whom, on the excellent authority of the Moscow journal *Bolshevik,* April, 1948, I am to be numbered, together with other "dark devils" such as Professor Flewelling, editor of *The Personalist.*

5. A possibility to this end involving a World Payments Union and perhaps a World Central Bank has been suggested with cogency by Mr. Frank Aiken, T. D., of Ireland in a speech before the General Assembly of the UN, Sept. 19, 1958.

6. This is the chief topic of my book *The Spirit of World Politics,* 1932, based on travel and study in the Near East and in Geneva during 1928.

7. A stabilizing role for the UN is not out of the question, in any case. The UN is neither vested with the financial resources for aid on a world scale, nor with the function of administering such aid. It might, however, act as an umpire.

In this capacity it could see that such aid is free from duress or bribe, and ensure that the neutrality of receivers is respected by both competitors.

Let me add that these lines were written prior to the important developments of November, 1958, in which the USA proposes to the General Assembly's Economic Committee a world-wide appraisal of all forms of aid, both public and private, to underdeveloped nations. This proposal calls for reports by all member nations of their current programs in this field, with a summons "to chart anew their courses of co-operative action"—the word "co-operative" is here especially pointed—and with special attention to education as well as to economy. This appeal, whatever its effect, is a welcome confirmation of the direction of our argument.

IX. *The Tangible Realities: 2. The Process of History*

1. In a statement published at New Delhi, Aug. 22, 1958, as reported by Reuters.

2. In a statement to the Senate Foreign Relations Committee, June 6, 1958. As further instancing the problem of freedom, Mr. Dulles indicated that satellite lands are growing in restlessness under the impulses of nationalism and individualism, and that the exodus of dissatisfied groups and individuals reaches formidable proportions. But he noted also a "therefore switch" to policies overtly friendly tending to "develop a vested interest in respectability," indicating that he recognized that Communism is a moving target.

3. The story of this tragedy and of its lesson have nowhere been so authoritatively told as by Arnold Brecht in his *A Prelude to Silence* (New York: Oxford University Press, 1944).

4. Dr. W. F. Ashe, in *Oberlin Alumni Magazine,* October, 1958.

5. Cf. *The Spirit of World Politics,* pp. 124 f.

6. Walter Lippmann, *The Communist World and Ours,* p. 51.

7. *The New York Times,* June 26, 1959.

X. *Foundations of National Strength*

1. Pavlov's "conditioning" is entirely genuine and useful, but a secondary principle: it must work without announcing itself. Tell me I am being conditioned, and I am instantly immune.

2. *Human Nature and Its Remaking* (New Haven: Yale University Press, 1929), pp. 94-100. Suffering in repute through its interpretation by Nietzsche, reminiscent of Hobbes, and partly rescued by Adler, the will-to-power has a wider significance than in any of these writers. Love itself—often set in opposition to ambition—is a manifestation of this will, as Plato saw, and Freud failed to see. For love, first sensed as an impulse toward merging-of-being with another, wins full self-understanding as a will-to-take-care-of that other, and to make of the common life a fruitful common task. It is a will to create, and to suffer in creation.

3. *Man and the State* (New Haven: Yale University Press, 1929), p. 116.

4. On this poinst see Gustav Radbruch's remarkable confession

for Germany in his preface to *Staat und Moral;* cf. my book *Experiment in Education,* p. 52.

XI. *Conditions of Justified Risk*

1. For further discussion of the issue of contrast between Law and Diplomacy in the international field, see Appendix II.

2. Michael Amrine, *The Great Decision* (New York: Putnam, 1959), p. 54.

3. This episode is related in detail in *Experiment in Education,* pp. 179-84.

4. There is a certitude of effect which, under certain conditions, accompanies the most presumptuous of human deeds. Some years ago I investigated these conditions under the title "The Prophetic Consciousness," ch. xxxii of *The Meaning of God in Human Experience.*

XII. *Moral Dilemmas of Peace*

1. See Gunnar Myrdal, *Economic Nationalism and Internationalism,* Dyason Lectures, 1957, Melbourne, Australia.

2. C. S. Braden, *War, Communism, and World Religions* (New York: Harper & Brothers, 1953).

3. *Op. cit.,* p. 260.

4. Cf. my *The Coming World Civilization* (New York: Harper & Brothers, 1956), Study I, "Impotence of the State."

5. *The Rebel,* p. 274.

6. *Man on His Nature* (New York: Anchor Books, 1953), pp. 240-91.

7. *Science and the Modern World* (New York: Macmillan, 1925), p. 125. Though he uses this appeal, in this passage, to support the view that we are *within* a world which extends beyond us in all directions, before and after in time, and outward in space, a view which he afterward modified.

8. It is now twenty years since I gave in Glasgow two series of Gifford Lectures. The theme of those lectures, in view of what I have here said of the contemporary philosophic task, may afford some explanation of the delay: the topic is "Fact and Destiny," with special reference to the obduracy of Fact, for any vision of a meaningful world. The period in which they were given included the Munich Pact and the premonitory rumblings of the second World War; in the Fall of 1938 gas masks were distributed to us in Cambridge, England. Later developments, both in event and in the world of thought, have required a deepened estimate of the portent of Fact for any philosophy holding that the world as a whole has a meaning. The present work, largely occupied with such an estimate, as a

crucial issue in the existing world split, may serve as a prolegomenon to the Gifford Lectures, which have so far appeared only in fragmentary outlines.

9. Cf. my *What Man Can Make of Man* (New York: Harper & Brothers, 1942), pp. 60 f.

Appendix I

1. Letter to *The New York Times,* March 1, 1959, from a former president of The Royal Academy.

2. *The Rebel,* pp. 274 f.

3. Cf. Walter Grossmann, "The Idea of Cultural Evolution in Schiller's *Aesthetic Education,*" in *The Germanic Review,* February, 1959.

4. *The Meaning of God in Human Experience,* pp. 13-26.

5. Fred Grunfeld in *The Reporter,* April 30, 1959.

Appendix II

1. *Human Nature and Its Remaking,* p 413.

INDEX

Absolute, 7, 51, 55, 77, 82, 93, 111, 113, 192, 206, 208, 215; as common sense, 86; moral absolute, 76-78, 82-85, 194; *see also* Relativity
Abstraction, 95; in art, 24, 30; in national aims, 80, 105
Absurd, the, 210
Acheson, Dean, 78-81
Act, as creative, 58, 187-89, 200
Activism, 141, 169
Adams, J. Donald, 18
Adventure as motive, 65
Advertising, *see* Publicity
Africa, 136, 143, 163
Aggression, neutralized, 164
Aid for underdeveloped, 146; principles of, 150-52; as business venture, 146-48, 150; role of neutrality, 146, 151, 202; role of UN, *see* UN
Alexander the Great, 161
Aloneness impossible, 194
America, *see* USA
Amur gold-rush, 103
Analogy in law, 181, 201
Anglo-Saxon, 167, 195
Animal faith, 218
Anti-Bolshevik campaign, 131
Anti-religion, 208-10
Appeasement, 13, 14, 127, 182
Arab, 130
Arbitration, 180 f.
Armament race, 2, 150, 154, 161, 180, 185
Art, 214; nature of, 26, 120; in diplomacy, 16; factor of national strength, 26-29; abstract, 24, 30; modern, 27; mood-changing, 199 f.; universality, 28; *see also* Appendix I
Artist, 120
Asia, 131, 144, 163
Aswan Dam, 151
Atheism, 126, 218
Atom bomb, 186
Australia, 153
Authoritarian rule, provisional function, 43, 159
Authority and Liberty, 158

Backwardness, 144, 149
Ballot-box, 114, 192
Barbed-wire, 32
Barker, Ernest, 21
Barnard, Chester, 74
Beatniks, 126, 208
Beauty, 212
Bellamy, Edward, 34
Berdyaev, N., 109
Bergson, H., 214
Berlin, 5
Bertalanffy, Dr., 40

Bill of Rights, British, 77; American, 110; Soviet, 49; UN Universal, 49, 112
Biology, 212
Bluntschli, 177
Body, the, 168
Bohr, Niels, 214
Bourgeois, 114, 184, 207
Briand, A., 81, 190 f.
Bribery, 92, 148
Bricklaying, 60
Britain, British Empire, Commonwealth, 85, 145 f., 151 f., 175, 182
Brotherhood, 58, 88, 100, 103, 195, 217
Bryce, James, 115
Buffer Zone, 131, 165, 204
Bureaucracy, 114
Bushido, 130
Business, American, 63, 74-76, 95; power in politics, 63; centralization, 75; morality of, ch. V
Byrd, Admiral Richard, 40

Camus, Albert, 3, 44, 78, 199, 209, 213
Canada, 153
Capitalism, 33, 58, 65, 114, 133, 184, and *passim*
Capitalism v. Communism as issue, 10, 33, 36, 41, 49, 124, 186
Centralization, 142
Certitude, 28, 31, 195, 196; as basis of risk, 166, 188
Change, as sign of life, 142
China, 104, 121, 139, 145, 174, 216; Chinese art, 28
Christianity, 107; begetting civilization, 74, 106; disclosing individual, 73; ultimate revolution, 73
Circle, Vicious, 128, 182
Civilization, 52, 124; Eastern, 104, 116; Western, 106; world-, 70, 144, 162; as ruling end, 82
Classless Society, 133
Class war, 60, 92, 121
Clark, John M., 92
Clay, Gen., 179
Cliburn, Van, 28, 120
Coexistence (*see also* Peaceful Competition), 134, 140, 183
Cold War, 3; *see* ch. II, and Armament race
Collectivism, 42
Colombo Plan, 151
Colonialism, passing, 145 f.
Coming World Civilization, 70, 144, 162
Committees, infertile, 191 f.
Common Law, 51
Common man, the, 27
Commonwealth, British, 145 f., 151; *see also* Britain

243

244 *Index*

Communication, 144
Communism, 10, 20, 144; as ideology, 206; in production, 35 f.; *see also* Capitalism v. Communism as issue, and *passim*
Community of purpose, goal, 167
Competition, 41, 56, 95, 151 f., 154; *see also* Peaceful Competition
Compromise, 127
Conant, J., 179
Conference, 195
Confidence, 200 f.
Confucius, 36
Conquest, right of, 2, 170, 203
Conscience, 108, 193
Consciousness, 211
Constantine, 77
Constitution, American, 110; Soviet, 209
Consumer, 41
Containment, 131, 165
Convergence, 15, 55, 186
Conversation as democracy, 195 f., 197, 198 f.
Cost of Aid, 146, 149; of Empire, 145
Counterfeit, 17
Court, World, 182
Creative Diplomacy, 16
Creative Risk, 165 f., 188, 196
Creativity, 78, 120, 162
Crime, 125, 177, 192, 203
Czechoslovakia, 84

Death, 126; racial, 198, 206
Democracy, ch. VI, and 7, 12, 19, 90, 119, 122, 177, 215; concept of, 110, 192, 195; aboriginal, 194; as *esprit de corps,* 110; as revolution, 116, 122; and leadership, 123; and regimentation, 48; counterfeit, 105, 123; curing own evils, 113; in autocracy, 137; indestructible, 122; of identical standards, 194; postulate of, 112, 157; in Germany, 177; in USA, 90, 96
Denazification, 177
Descent into Hades, 210 f.
Destiny, 216
Dewey, John, 9
Dialectic, 55, 85, 119, 122, 138, 157 f., 186, 217; economic, 50; of idea, 157 f.; of the Demos, 118
Dictatorship, 43, 118, 122, 153
Diplomacy, ch. I, and 129, 134 f., 142, 169, 185; third type, 14, 187; man-to-man, 196; as improvisation, 181, 196; *see also* Appendix II, Diplomacy and Law
Disengagement, *see* Buffer Zone
Distribution, 35, 37, 92; principles of, 61 f.
Distrust, Vicious Circle, 129, 182-88
Divided Mind, 129, 164 f., 180
Djilas, 46
Double Morality, ch. V, and 193
Dream, 130
Dresden, bombing of, 125
Dulles, Sec'y. John Foster, 156
Duma, 44

Earning, 57, 64
Economic, -s, 10, 20, 40; determinism, 10, 121, 141, 155; nationalism, 205; not a closed science, 96; solutions, 96, 154
Economy, 33, 141; and culture, 96; and morality, 97; self-adjusting, 60, 64; world pattern, 52; *see also* ch. III
Education, 6 f., 16, 18-22, 177, 215; in history, 177; tough disciplines, 20; Mass Education Movement, 18, 143
Egypt, 148, 160
Einstein, A., 214
Eisenhower, President, 151
Émigrés, 132
Empire, 142, 145, 174, 184; *see also* Imperialism, Colonialism
Empirical scope, 214
Encirclement, 131, 165
Energy, concept of, 212
Engels, 130; *see also* Marx
Enmity, 196
Equality, 19, 58, 61, 194; and Liberty, 57 f.; *see also* Justice
Esprit de corps as essence of democracy, 98
Ethical impulse, 217
Every man a whole man, as driving force of democratic goal of history, 19, 58, 61, 194
Evocable will of nation, 164
Experience as requisite of knowledge, 30, 156, 181 f., 210, 213; nuclear, 198, 208
Experiment, 42
Exploitation, 61, 78, 114

Fact, 3, 211, 213, 215
Fait accompli, 2, 72, 170, 203
Faith, 166, 216
Family, the, 121, 208
Farm, -ing, 89
Fear, 15, 128, 162, 189, 210; as motive, 130, 132
Feeling, 18, 24, 26, 212, 214
Feis, Herbert, 95
Feuerbach, 210
Fine arts, *see* Art
Foch, Marshal, 158 f.
Foreign Policy, 168; *see also* Diplomacy
Fortune, 57, 64
France, 146 f., 189
Fraternal group, as Claimant, 86-91; as Combatant, 91-96
Fraternity, 58, 195; minimal, 124, 127
Freedom, 169; absolute, 111; extension of concept, 196; of speech and press, 111, 156 f.; pattern of, 10, 48; revolution and, 159; *see also* Liberty
Free enterprise, 13, 31, 39, 42, 48, 49, 93, 142; export of results, 42
Freud, S., Freudian movement, 40, 216
Frost, Robert, 32
Futility as root evil, 171
Futurity as present, 198

Gamble, 196